Literary Practices as Social Acts
Power, Status and Cultural Norms in the Classroom

Literary Practices as Social Acts

Power, Status and Cultural Norms in the Classroom

Cynthia Lewis
Associate Professor
Language, Literacy and Culture
University of Iowa

LAWRENCE ERLBAUM ASSOCIATES, PUBLISHERS
2001   Mahwah, New Jersey   London

Lawrence Erlbaum Associates, Inc., Publishers
10 Industrial Avenue
Mahwah, NJ 07430

Cover design by Kathryn Houghtaling Lacey

Cover art © 2001 Artists Rights Society (ARS), New York / VG Bild-Kunst, Bonn Paul Klee, "Ohne Titel (Captive)," 1940

Library of Congress Cataloging-in-Publication Data

    Lewis, Cynthia (Cynthia J.)
Literary practices as social acts : power status and cultural norms in
    the classroom / Cynthia Lewis.
            p. cm.

    Includes bibliographical references and index.
    ISBN 0-8058-3677-2 (cloth : alk. paper)
    ISBN 0-8058-3678-0 (pbk. : alk. paper)
    1. Literature—Study and teaching (Elementary)—Social
aspects—United States—Case studies. 2. Reading (Elementary)—
Social aspects—United States—Case studies. I. Title.
    LB1575.5.U5 L49 2001
    372.64'044—dc21   00-067770
                                                                    CIP

Printed in the United States of America
10 9 8 7 6 5 4 3 2 1

*For my parents, Rose and Max Lewis,
my first and best teachers*

Contents

Preface

To understand the ways that the literary culture of a classroom is created within the interwoven social contexts of classroom and community, I conducted a year-long ethnographic study in a fifth-sixth-grade classroom in 1993–1994. This book follows five students as they read and responded to literature during key events with their teacher and classmates. In telling this story, I focus on four classroom practices involving literature: read-aloud, peer-led literature discussions, teacher-led literature discussions, and independent reading. The reader will see how these practices were shaped by discourses and rituals within the classroom and by social codes and dominant cultural norms beyond the classroom. Given the widespread adoption of literature-based reading programs in elementary classrooms nationwide, this in-depth look at what it means to read and discuss literature in one upper elementary classroom has important implications for classroom practice and future research.

Reading education is a high national priority, yet most studies focusing on reading practices or reading interventions are targeted toward early readers. On the other hand, studies related to literature are most often conducted in secondary schools where "English" is typically a code word for literary study. Reading comprehension and literary interpretation are separated as though comprehension is a developmental stage or level one must reach before interpretation is possible. Although scholars have pointed to the connections between literary response and reading comprehension (Dias, 1990; Harker, 1987), few studies focus on the uses of literature among elementary students, and those that do have focused primarily on student–text interaction (Cox & Many, 1992; Galda, 1982; Lehr, 1988; Purcell-Gates, 1991). Recent work by Johnston, Guice, Baker, Malone, and Michelson (1995) examined assessment practices in literature-based classrooms and found them to be profoundly influenced by social and institutional contexts. Yet, studies of interpretation in literature-based elementary classrooms have not taken this path. Even work focusing on the classroom contexts of literature instruction (Langer, 1995) tends to define interpretation in terms of interaction between reader and text. By contrast, in this volume I argue that interpretation itself is a deeply social act. Through such examination, status and power negotiations become clearly visible, underscoring the critical role of the peer dynamic and posing a challenge to the concept of the classroom as a unified learning community so often idealized in educational literature.

The classroom I studied used a literature-based reading curriculum, one in which students spent most of their time in small groups discussing journal responses to the literature they read. Just as Lensmire (1994) and Finders (1997) entered into their studies with positive expectations for a student-centered, process-based literacy pedagogy, I brought a similar set of assumptions to my study. Much like these authors, I left this fifth-sixth-grade classroom with a less facile, more complicated view of such pedagogies, particularly in regard to the role that power and status play in the discussion and interpretation of literature. However, whereas this book makes clear that social conditions worked to position students as more or less successful in relation to others within the classroom culture, a closer look at students' multilayered performances calls into question any easy conclusions one might draw. Looking closely at moment-to-moment interaction, I document the shifts in power and status that shaped and changed the classroom culture as described in the chapter summaries that follow.

PLAN OF THE BOOK

Chapter 1 explains the sociopolitical and performative theory that framed my study of four literary practices. It includes the dominant meaning of each literary practice within the overarching umbrella of cultural practice and a brief description of methodology, focusing primarily on my role in relation to the students and their teacher.

Chapter 2 includes detailed descriptions of places and people to provide the backdrop for the literature events depicted throughout the rest of the book. Here, I introduce readers to the nested contexts of classroom, school, district, and community, to address the reading and language arts curricula as well as issues related to social class, race, and gender in the school and surrounding community. Readers will meet the five focal students who figure most prominently in the book.

Chapter 3 starts with a description of social and interpretive expectations in the classroom before introducing the first of the four literary practices—the read-aloud. In describing the read-aloud practice, I focus on its ritualized meaning in terms of its relation to the shaping of a classroom culture. The focus of this chapter is on the local culture of the classroom as it exists within the community.

Chapter 4 begins with a description of conditions in the classroom that disrupted an idealized enactment of community, including the nature of grouping practices related to literature. The chapter then explores the relation between social and interpretive expectations and the positions students took up during literature discussions with their peers. During these discussions, students negotiated social positions and commented on the meaning of social and interpretive competence, focusing the research lens, once again, on the local cultures of classroom and community.

Chapter 5 examines teacher-led discussions and reveals how Julia Davis, the classroom teacher, encouraged students to probe and, at times, resist the ways that dominant cultural assumptions and textual ideologies shaped their readings of texts and experience. In this chapter the focus shifts to cultural norms and symbols beyond the classroom.

Chapter 6 examines the practice of "independent reading," a time set aside daily for students to read books of their own choosing and discuss them on a voluntary basis. Students viewed independent reading as an opportunity to appropriate and reinvent elements of dominant and popular culture for social uses within the classroom. This chapter brings to the foreground the ideological construction of what educators have dubbed "free-choice" or "independent" reading.

Finally, Chapter 7 elaborates the function served by each literary practice as it was shaped by the local culture of the classroom and by cultural norms and symbols beyond the classroom. In this chapter, I also suggest implications for classroom practice to better understand how readers, texts, and contexts intersect for particular interpretive purposes and interests.

ACKNOWLEDGMENTS

I am grateful to the teacher who opened her classroom to me during the year of this study. I admire her belief in the power of talk, text, and critical reflection, and I am indebted to her for allowing me to learn from her work with her students. While conducting this study, I would often remark to friends that my focal students ought to be the ones to analyze the data, so rich were their insights. I thank them now, many years later, for their enthusiasm and wit.

I am indebted to the exceptional committee of researchers and teachers who guided me through this research, which began when I was a graduate student at the University of Iowa. I am deeply grateful to Carolyn Colvin, who continues to be an inspiring mentor, colleague, and friend. Her guidance throughout this project was both supportive and challenging in the best possible ways. I am grateful also to Anne DiPardo, Linda Fielding, Jim Marshall, Cathy Roller, Bonnie Sunstein, and Mary Trachsel, who each offered key insights into this project and whose collegial insights I continue to treasure.

I owe a debt to Bettina Fabos, whose expert and meticulous help on my other research projects allowed me the space to work on this book. Without the help of Laretta Henderson and Jill Heinrich, graduate assistants on this project, the book would still be in process, and I thank them for their dedicated work.

I would also like to thank the family, friends, and colleagues who have had an impact on this book and who have sustained me in many ways: my grad school sisters, Julie Cheville and Peg Finders, whose words and thoughts intermingle with mine throughout this book; Pat Enciso, friend and collaborator, whose own research has intersected with and influenced mine from the start; Steven Athanases, Min-Zhan Lu, and Bruce Horner for abiding friendship and professional inspiration; Roberta Lewis, Jeffrey Lewis, and Jordan Lome for their love and genuine interest in this project.

For many years, I have been profoundly influenced by the ground-breaking scholarship of Donna Alvermann, Jim Gee, and Allan Luke, and I hope this book bears the mark of that influence. I thank them all for their generous support of my work. I consider myself very fortunate to have had early chapters of this book reviewed by two eminent researchers in the field of literacy. I would like to thank Rick Beach and Susan Hynds for their careful reading and unerring advice.

Naomi Silverman, my editor at Lawrence Erlbaum, provided expert guidance and support throughout the process. Her input made for a stronger book. I appreciate as well the careful attention and expertise that production editor Marianna Vertullo gave to this project .

I would also like to thank the University of Iowa for the Old Gold Fellowships that enabled me to devote my summers to this work. Thanks also to Jay Semel, director of the Obermann Center for Advanced Studies at the University of Iowa, for providing the quiet space to complete this book.

My deepest love and gratitude go to my sons, Jacob and Alley, for inspiring my work and invigorating my life and to Thom Swiss, whose critical eye, poetic ear, and loving support never fail me.

Foreword

This book, *Literary Practices as Social Acts,* by Cynthia Lewis, is important. Of late there have been a great many case studies of students and teachers and thick descriptions of classrooms. Too many of these have missed the forest for the trees. The significance of this book is that, though we get loving portraits of the trees, Lewis clearly shows us the shape of the forest. Her case studies and descriptions give substance to a specific perspective on literacy, one that I discuss a bit later. More significantly, Lewis's work indicates that a good many people concerned with reading and reading test scores today have missed both the trees and the forest. Let me explain.

Reading has been in the public limelight for some time now. Reading test scores are published in newspapers and used to judge teachers and schools. Public reports proliferate, calling for early training in phonemic awareness and overt, often scripted, instruction on phonics. Nearly all this attention has focused on early reading, where reading is defined narrowly as the ability to decode print. Literacy is viewed almost exclusively in terms of mental processes and individual skills. Learning and lifetimes are left out of this perspective, save for the facile and empirically false assumption that children who learn to decode early and well will necessarily be successful later in school and society. This assumption is contradicted by the long-term and well-documented problem of the "fourth-grade slump," the phenomenon whereby many children, especially poor children, pass reading tests early, but thereafter fail to be able to learn content well in the later grades.

Given all the attention to reading in the United States today, it is paradoxical that U.S. children score very well on international comparisons of reading. However, they do not perform as well on international comparisons of content learning, for example in the areas of science and mathematics, although there are controversies over how meaningful such comparisons are. At any rate, if we have a crisis in our schools, it would seem not to be a crisis of early reading, but of using literacy to learn content, early and late, in and out of school. However, I point out that I do not think this is exactly the right way to put the matter either.

Everyone concedes that there is a great disparity in how early and how well poor and rich children learn to read in our schools. Nonetheless, current debates over reading have focused on teaching methods and tests, not on poverty and inequality, despite the fact that it has long been known that although teaching methods are important, they are outweighed by out-of-school factors. The focus on methods and tests, rather than poverty and inequality, is due, perhaps, to the fact that so many people in the research field of reading see literacy in terms of mental processing and individual skills. They feel they can talk about cognition and skills as scientists, but about poverty and inequality only as citizens.

Nonetheless, from another perspective on literacy, one I discuss later, it is not altogether unreasonable to see poverty as a variable central to "reading science." One empirical argument would go as follows: It is now a well-known fact that from the late 1960s to the early 1980s, the Black–White gap in IQ test scores and other sorts of test scores, including reading tests, was closing fast. This heartening progress, especially in regard to achievement tests, ceased in the 1980s. Clearly, the factors that were causing the Black–White gap to close so quickly were, whatever else they were, powerful reading interventions, as they significantly increased the reading scores of "at-risk" children. The factors that made this progress stop are, too, powerfully related to reading, as they are clearly related to reading test scores, whatever else they are related to. Ironically, the progress made on reading tests during the time the Black–White gap was closing was greater, in quantitative terms, than the results of any of the interventions (e.g., early phonemic awareness training) that recent reports discuss and advocate.

We do not actually know exactly what the factors were that were causing the Black–White gap to close. We do not know what the factors were that caused that gap to stop closing. The matter has been little studied by reading researchers, debated more often by psychologists and policy analysts. Nonetheless, it is obvious that these factors are connected to larger social, cultural, and political changes; for example, the fact that segregation waned in the years following President Lyndon Johnson's "War on Poverty" and increased following the neoliberal hegemony that spread across much of the developed world with Margaret Thatcher and Ronald Reagan.

There is another way to look at literacy beyond seeing it in terms of mental processing and individual skills. This alternative perspective, the perspective so well developed in this book, does not leave the social and the political out of the picture. In this perspective, reading and writing are not primarily mental acts; they are primarily socially situated acts. From this perspective, there is no such thing as writing and reading in general. We always read and write within a specific social practice. A child presenting a summary report of a small group collaborative science project to his or her class is engaged in a different literacy-related social practice than is a child who is writing in a personal journal that will be responded to by his or her teacher. There are a myriad of other school-based, literacy-related social practices. An African American child creating a metaphor-filled rap is engaged in a different literacy-related social practice than is another child who is pretending to read a book by making up a booklike story. There are a myriad of home- and community-based, literacy-related social practices.

The change of focus from private minds and individual skills to social practices profoundly affects how we look at literacy. For one thing, it immediately connects literacy to learning and participation, indeed, learning as participation. To see this, consider the following argument: Literacy-related social practices almost always involve a good many other things besides written language. They almost always include and integrate, along with written language, specific and characteristic ways of talking, acting, interacting, feeling, thinking, valuing, and using various sorts of symbols and tools (e.g., computers). Literacy-related social practices are a package deal. Think, for instance, of the ways with words, deeds, and values a child must recruit to do "hands-on" small group science, as a full and valued participant, as opposed to those used when doing personal journal writing with a teacher.

Here is where and how learning and participation come into the picture: Learning involves engaging in a process whereby one progressively becomes a fuller and more valued participant in a specific social practice. Obviously, if one has acquired literacy skills, but cannot use them to participate in any specific literacy practice, these skills are worthless and not, in any real or important sense, an instance of learning. But here is the rub: Starting the process of becoming a participant in a specific social practice, when one is just a beginner, and, thus, not yet adept at the practice, takes trust. Becoming a participant in a specific social practice requires access offered by those already adept at the practice or those who "own" and control it. Achieving fuller and fuller participation in a specific social practice requires active affiliation with the values and norms inherent in the practice and with the other participants in the practice. Thus, it is clear that, in this view of literacy, we cannot separate literacy from trust, values, access, and affiliation. We cannot separate literacy, and the cognition involved in literacy, from affect, from society, from culture, or from politics in the sense of equal and fair access to social participation and power.

When people treat reading or writing as mental skills, they think of literacy in much the same way we normally think of thoughts in our head. Literacy becomes something that is primarily private and one's own responsibility. When people think of reading and writing in terms of situated, literacy-related social practices, they think of literacy in much the same way we think about tools. A tool, like a hammer, is perfectly meaningless all by itself. A hammer takes on different significances in different practices (e.g., hammering nails vs. straightening bent metal) and there are different types of hammers suited for different jobs.

Tools—and different types of literacy—mediate between a person and a specific practice in which a person participates. Tools and literacy are out there in the world, not inside people's heads. Furthermore, a person with a hammer (of a specific sort) is a different sort of person (one with different powers) than a person without a hammer. So, too, a person with a specific type of literacy, suited for participation in a specific social practice, is a different sort of person (one with different powers) than a person without that specific sort of literacy.

In my view, we do not have a reading crisis in our schools. Rather, we have what I would call an affiliation crisis. For anyone to participate in any social practice (including any school-based, literacy-related social practice) requires that, at least for a time and a place, that person is willing and able to take on the sort of identity this practice demands. To take on such an identity means to participate fully in the attitudes, values, and norms the practice requires. In this sense, it means that the person, for a time and place, is able and willing to affiliate with the practice and through the practice (and other related ones) to affiliate with the institution (e.g., schools) and the people (e.g., teachers, special educators, reading resource teachers, etc.) whose practice it is.

Lots and lots of children will not or cannot affiliate with specific school-based, literacy-related practices. The problem is worse later in school than earlier, despite our emphasis on early reading. Many school-based, literacy-related practices assume the sorts of backgrounds and preparations that only privileged children tend to have, but teachers do not admit this and explicate what these backgrounds and preparations are. Many operate by values and norms that are, at best, foreign to children from some families, and at worst, perceived to be hostile to these families' own values and norms. Many school-based, literacy-related practices, early and late, claim to be related to worthwhile learning and to futures in a changing world, but, at a deeper level, they are perceived by students (rich and poor) as simply forms of "doing school" connected more to getting through a gate than to learning of futures. For a great many children the evidence of their lives demonstrates the centrality of inequality and unfairness in society as schools ignore inequality and unfairness in the name of "disinterested" knowledge and "scientifically proven" methods.

A focus on literacy as mental skills misses all this, renders it invisible. How can we make it visible and, in the act, actually speak to the affiliation crisis? We can do so by taking our gaze away from reading and writing "in general" and turning our gaze to specific sorts of reading and writing, coupled with specific sorts of ways with words, deeds, actions, interactions, values, feelings, symbols, and tools within specific social practices. This will bring issues of trust, values, access, and affiliation to the forefront of consciousness and research. We will begin the process of producing lifelong learners who can use and critique literacy within specific social practices, including new ones in the future, to change themselves and society.

This book is a careful study of literacy-related social practices and the ways in which they do and do not recruit children's affiliation. It speaks, as well, in crucial ways to how class works in regard to such affiliation, an issue that has been heretofore badly confounded with race in educational studies. In treating literacy in terms of value-laden social acts, it has the capacity to place the public discussion of literacy back where it belongs.

—James Paul Gee
University of Wisconsin, Madison

I

Contexts

1

The Social Politics
and Performance
of Literature

[Nikki] was really excited about talking about books. And I think this was her first teacher—probably the first teacher that she's had—where the literature came first. Now we're going to teach literature as opposed to reading. (Nikki's mother)

This book is about the literary culture of a fifth-sixth-grade elementary classroom—a classroom where, as Nikki's mother put it, the literature came first. Nikki was a student participant in my study of this classroom, where I spent a school year watching 10- to 12-year-olds read and talk about literature.[1]

Nikki's mother was clear that she did not view the teaching of literature to be the same as the teaching of reading, and this would be her daughter's first experience with a teacher who did not use literature in the service of reading. Of course the fact that literary texts are most often taught through the language and technology of reading comprehension is not surprising, given that most elementary teachers receive little training in literary genres, theory, or pedagogy compared to that which they receive in reading (Walmsley, 1992; Wolf, Mieras, & Carey, 1996). Yet, despite the fact that the teacher whose class I studied was not an exception to this rule, she

---

[1]All names of people and places are pseudonyms. The five focal students and teacher chose their own pseudonyms.

worked in consort with many of her students to create a different sort of literary culture in her classroom, one that sustained students like Nikki.

My principle argument in this book is that the meaning one gives to literature, including its function and interpretation, is, above all, a social act. When I say that literary activity is social, I do not mean merely that it involves people constructing knowledge together through social interaction, although this is often the case. I mean, in addition, that it involves readers who have been constructed through social codes and practices that shape their relationships to texts, including literary texts and how such texts might be defined. Hence, the literary culture of any classroom is—to say the least—complex.

Throughout this book, I read the literary culture of classroom and community through a sociopolitical lens. My lens is social because literary practice is enacted not only through social interaction among people who have social histories and statuses, but also by readers who have been constructed through social codes that shape their relationships to texts. My lens is political because these histories, statuses, and codes carry differential power in the classroom and beyond. In this book, readers get an up-close look at the social politics of a classroom as it shaped and, in turn, was shaped by literary practices.

THE STUDY

This yearlong ethnographic study focuses on four classroom practices involving literature: read-aloud, peer-led literature discussions, teacher-led literature discussions, and independent reading. As the story unfolds, the reader will see how these practices were shaped by discourses and rituals within the classroom and by social codes and dominant cultural norms beyond the classroom. Emerson School was an elementary school situated in an older neighborhood of mixed-income residents. I chose a multiaged classroom because of my interest in how age differences and classroom histories shape classroom context and literature discussions. For nearly all the sixth graders, this would be their second year with their teacher, Julia Davis. In deciding on the classroom site for this study, I looked for a teacher whose pedagogy would allow for much peer-led discussion, student decision making, and collaborative work, and who herself would have a strong identity as a reader and writer. Julia met these criteria (described fully in chap. 3).

The five focal participants represent contrasting characteristics in terms of gender, age, social class, perceived ability, and peer status. As participant-observer, I used ethnographic tools to determine broad status hierarchies in the school, classroom, and community (see chap. 2). Not surprisingly, status was evident not only through markers of social class and achievement, but in the daily rituals of life in school—in who gets included or excluded from tables in the cafeteria or from games in the schoolyard; in the volleying of conversational turns during a literature discussion or an animated discussion about an upcoming sleepover party. The field notes I took to record my observations became my most consistent and revealing data source.

I wanted my study to include both working-class and middle-class students because social class is often a prominent marker of difference in Midwestern schools located in predominately White communities like this one. Initial conversations with parents, school personnel, and community members indicated that social class would be a salient feature. For instance, when I asked the coordinator of the community's neighborhood association how she would represent the socioeconomic status (SES) of the community, she reported that the community is one where middle-class and working-class people live side by side. I received a similar response from the literacy specialist who added that Emerson School was the most diverse school in the district in terms of the wide range of income levels represented.[2] At the time of my initial phone call to the teacher, she too described the school as a place where "kids who are low SES and low achieving are best friends with kids who fly to Europe at a moment's notice." She added that parents in this neighborhood generally taught their children "to respect idiosyncrasies" in a way that created what she described as a "classless" classroom. Intrigued by these characterizations of social class in the school and community, I wanted to see how it played out for individual students.

Although social class is a constructed category due to its ambiguous relation to income, occupational status, taste, and lifestyle (Swartz, 1997), the way that it is constructed is important to this study. For instance, Jason, a focal student whose father was a plumber, was viewed as working class by the teacher although his family's income may well have exceeded that of the families of other students viewed as middle class. Julia was aware of the

---

[2]When I inquired about two other schools in the district, one with more ethnic and racial diversity and one with many low-income children, the literacy specialist pointed out that neither of those schools had students from both ends of the socioeconomic spectrum and reminded me about the families who lived in large homes two blocks from the school. I couldn't help but compare it to more diverse schools in the urban center where I once lived. However, despite its relatively small number of racially or ethnically diverse students (12.8%), Emerson's community was not homogeneous.

constructed nature of social class; yet like many of us, she marked social class in fairly typical ways (see descriptions of students in chap. 2).

Perceptions related to gender and power in the classroom were also important to this study in that many students and parents felt that girls were favored in the classroom. The teacher was well aware of these complaints and had strong beliefs about countering the lack of power she believed girls too often experience. Her classroom was a place where girls were often given leadership roles and challenged intellectually. The literary culture of the classroom was one in which the performative norm for girls' reading and response practices were established as the norm for competence. That is, the kinds of responses to literature that were valued in this classroom were related to the ways that girls often perform their readings of texts—attending to experiences, characters, and ideas rather than to plot and action (Cherland, 1994; Simpson, 1996). Of course, girls in this classroom took up complicated stances relative to the normative roles in which they were cast. Tobin's (2000) explanation along these lines is instructive here: "Following Butler (1990, 1993), I view gender—and, by extension, race and ethnicity—as awkwardly written social scripts that people, once they are cast in a part, perform with as much enthusiasm and conviction as they can muster, but never totally convincingly" (p. 14). In coming chapters readers will see the girls and boys in Julia's class performing gender in ways that both reinforce and contradict gendered norms and interpretive expectations.

Research Stance

As a participant-observer in this classroom, my level of involvement was moderate, defined by Spradley (1980) as "a balance between an insider and outsider" (p. 60). Because my focus depended so much on understanding the culture of the classroom as constructed by Julia and her students, I believed that my participation in literature discussions might have been intrusive and caused students to be guarded in sharing their beliefs with me. Given the challenge of researching children, I decided to establish myself not as an authority figure and not as a peer, but as a "quasi-friend" or "tolerated insider in children's society" (Bogdan & Biklen, 1992, p. 88). Within the first month of the study, I began to eat lunch with students and talk with them as they gathered on the playground. This level of involvement helped me to understand the nature of the students' friendship circles within and beyond the classroom and eventually to choose focal students.

Responses to my participation varied. One fifth-grade child asked me as I sat across from her in the cafeteria if my mother had packed my lunch for me that day and later invited me to join her as she rolled down a hill on the playground. Other children stiffened as I sat down on the cafeteria bench near them. Apart from these forays into the children's world, however, my early stance in the classroom would more aptly be characterized as that of an observer rather than participant. My presence was acknowledged in many ways, including attention from the children, but during this time I never spoke during book discussions, and I rarely discussed pedagogical issues with Julia. Beginning my study as more of an observer than a participant allowed me to bathe in the culture of this classroom until I became familiar with its shared practices, beliefs, and expectations.

Early on, I suggested to the teacher that I might read aloud to students on occasion, reasoning that this would help me to establish a relationship with the students without placing me in a teacherly role. On a day when Julia was going to be absent, the students were to discuss books in peer-led groups, and Julia asked me if I'd keep an eye on a student (one of my focal students) who rarely participated during small-group discussion. I reminded her that I didn't feel I could say anything to encourage his participation but would let her know what I observed as I watched the group. After our conversation, I questioned whether it was possible, even desirable, to define myself as an outsider observing a "natural" setting when I clearly had become a part of the setting. It was natural for me to be there as a person, an adult, a "quasi-friend" and "tolerated insider." Although I did not become a full participant in the classroom, over time the students often requested my responses, not only during literature discussions but during routine social exchanges as well. I began to acknowledge my personhood in the life of this classroom and my potential influence on the students' public performances.

Literature Events

Because the connection between social contexts and literary practices was central to this study, I focused on the interdependent social events in the classroom that were related to literature. Deciding to focus on contextualized events meant narrating interactional contexts rather than describing each focal student as a particular case (chap. 2 includes a portrait of each child to serve as a backdrop to these events). I focused my closest analysis on two categories of events: (a) key events—those that research participants characterized as particularly significant, and (b) illustrative events—those that depicted performative roles that were repeatedly documented in field notes and audiotapes (Lewis, 1997;

Lewis, Ketter, & Fabos, 2001). In writing about these events, I have framed each with the sociocultural conditions of its occurrence, including the social and interpretive competence of the key players in the discussion, as well as information gleaned from interviews about home and community contexts. I've done so in keeping with Goffman (1981), who argued that analysis of the social conditions that shape spoken interaction must be "identified and mapped with such ingredients as are available to and in local settings" (p. 193).

To extend beyond the local setting and examine how the text of students' literature discussions supported particular social identities and institutional interests, I used approaches to examining discourse based on work by Gee, Michaels, and O'Connor (1992a, pp. 233–250). I analyzed, at the level of "sociocultural setting" (p. 233), the activity system and ideological underpinnings of the discourse and formulated, at the level of "discourse structure" (p. 239), an interpretation of the event that took into account its "sensemaking" (p. 249).

Finally, I characterized the dominant meaning of each literary practice within the overarching umbrella of cultural practice and devote a chapter of this book to each. In interpreting the data, I began to see that each literary practice was shaped by both the local culture of the classroom and community and by the larger culture, by which I mean broad cultural norms and symbols. These two categories—local and larger culture—helped me to frame my analysis and focus on the ways that the social discourses of each were at times set in opposition to one another. I want to emphasize here that local cultural norms and symbols cannot be divorced from those of the larger culture. Local norms are shaped by larger cultural norms in ways that this study illustrates. Yet, two practices (read-aloud and peer-led) were shaped more by local cultural norms that governed the immediate social situation, whereas the other two practices (teacher-led and independent) were shaped more obviously by dominant cultural norms. Figure 1.1 lists each literary practice and two features of the practice. The circles that symbolize each practice overlap to represent their interrelated nature. First, I identify each literary practice (bold); second, I include what I came to see as the dominant function or meaning of each practice (underlined); and, third, I pose a question that serves to foreground the issue that was most salient within each practice (italics).

The dominant function of the read-aloud practice was to enact a classroom culture. The question at the root of this practice was "What do we have in common?" Given this emphasis on the classroom community,

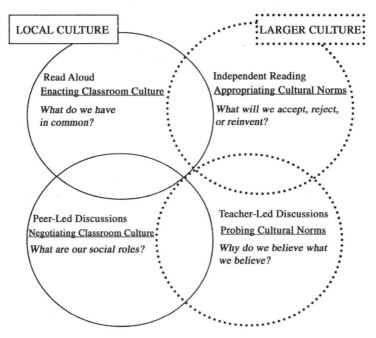

FIG. 1.1   Literary practices and their meanings.

read-aloud was shaped most directly by the local culture and immediate social situation.

The dominant function of peer-led literature discussions was to negotiate classroom culture. The question at the root of this practice was "What are our social roles?" Again, the emphasis here was on the immediate social situation as governed by local cultural norms.

The dominant function of teacher-led literature discussions was to probe cultural norms. The question at the root of this practice was "Why do we believe what we believe?" The most notable feature of this practice was its examination of larger cultural norms and assumptions.

The dominant function of independent reading was to appropriate dominant cultural norms (often popular culture). The question at the root of this practice was "What will we accept, reject, or reinvent?" The emphasis here was on larger cultural norms and symbols (although often in relation to the immediate social situation).

To examine the various discourses that constitute the meaning of literature in the classroom, I draw on a theoretical framework that views all literacy as social practice (Gee, 1992, 1996; Heath, 1983; Luke, 1991; Luke &

Freebody, 1997; Street, 1993). The next section explains the theoretical grounding for this study in theories of literacy as social practice involving ritual and performance. The chapter concludes with a discussion of the sociopolitical nature of literary response.

LITERACY AS SOCIAL PRACTICE

Informed by theories of literacy as a social practice, researchers from a range of disciplines have considered the social dimensions of literacy. This branch of literacy research has shifted the focus from models based in psychology that emphasize individual cognition to models based in sociology, linguistics, and anthropology that focus on the social and cultural contexts of literacy (Freebody, Luke, & Gilbert, 1991; Gee, 1992, Lankshear, 1997). In a recent edited volume (Barton, Hamilton, & Ivanic, 2000), Barton and Hamilton (2000) delineated several principles that undergird a view of literacy as social practice. Among them are two principles central to this study:

- Literacy practices are patterned by social institutions and power relationships, and some literacies are more dominant, visible, and influential than others.
- Literacy practices are purposeful and embedded in broader social goals and cultural practices. (p. 8)

In keeping with these principles, sociolinguists and ethnomethodologists have studied how interaction defines what counts as reading within elementary classrooms (Baker, 1991; Baker & Freebody, 1989; Bloome, 1983; Bloome & Egan-Robertson, 1993; Green & Meyer, 1991; Heap, 1991; McDermott, 1977). These studies revealed the micropolitics of reading in particular contexts, demonstrating how social status and institutional power legitimize particular ways of reading over others. However, this perspective on literacy has rarely been applied to the study of literary response and interpretation as it is in this book.[3]

In discussing literacy as social practice, I align myself with theories that view cognition and activity as constructed by the social world rather than embedded within it. To bring this distinction to light, Hruby (2001) ana-

---

[3]A notable exception is Cherland's (1994) study examining the role that popular fiction plays in constructing the gendered identities of sixth-grade suburban Canadian girls. However, Cherland's primary focus is on the sociopolitical contexts outside the classroom rather than the classroom scene where interaction occurs.

lyzed the difference between social constructivism and social constructionism. Social constructivism, he argued, is grounded in the epistemology of psychology, which "pays more attention to the social scaffolds and frameworks that promote the fashioning of such internal structures in a manner reasonably cohesive with an individual's social surround" (p. 48). Social constructionism, on the other hand, is grounded in the epistemology of sociology, which attends to "the way knowledge is constructed by, for, and between members of a discursively mediated community" (p. 48). Hruby placed Vygotsky's sociohistoric theory and Vygotskian-influenced activity theory within the social constructivist paradigm. Similarly, Hynds (1997) chronicled the evolution of literacy education and her own theoretical orientation as one that moved from constructivism to social constructivism to sociopolitical constructivism. She defined constructivism, in Piagetian terms, as an approach that centers on the individual in interaction with the object of learning, in this case the text. Hynds moved next to a social constructivist view based on the work of Vygotsky, but eventually came to the conclusion that neither perspective helped her understand the complicated social and power relations at work in the classroom she studied. Others, however, have noted that Western notions of the individual lead to an interpretation of Vygotsky's work that ignores his concept of "a self that is social, constructed, and formed by symbolic action" (Zebroski, 1989, p. 153).

Recent perspectives on literacy as social practice that draw from social constructionist and poststructural concepts of language and subjectivity are more relevant to this study than social constructivism. In her work on situated cognition, Walkerdine (1997) argued that sociohistoric activity theory (based in Vygotskian theory) does not adequately explain how subjects are produced through language and discourse. Its focus on individuals "thinking in different contexts" (p. 65) to accomplish activities in practical settings does not account for the production of subjects through discourses that regulate practices and rationalize actions and events.

To illustrate with the example of Nikki and her mother, their embodied literary practices were regulated through discourses related to social class, education, and disciplinary institutions. The meaning Nikki's mother gave to literature can be viewed, in Bourdieu's (1990) terms, as "habitus" for Nikki, a social field about which she formed (through the social codes that were available to her) embodied perceptions, tastes, and actions relative to literary texts. It is a habitus that served her well in that it aligned with her teacher's "ways with literature" and allowed Nikki to shape the literary culture of the classroom along with her teacher. (Readers will see this process at work related to Nikki and other students in subsequent chapters.) Furthermore, Nikki's mother's discourse was constituted within larger institutional discourses as well. For example, the meaning of literature shared by Nikki, her mother, and her teacher opposes the way that literature is usually viewed within elementary school contexts, but coincides with particular disciplinary discourses about literary knowledge that are more associated with secondary and postsecondary education. Thus, the connection that Nikki's mother implicitly makes to literature as interpretation rather than comprehension, aesthetics rather than utility, carries a certain legitimacy within and beyond her classroom.

This way of theorizing subjects and settings informs my study because it makes clear that discourse is more than talk in classrooms—more, too, than the language of social and power relations within the classroom. As Gee (1992b, 1996) outlined in his well-known distinction between Discourse and discourse (D/d), identities are constructed through institutional and ideological worldviews. Indeed, methods of critical discourse analysis (Fairclough, 1989; Gee, 1999; Luke, 1995) have been developed to examine the ideological and institutional aspects of discourse as they connect to social relations and identities.

Given the degree of normativity in terms of what is expected, accepted, and valued in any classroom, the theoretical framework that informs this book includes a view of classroom life as a temporary culture with a 9-month life span. Viewing the classroom as a culture is useful in that it provides a context for examining discourse and ritual as they represent group life and, in this case, define what it means to read and discuss literature. *Discourse,* as I use it throughout this book, includes not only classroom interaction, but also the worldviews and ideologies that regulate and define particular social contexts and activities (Brodkey, 1992; Gee, 1996; Weedon, 1987). Rituals are enacted and reenacted as practices that shift in meaning from setting to setting but exist within the boundaries of social and interpretive competence established by the members of the classroom culture. Rather than a cohesive system of beliefs, actions, and evaluations (Goodenough, 1971), culture is defined here as a dynamic system within which social relations and identities are continuously negotiated and power is asymmetrical (Cazden, 1988; Giroux, 1992; Pathey-Chavez, 1993; Rosaldo, 1989). As Bruner (1986) defined it, "A culture is as much a forum for negotiating and renegotiating meaning and for explicating action as it is a set of rules or specifications for action" (p. 123).

A Performative View of Self and Context

To better understand the social positions from which particular students speak and act and the power relations represented by those social positions, I turned to the interdisciplinary field of performance studies. Performance studies view all social action as performative. From this perspective, speakers and writers take up positions in relation to the expectations of others and the social codes and discourses available within a given context (Bauman, 1977; Bauman & Briggs, 1990; Conquergood, 1989; Davies & Harré, 1990; Lewis, 1997; Lewis et al., in press). Individual and group identities are defined through repeated performances (ways of talking, listening, writing, and using one's body) as participants "perform the self," which is always in relation to the group (Butler, 1990; Dyson, 1992; Enciso, 1998; Kapchan, 1995; Newkirk, 1997; Tobin, 2000).

In the hypothetical case of a voracious sixth-grade reader discussing a text with a reluctant fifth-grade reader, the positions each student takes up may change as the discussion progresses. The fifth grader might take up a position of resistance as well as compliance, and disinterest as well as engagement in the course of one discussion, for instance, depending on the context of that interaction. Let's imagine that the sixth grader begins the discussion by performing the role of a teacher, and the fifth grader dutifully conforms. Later in the discussion, however, the older student shifts to an engaged stance in relation to the text and the discussion, causing the younger student, a reluctant reader, to become disruptive and to avoid interaction. These performances depend not only on the moment-to-moment shifts that occur during the interaction, but also on the relationship established between these students in and out of the classroom; each student's position and status within the classroom and neighborhood may play a role as well, as do their relations to discourses within the classroom and to larger cultural norms. Adopting a theoretical framework that views all social action as performative provided me with a way to understand the fluid nature of social interaction during literature discussions in the classroom site for this study.

This performative view of self and context coincides with Bakhtin's (1981) argument that what may appear to be an individual utterance is constituted in social interaction. In their glossary entry for Bakhtin's concept of "heteroglossia," Emerson and Holquist (cited in Bakhtin, 1981) underscored the importance of context:

> [Heteroglossia] is that which insures the primacy of context over text. At any given time, in any given place, there will be a set of conditions—social, his-

torical, meteorological, physiological—that will insure that a word uttered in that place and at that time will have a meaning different than it would have under any other conditions. (p. 428)

A performative view of classroom context complicates a central tenet of social constructivist learning as it has been represented by literacy researchers and educators in recent years—that classrooms should serve as unified learning communities. Such classrooms are "student-centered," the literature suggested, sites where students can share their voices equitably in talk and writing about texts. However, some literacy theorists have questioned the reality and even the desirability of such classrooms, warning that within them social conflict and difference are often masked (Dyson, 1992; Finders, 1997; Hynds, 1997; Lensmire, 1994). Pratt (1987) criticized the utopian nature of this view, arguing that speech communities are not linguistically or socially unified. An idealization of community works against the processes that need to take place in classrooms where language should be used both to critique and produce social relations (see also Phelps, 1988). Harris (1989) also called for rethinking the concept of community. Drawing on his own ambiguous identities related to social class, he described the "tense plurality of being at once part of several communities and yet never wholly a member of one" (pp. 11–12). Extending this argument to the classroom, Harris proposed that classroom discussions should focus more on how competing discourses shape social practices than on achieving community consensus.

Rather than being conflict-free, classroom communities are subject to the everyday tension and the regular give and take of conversation between members of a community who have differential needs, beliefs, patterns of interaction, and positions of power or status—members who must share certain norms and standards of the classroom culture, but who are themselves participants in cultures beyond the classroom. Turner (1969, 1982) referred to conflicts within communities as social dramas that grow out of the multivocal nature of rituals and their meanings. Social dramas, he argued, have the potential to shape subsequent performances and lead to cultural growth. In this way, through conflict within communities, context is dynamic.

Turner (1974) used the term *communitas* to represent the dialectical relationship that exists within social groups between unity and disunity, similarity and difference, and conservation and reformation. Communitas rather than community embodies the social drama and struggle that can lead to cultural growth. Such social drama often occurs in liminal spaces, existing between social worlds. Schechner (1988), an anthropologist whose work was influenced by Turner, used the term *creases* to describe these liminal spaces—spaces where, for example, the unofficial world of unsanctioned literacy might overlap with sanctioned literacy. Rejecting the discourse of marginality, Schechner (1988) insisted that such creases are "places to hide, but more importantly they signal areas of instability, disturbance, and potentially radical changes in the social topography" (p. 164).[4]

Two ethnographies of education that use a performance and ritual framework have had a particular influence on this study. The first, by the anthropologist Foley (1989), is a study about youth in a predominately Mexican American town in southern Texas. In this study, Foley viewed ordinary classroom speech events as performances that reproduced or resisted dominant cultural codes in the community. The second, by McLaren (1993), is similar in its close examination of classroom ritual as it is constituted within broader cultural systems. Although McLaren argued that Turner's later work broke with structural-functionalism, McLaren's study is organized around Turner's (1969) early binary opposition of structure and antistructure. McLaren's study, which focuses on Portuguese students in a Toronto Catholic high school, equated classroom conformity with structure in Turnerian terms, and resistance with antistructure. Within these categories, however, his analysis is nuanced as it reveals the way that resistance can cause shifts in power and status.

Given a dynamic, shape-shifting view of context, Bauman and Briggs (1990) argued that researchers must attempt to "discern how the participants themselves determine which aspects of the ongoing social interaction are relevant" (p. 68). Whether students perform for the teacher or for particular peers during a literature discussion, for instance, might shift depending on a student's intellectual engagement or relationship with teacher and peers. Moreover, the ways that a student performs may relate to the degree to which the contextual discourse is authoritative in that it does not invite addressivity or transformation (Bakhtin, 1981; Bauman & Briggs, 1990). A central notion in Bakhtin's (1986) work is the sociocultural constitution of utterance, with a speaker's utterance embedding prior and anticipated utterances.

Within a performance perspective, Bakhtin's work is invoked in the work of anthropologists Bauman and Briggs (1990) as they discussed the nature of

---

[4]One sees these "creases" at work in Dyson's (1997) description of how two African American girls, marginalized by European American male classmates, used sanctioned literary practices to rewrite their stories and revise their positions in the classroom.

speech events (see also Bloome & Egan-Robertson, 1993; Brooke, 1991; Dyson, 1992). Their work underscores the Bakhtinian theory that features of one social language embed in another—what Bakhtin called *interanimation*. Wertsch (1991) pointed out that Bauman and his colleagues developed notions about speech genres that follow Bakhtin's in that they, too, highlight the emergent quality of speech performances. A performative view of literacy sees context as dynamic and manifold in its relation to performers. An individual or group performance is created by context that is re-created by the performance. This study is grounded in a theoretical framework that accepts such dynamic interplay as central to classroom life, and this dynamic context will be evident throughout the book.

The Sociopolitical Dimension of Reader Response

Aligned with a performative view of context is a perspective on response to literature based in the social stances (Beach & Lundell, 1998) of readers and texts. These social stances, positioned as more or less powerful related to each other and to broader social structures, are central to my understanding of the literary culture of the classroom I studied. Whereas reader response theory is often associated with private, internal response, the reader–text relation has long been framed in more sociopolitical terms. For instance, according to the literary theorist Bennett (1979), it is a relation that involves readers who are formed as particular subjects and texts that are formed in ways that promote a set of available readings. Similarly, Bakhtin (1981) situated ideology at the core of textual interpretation, asserting that "a particular language in a novel is always a particular way of viewing the world, one that strives for a social significance" (p. 333). Ideology as embodied in texts is especially significant in discussions of children's literature, in light of the socializing and enculturating functions such literature often serves (Hollindale, 1988; Nodelman, 1996; Taxel, 1989). With this enculturating function in mind, Enciso (1998) argued that it is important to teach students to "talk back" to texts and to each other as they take up positions in relation to the text and their classmates.

According to critical theorists, literature instruction should invite students to question the discourse that shapes their experiences as well as to resist textual ideology that promotes dominant cultural assumptions. Feminist and multicultural theorists have long espoused this position. Early work by Fetterley (1977) argued that readers must engage in resistant readings to contest normative patriarchal tendencies embedded in the text. In more recent work, Felman (1993) acknowledged the function of resistance in feminist readings, but argued that readers must resist from inside rather than outside the text, reading for competing positions that represent forms of resistance within the text. hooks (1991), in discussing what she saw as critical fictions, stories that challenge dominant discourses and reading practices, argued that the imagination should not be viewed as "pure, uncorrupted terrain" (p. 55) but as colonized by dominant discourses. Notwithstanding these perspectives on reader response, few studies of literary response in elementary classrooms derive from a critical stance.

Although reader response theory takes many forms (Beach, 1993; Tompkins, 1980), including the sociopolitical, the way that it has been practiced in schools—largely in opposition to New Criticism—is to highlight the life of the reader through personal response. Rosenblatt's (1978, 1995) work on reader response is most often cited to support this focus, despite the insistence of many scholars that her work does not easily fit that mold given its focus on the dialogic relation between the reader and text (Cai, 1997; Pradl, 1996; Willinsky, 1990). However, Rosenblatt (1988) acknowledged that her view of the transactional does not include a "reading" of the ideological content of the text. The primacy of the individual reader is clear in Rosenblatt's (1991) own words about her transactional theory: "The importance of the cultural or social context is stressed, but transactional theory sees the convention or code, as, e.g., in language, as always individually internalized" (p. 60). In his recent review of research on response to literature, Marshall (2000) made the important point that misrepresenting the nuance and breadth of reader response theory and criticism limits the potential of its classroom application.

A growing number of researchers and theorists note that reader response as it has been applied to English and language arts education fails to acknowledge the sociocultural constitution of textual interpretation and evaluation. Freebody et al. (1991) objected to the valorizing of what reader response advocates refer to as the reader's "personal response," asserting that these presumably internal subjective responses are instead constructed within cultural ideologies. These critics (and others, including Baker, 1991; Corcoran, 1994; Edelsky, 1994; McCormick, 1994; Morgan, 1997; O'Neill, 1993) all share the view that by valorizing the personal, educators ignore the ideological. Because ideological positions are often naturalized within a text, students encouraged to respond personally are not likely to consider the multiple subject positions one could take in relation to the text (Davies, 1993a). A more important response to engender in students, these critics claim, is an awareness of the text as constructed world. Indeed, Knoblauch and Johnston (1990) suggested that from early schooling on, the constructed nature of the text and the talk should be a primary focus of the curriculum. In a similar vein, Millard (1994) argued for a pedagogy that makes visible to students the constructed nature of interpretive conventions, a pedagogy that teaches students that particular ways of reading are, indeed, conventions rather than natural processes.

As this chapter underscores, the reading and discussion of literature are socially and culturally defined practices. Understanding the nature of such practices within a specific classroom requires an analysis of the performative roles enacted during literature discussions and a careful rendering of the social and interpretive norms and expectations at the site. *Literary Practices as Social Acts* takes on this project.

2

A Social Geography
of the Classroom
and Surrounding Community

This chapter weaves data from interviews together with observational field notes to re-create the individual threads of participant voices within the fabric of the school community.[1] First, I start with the focal students who were central to this study, closely examining their lives through the lens of status, both social and academic. For each student, I include the student's social class and ability level as perceived by their teacher (see Table 2.1) and then augment this perspective with additional ethnographic data about the student's social and academic identities within the school, classroom, and community.[2] Second, I consider the larger context that shaped who these students were, examining the school and surrounding community. Third, I focus on how literacy education was discursively constructed in the district and the school, and how the practices surrounding literature were arranged in Julia's classroom.

---

[1]The following conventions are used in the presentation of transcripts: [text] indicates descriptive text added to clarify elements of the transcript; *text* indicates emphasis; text indicates overlapping utterances; ( ) indicates unintelligible words; … indicates extracts edited out of the transcript; / indicates interrupted or dropped utterances.

[2]I decided to foreground the teacher's point of view because my research questions focus on how meanings within this classroom have been discursively constituted. Although the designation of one's social class background and ability are not constructed entirely through the teacher, the teacher has a primary role in shaping the authoritative view of student identity in the classroom.

TABLE 2.1

Research Participants

Focal students (Each student chose his or her own pseudonym)				
Name	*Grade*	*Socioeconomic Status (Teacher-Rated)*	*Ability (T)*	*No. LDG Observed*
James	Fifth	Working class	Low	4
Jason	Fifth	Working class	Middle/low	4
Nikki	Fifth	Middle class	High	5
David	Sixth	Middle class	High	4
Mackenzie	Sixth	Middle class	High	5

Teacher

　　European-American and middle class; late 40s.

　　Literature-based reading program.

　　Strong identity as a reader and writer.

　　Strong commitment to literacy learning and teaching.

　　Emphasis on student decision-making and collaborative work.

Parents of focal students: Secondary sources

　　James's mother.

　　Jason's mother.

　　Nikki's mother and father.

　　David's mother and stepfather.

　　Mackenzie's mother.

Administrators: Third-Level sources

　　Principal of Emerson School.

　　District director of curriculum.

　　Literacy specialist (for three schools).

Note: LDG=Literature Discussion Groups

THE FOCAL STUDENTS

Here, I present a detailed portrait of each focal student to help readers understand how these students have been constructed through social conditions and practices that shape their relations to texts and their interactions with their teacher and classmates. These portraits provide a basis for understanding the complexity of the literature events depicted throughout the book. I start with a discussion of each student in terms of teacher, parent, and self-perceptions of classroom and community status and academic standing. Each student is characterized by a section title that includes a phrase spoken by another participant in the study. Most often, the speaker was the classroom teacher, whose characterizations were very important in representing how each student was positioned as a member of the classroom community. On two occasions, however, the most revealing characterization of a child came from his or her parent.

I begin this section with portraits of two sixth graders who were powerful both socially and academically, David and Mackenzie. I turn next to Jason and James, two fifth graders who were not academic and social leaders, but who spoke, sometimes with power, from the margins. Finally, I present Nikki, a fifth grader whose power ebbed and flowed and whose role within the classroom remained in flux.

David: "The Head That Wears the Crown"

The title of this section refers to the phrase Julia used during one of our interviews to describe David, a phrase that underscores his position as leader among his fellow students. David, a sixth grader designated as middle-class and high-ability, held high status within the classroom and the community. He lived with his mother and stepfather in a split-level home just outside the Emerson district. His stepfather was an attorney and his mother was employed by an educational firm. His father, with whom he shared a close relationship, was an artist who provided him with much exposure to the art world. David's mother loved to read and enjoyed discussing a wide range of topics with her son. Whether discussing work or David's experiences at school, books or politics, David's stepfather told me, "There just isn't anybody that's better company" than David.

David had short, sculpted hair and delicate features. Like many kids his age, he used clothing to establish his identity. He wore knee-length shorts even on cool days in late fall and early spring, pairing them with an oversized t-shirt and an unbuttoned flannel shirt. He and one of his closest friends wore oversized striped stocking caps in the fall and winter, which David would hang from his belt loop during the day because he was not allowed to wear a hat in school. David often asserted his individuality. He preferred reading books that most of his peers did not read, and he was annoyed when his passion for the *Redwall* series (Jacques, 1987) caught on among most of the sixth-grade boys.

During my first formal interview with Julia, she noted with pleasure that David "never is not on my side." My field notes are full of examples of David's helping other students, actively participating in discussions, doing the work he was asked to do, and generally fulfilling the role adults in his life would want him to fill, yet I learned that he often got into trouble outside the classroom for talking back or fighting. David was able to manage multiple performances, including adult-pleaser, engaged learner, and rebellious youth, while retaining his leadership status. He might, for instance, pose an intriguing question about a book during class discussion, then lean toward a friend to whisper and laugh. Or he might poke and tease a friend, then shift effortlessly back to the discussion as though he had known, all along, that learning meant more to him than goofing off.

When I asked David during our final interview how he would describe his role in the classroom, he first said that he was always "goofing off," but then added that "Mrs. Davis always says that I'm a leader." His self-defining discourse, then, matched the good boy–bad boy dichotomy that seemed central to how others viewed him. Julia would often joke about David's power over other boys in the class, how they would ask him if they could come to his house after school and follow him wherever he led them on the playground. One of his peers, in an end-of-year awards list, bestowed on David the title of "Best Male Leader."

Having had David in her class since fifth grade, Julia felt comfortable in her relationship with him. Commenting on his strengths, Julia noted that, "Even after he's done something dreadful he talks well to adults," adding that for David, communication was important; he rarely shut people out.

By the end of the year, however, Julia experienced the harshness of his judgment when David decided that she was too controlling and "sexist" in favor of girls (letting them off the hook, he felt, in ways that she would never let off boys). During our final interview, Julia told me about one way she felt David had changed over the year. "He decided we [teachers] were the enemy. And that to be cool with the guys, he had to choose between his relationship with me and his relationship with them."

Once during a book discussion, David mentioned that kids were power-less in school. "What would make it better?" I asked. "Nothing—there is nothing you can do as long as there is a teacher in the room. They have every single power over you. So that's what makes kids powerless."

His parents felt that David was simply ready to move on to junior high, and believed that he had been well served by his 2 years with Julia, whom they felt had challenged him to work hard and think critically. They thought that at times David could be "unforgiving," and believed that had he ended up with a teacher for whom he had less respect, he might have given that teacher a difficult time.

Although David did well in school, he believed that Julia picked on him more than she did other kids, perhaps because she expected more out of him. David's mother, on the other hand, felt that Julia challenged David and his classmates academically: "Julia doesn't talk down to children at all. It's real adult vocabulary, kind of like almost as if she were talking to an adult. I think that that is something that David really responds well to."

Throughout the year, Julia emphasized to David that "what he does mat-ters because he is hero worshipped by a lot of kids," and so she was disap-pointed when in February he dropped a less academically and socially successful boy, James (another focal student), from his circle of friends. When Julia encouraged David to give James another chance, he com-plained that James pirated writing from other students' computer disks in the writing center and continued to brag about not doing his homework, even though David told him that such bragging was "stupid." Julia ex-plained to David that because James cared about him, his messages to James might eventually make a difference. Toward the end of the year, when one of David's official roles in his class was to act as a kind of tutor and support person for James, they renewed their friendship.

David's popularity extended to girls as well. During his final interview, he mentioned that the most memorable experience of sixth grade was hav-ing become friends with girls and having had two girlfriends during the course of the year. Early in the year, Mackenzie (another focal student) told me that last year's sixth-grade boys were a better group. When I asked if she was friends with David and a few other boys, she said that David was popu-lar, but she didn't like him because he didn't "hang around with a nice crowd." By the end of the year, however, Mackenzie's mother mentioned her daughter's closeness to many of the sixth-grade boys, identifying David by name as one with whom she was close, and I often saw David in the schoolyard after school with a large group of sixth-grade boys and girls.

David's status in the community outside of school matched his status in the classroom. His mother called him a "social leader," the friend who most often made the plans and set the agenda. He spent most days after school with his friends and occasionally participated in sports or various lessons. He had a friend for each of his interests: Dungeons and Dragons, building with Legos, reading, and collecting comic books. Both David's mother and stepfather described David as an intelligent and curious child with many interests and talents. In addition to reading and writing, David loved to produce art, particularly sculpture. His drawing graced the cover of the class literary journal and he was called on whenever an art project surfaced in the classroom. David's other well-known interest was anything medieval. He had a great deal of knowledge on the subject, particularly in the area of medieval weaponry, and so he served as the class expert during two related units, one in which the students read novels that took place in medieval times and one in which students researched topics and wrote reports about the Middle Ages, culminating in an elaborate medieval feast.

David answered my question about how he would describe himself by saying, among other things, that he thought he did well in school ("at least that's what my mom says"). Indeed, according to his parents, he always did his homework without complaints, and, from my perspective, he wrote thoughtful journal entries in response to literature. During the time of this study, David won third place in a citywide writing contest, and his responses during literature discussions were appreciated by his teacher and several of his classmates. Nikki and Mackenzie both mentioned his comments as being particularly thought provoking, not ones with which they always agreed, but ones from which they learned. At the end of the year, Emerson School participated in a Presidential Academic Fitness program, initiated during President Clinton's term in office, and David was one among several students nominated by classmates to represent his classroom as an academically fit student. When David's mother heard that he was invited to be part of this study, she told him that he must be a good reader for a researcher to be interested in his reading. David told her that I wasn't choosing only good readers because I had chosen James as well, demonstrating his awareness of who had academic status and who did not.

Mackenzie: "Socially Literate"

Many of my conversations with Julia about Mackenzie, a sixth grader designated as middle-class and high-ability, centered on her social power.

Mackenzie was described by her teacher as "socially literate" and someone
for whom "social power was all that mattered." Her mother described her
daughter as "powerful."

As I write about Mackenzie, her social power looms large in my mind as
well. Mackenzie led, organized, facilitated, and, at times, controlled her
peers. A tall girl, she wore neatly coordinated outfits, usually leggings and a
long top or tunic. Most often, she wore her hair tied back with a bow to
match her outfit. Mackenzie could be helpful and solicitous of others—asking a non-native-speaking student if he needed help, for instance—or she
could be exclusive—telling another sixth-grade girl that she wasn't invited
to a party. Many of the fifth-grade girls found Mackenzie and Brooke (one
of her closest friends and another powerful student in the class) to be unwel-
coming. Nikki, also a fifth grader, told me that "Emerson has always had its
popular kids," and she named Mackenzie among this group that "always
wear these perfect little, new clothing, matching," adding indignantly that
"the people in that group are favored by the teachers."

At the end of the year, the sixth-graders wrote essays about what had
been most memorable for them in their years at Emerson. In writing about
fifth grade, Mackenzie remembered her fifth-grade boy–girl party, the first
mixed-gender party for her age group. It had been the talk of the school, and
I heard quite a bit about it during my time with the sixth-graders. As Julia
described it, "She invited hundreds of people and created romances....
[She] perceives herself as getting couples together, as maneuvering other
people's personal lives. So she's a terrific social force."

Mackenzie's social awareness extended to me. Of all the focal students,
Mackenzie was most aware of my presence in her world. She was the only
one who went out of her way to talk to me during free time, lend me books
that she thought I ought to read to my sons, and make efforts to show me
photos and other emblems of her world without my asking. At times she
wore my interest as a badge of honor, mentioning in front of another student
who had wanted to be part of the study that her mother planned to have me
over for dinner (which never occurred) and telling her friends of our upcoming interviews.

Mackenzie, of all the focal students, most obviously valued adult conversation. She sought it from me and from Julia (much preferring literature
groups with Julia present, for instance). Her relationship with Julia was so
important to her that she started the year in a state of despair over what she
saw as the change Julia had undergone since the previous year. According
to Mackenzie, Julia so pined for the group of sixth-grade girls who had left

for junior high that she now seemed sad all the time. When I pointed out that she didn't seem sad to me as a newcomer to the class, Mackenzie said that this was because I hadn't known what she was like last year when that particular group of sixth-grade girls was able to make her laugh all the time. To me Julia seemed perfectly happy with her class, although it is true that she often talked about the particularly intelligent group of girls from the year before whom she had enjoyed immensely and thought would go on to do great things. All year, it was important to Mackenzie to compete with the shadows of the girls who had gone on to junior high. When it was time to publish the class literary journal, Mackenzie told me that she had met her goal to have as many stories in the journal as her friend had had last year (never mind that several were less than a page in length). Mackenzie had had a special relationship with another adult at the school as well—the former media specialist from whom she had won a special award at the end of her fifth-grade year for having read the most library books of all the students in the building.

Mackenzie's family lived in an older, brick, two-story home near the school. Her father worked in sales and her mother was completing an undergraduate degree at the nearby university. Her mother told me how much the family enjoyed their time together. "We're all activists in our own way," she explained. "We all have, um, issues—community and world issues—that strike us at different levels, you know." Mackenzie's mother initiated much talk at home about feminist issues and social dynamics, and the whole family, including the children, gave their time to various social action organizations. On occasion, Mackenzie's mother shared feminist texts with Mackenzie and took her to hear feminist speakers. In fifth grade, Mackenzie decided to add her mother's family name to her own last name. Julia talked about Mackenzie's family in terms of dreams fulfilled.

> [Mackenzie's] parents see themselves very much as children of the sixties, who have been lucky in love, lucky in family. They have chosen wisely. They have chosen each other wisely. They have been very lucky in having very strong families. They are both from very strong families, and have been successful at doing their own thing, getting what they wanted. Their house is adorable. Mackenzie said, you know, it is their dream house. They often talk about dreams being fulfilled in that family.

Mackenzie openly referred to her family's closeness. Once, when Julia asked students what they would miss most if they were on the ocean for an extended time, Mackenzie said "My house and the safety I feel there." Mackenzie and Chelsea (another of her good friends) were to attend space camp together over the summer, but Mackenzie was worried that she would miss her family too much. Her mother told me that the entire family might take a trip to Florida at that time to be close to Mackenzie while she was at camp. Secure relationships were very important to Mackenzie. During my first foray into the cafeteria, I sat with the sixth-grade girls who felt responsible for acclimating me to their world. Brooke, one of Mackenzie's best friends, dramatically swept her arm across the row of girls, proclaiming, "These are all my best friends; they all live near me." Then, with no provocation, Mackenzie recited all the last names of her classmates from her kindergarten class in alphabetical order—a smooth and apparently accurate recitation. The underside of Mackenzie's hinged desktop at school was plastered with photographs of friends, many of them in Julia's class, taken at sporting events and parties.

Mackenzie's status in the classroom was evident throughout the year: She was one of two students, both girls, elected to student council after Julia gave the class the direction to elect someone whom they could trust to speak for them. She was the student coordinator for the school's conflict resolution program. She was ordained queen of the medieval feast, presiding in a blue velvet gown her mother had found at a consignment shop. She and Brooke were nearly always self- or teacher-selected leaders during peer-led literature discussions. When I asked Mackenzie how she would characterize her role in her classroom, she said, "To talk when no one else will. I'm right behind Brooke in that." Mackenzie made her preferences known, as when she was going to be out of town for one of two end-of-the-year class parties and tried to insist on holding the one she most wanted to attend on the day she would still be in town. In May, Mackenzie's family took a trip to Switzerland to visit neighbors who were there for the year. While she was gone, Julia and I both noticed that the sixth-grade girls spent less time huddled together and more time talking to others in the room. When she returned she brought initialed lace bookmarks for her best friends, showed them photographs from her trip, and drew them all together again.

Mackenzie excelled both socially and academically. She was enrolled in the school's program for "talented and gifted" students. During the year of this study, she completed a project on the Holocaust, about which she had read many books, both fiction and nonfiction. As I mentioned, Julia often asked her to facilitate small groups, and even when she was not formally in charge, she would take on the privilege and the responsibility. Once, at the very start of the year, I observed her enter a "cooperative learning" group of three other students. The two girls in this group, Mackenzie and a fifth-grade girl, proceeded to work together to complete the project, barely acknowledging the two fifth-grade boys in the group (both of low status socially and academically in this classroom). Realizing that perhaps she should include the boys, Mackenzie asked "Do you guys know what we're doing?"

Indeed, Mackenzie viewed the girls in the class as being academically superior to the boys: "I've noticed that mostly girls are in the higher reading groups. I just realized something. The one group that I rated the nine [a high rating] is all girls." Mackenzie's perception of ability groups for reading is particularly interesting in light of the fact that Julia did not form reading groups according to ability. (Chapter 4 explains reading group formation.) When, during our final interview, I asked Julia to talk about how she thought Mackenzie had changed during her sixth-grade year, she said that she had become more equitable socially and more organized intellectually.

Jason: "School Is School" and "Home Is Home"

Jason, a fifth grader designated as working-class and medium to low ability, did not engage his family in school activities. His mother told me, "I guess school is school and that is left there. And home is home."

My first interview with Jason's mother took place in November, just before the medieval feast. The majority of students and many of their parents were very involved in the planning and production of the feast: Students created coats of armor, planned the menu, practiced their play, wrote invitations, and enlisted their parents' help in making or buying costumes. Yet, when I spoke to Jason's mother, she said that she remembered a note coming home about the feast and had asked Jason about it, but he didn't seem to know much about what was going on, so she dropped it. When the feast took place, Jason's parents weren't there, and he had no costume prepared. Jason had opted not to be in the play, but there were other activities that involved being in character, and the entire feast was to take place in costume with "authentic" food. On the day of the feast, some students came with parents, stepparents, and grandparents, elaborately decked out in long velvet gowns or cloth tunics. Julia had suggested easy peasant costumes for those who did not want to spend much time on preparation, but Jason and a few other children in the class came without costumes. Julia came prepared with burlap, however, and fashioned peasant-wear on the spot (although I doubt that the irony of status escaped her).

A husky boy with broad shoulders and a tentative smile, Jason was quiet and accommodating. When he was asked to contribute to class discussions, he would quietly respond or say "I don't know." During interviews, Jason did not use my questions to springboard into issues of concern to him as did most of the focal students. Instead, he paused after each question, answering briefly but thoughtfully. When I asked specific questions about his position in his class, he explained, sometimes poignantly, what made him feel confident or insecure, excluded or included.

Jason's status in the classroom ranged from medium to low. Socially, he did not have close friends in the room, but he was not an obvious outsider. In an early field note, I noted that whereas other boys had begun to group together, Jason remained unattached and somewhat disengaged from others in the class. He was one of two students who took the bus to school, which meant that he had to leave class 10 minutes early and could not gather with the others in the schoolyard after school. As the year progressed and spring arrived, this gathering of friends took on an even greater importance. Emerson students tended to stress the importance of living nearby and knowing each other for long periods of time. Once, during a discussion about the school logo, I heard two girls inform two boys that the boys wouldn't have anything important to add because they had just started at the school that year. The girls then tried to outdo each other with the lengths of their own residences in the community.

Jason came to the school in third grade and lived in a ranch home in a rural area outside of town. His father was a plumber and his mother worked as a sales clerk in a store at the mall. His mother liked to read, but often only had time for the newspaper. She wished Jason would read more at home, noting that he only read at home when required. The men in the family liked to hunt and Jason and his brother were active in sports. When I asked Jason what his role was during literature discussions, he told me he was "a listener." At home, his role was to "kind of play sports."

Julie explained that during a conference, she had taken Jason's mother to the school library to look at the books that Jason could and could not read. Julia had the sense that Jason's mother thought she could just bring home the right books and fix the problem immediately, and connected what she saw as a lack of knowledge about educational issues to her perception that the family privileged sports over academics:

> It is perfectly all right with her because his brother plays football. His brother has those pins made with his picture on them. Jason is going to fol-

low in his footsteps. He's going to be fine. I mean Jason is going to be perfect for what they want of Jason.

On occasion, when Julia spoke to me, she was interested in getting a strong message across quickly, and so would speak dramatically about a child's situation in the class or at home. This was such a case. Other statements that Julia made about social class issues were far more complicated in that they considered the competing influences of income, education, and individual characteristics. In this case, however, Julia's words suggested a reification of Jason's status in the room based on what she had inferred about the family's embodied dispositions toward schooling (Bourdieu, 1990).

Of all the focal students, Jason was the only one whose academic ability Julia readily labeled. She mentioned several times, for instance, that Jason was good at "going through the motions" with very little content to back it up: "He can't make a contribution to a group. He can look like a member of a group really well, without ever having any investment or being able to make any contribution. And he kind of knows it, so that is a little scary." For the first small group literature discussion of the year, Jason chose to read *Alanna: The First Adventure* (Pierce, 1983). Of the 10 students in that group, 4 were fifth graders, the rest were sixth graders. All except Jason and one other student were verbal and confident. Jason was most often silent during the group discussions, to the point that his silence became an issue of discussion. Julia's interpretation of Jason's experience in the group was that he was "way too silent," and that the reason he was way too silent was because he often didn't understand what he was reading.

> He has school behaviors in the classroom.... He's just not a very thoughtful kid. And I think it's been, he's been swimming out of his depth for so long now that he doesn't, he doesn't know what it is to own something, to have it matter to him.

Julia often attributed to Jason a lack of self-knowledge that was not evident in my interviews with him when he would often explain his specific likes and dislikes during literature discussion groups. He was intimidated when sixth graders were in his group, perhaps due to his first negative experience with *Alanna,* and strongly preferred fifth-grade groups that focused on individual novels rather than on one group novel. Although he never attributed his anxiety about sixth graders to sixth-grade girls in particular, the truth is that it was the sixth-grade girls who were, by and large, successful and verbal students in leadership positions (see chap. 4). They were the ones who led the book discussions and, at times, reprimanded others for not completing their work or remaining attentive. Jason's favorite book group of the year had been an all-boy group at the end of the year for which the boys read individual books of their own choosing and engaged in animated discussions about scary plots. When I asked him if he liked it when others (often the girls) talked about ideas during book discussions, he said it was okay as long as it didn't take too long.

Julia tried, throughout the year, to offer Jason support for his ideas when he offered them to the class. Often when he initiated a comment during a group discussion, Julia tried to affirm or extend it (see chaps. 4 and 5). Once when Jason read from his journal during a discussion of *Alanna,* Julia pointed out that Jason had "picked up on something interesting" and went on to address his comment. So Julia tried, by word and action, to raise Jason's status in the classroom. She also attempted to make him feel more comfortable in her private communication with him. Jason wrote in a journal he shared with Julia that after school he would "go home and do nothing." Julia responded, "I'm sorry you 'do nothing' after school. How about staying to help someday? I buy pop, and we chat while we work." Here, she was referring to the time she spent after school with students who chose to stay and help her. Most of those students were sixth-grade girls, and Jason never joined them.

The students were aware that Jason wasn't performing to Julia's standards, particularly in the *Alanna* group, and three of my focal students speculated as to why he remained silent throughout most of the group. Their consensus was that although Jason might not have understood the book as well as others in the group, he learned just from listening, and was satisfied to listen. Jason told me, however, that he felt left out during *Alanna,* and that although the girls eventually invited him to speak, they didn't do so until everything he wanted to say had already been said. Jason perceived himself as a "medium" reader compared to others in the class and believed that his teacher and his peers also held that perception. My conversations with both the teacher and other students suggest that they saw him as somewhat less than a medium reader, not in terms of decoding print, but in terms of the expectations for discussing and interpreting texts that dominated this classroom, the interpretive competence I describe in chapter 3.

Jason's view of teaching and learning was traditional despite his experiences with student-centered classrooms at Emerson. Jason believed that his teacher's main interest was in correcting students when they made mistakes, and in turn, his main job was to be corrected. This view of learning extended even to his perception of the meaning of literature discussions. When I asked Jason why he thought his teacher wanted students to discuss books with other students at school, he told me that her purpose was "to make sure you read it." When I asked him if the discussions were helpful to him, he said, "Well, yeah … to correct things." In other interviews, when I asked more probing questions, Jason was very specific about the kinds of book groups he preferred and why, suggesting to me that he gave other meanings to and saw other purposes for literature discussions. In book groups where each student had read a different book, for instance, he liked finding out about new books and getting caught up in the plot of a book he hadn't yet read; however, when I asked questions about what teachers and students were supposed to be doing during these groups, his answers always referred to issues of correctness. For Jason, then, the manifest meaning of literature discussions was one of academic authority and control, despite whatever tacit meanings he found in them.

By the end of the year, Julia did think that Jason had grown, noting that "he saw school as less of a game. I mean I think it did matter to him what they [other students] thought." She told Jason and another fifth-grade boy that they were to be her leaders next year. (She attempts each year to recruit the sixth graders as model leaders and good examples for the fifth graders.) By contrast, in conversations with me, Julia bemoaned the fact that there were no fifth-grade boys that she could envision as sixth-grade leaders, much as David had filled that role during the year of this study.

Whereas Julia did think that Jason had made some progress academically over the year, his mother worried that Jason had regressed academically and socially. In my final interview with her, she told me that his teacher must not have thought he made much progress in reading because she had recommended him for a summer reading program. During our first interview, Jason's mother had mentioned that she was surprised to learn from Julia that Jason didn't talk much in class for social or academic purposes because his teacher last year had complained that Jason had done too much socializing. By our final interview, she expressed concern that Jason had lost his friends from last year without having made new ones. "He doesn't seem to care," she added and went on to explain that he was busy playing baseball and spending time with his family.

James: "Life Is a Job for This Little Kid"

James, wearing a T-shirt and print harem pants, rested his right knee on his chair, but kept his left foot on the ground. He leaned forward, elbows on his desk, his tousled hair in his eyes. Every few seconds, he glanced at the clock. In a few minutes, he would spring from his seat and be the first out the door at the sound of the bell. This was the James I saw on a particular day in October and, characteristically, throughout the year.

The title of this section refers to a phrase Julia used to describe James, a fifth grader designated as working-class and low-ability. It is a phrase that underscores his difference from other students in Julia's class. James lived with his mother and younger brother in an apartment on the first floor of an older home. His mother's fiancé lived with them occasionally as well, and stayed with the boys twice during the school year when James's mother was enrolled in a substance abuse program. During my first interview with James's mother, she had a job cleaning residential homes, but hoped to go to school or get job training some day. By our final interview, she was pleased to have started a job as a custodian for the nearby university, one that would provide her and her sons with benefits and insurance.

The first time I spoke to James's mother, she had just come out of a drug rehabilitation program and was trying hard to make changes in her life.

> James and I really don't have enough time together alone, but when we are to-gether alone, we talk a lot. He, uh, he opens up to me.... I think we have a pretty good relationship.... I think James is realizing more and more now that Mommy's getting better, and ... I see a new kid opening up and blooming.

By the time Julia was able to get in touch with James's mother for the first time it was November, but once they made contact they discussed James regularly. James had not been doing his homework, so Julia and his mother decided to put him on a reward system: For him to take wrestling lessons, he would need to complete his assignments. It was clear to Julia that James's mother wanted to do what she could to help James succeed at school, and she tried to welcome this interest and enlist her help. Julia was pleased to see that the family felt comfortable enough with her to let her know, by way of a note, that they couldn't afford the fee required to attend a class field trip, thus allowing Julia to request money from school funds so that James could attend.

By the end of the year, James's mother felt so good about her son's rela-tionship with Julia and his peers at Emerson that although the family was going to move, she intended to keep James at Emerson for his last year of el-ementary school. Emerson had been James's third school in 4 years, so she felt the stability would do him good, and her son had told her that he wanted to stay. She also felt that Julia really cared about James and that he had con-nected to some children for whom school success was a priority. She appreciated that James was not just being pushed along, but that his learning difficulties were acknowledged and addressed. There had been times when she thought Julia may have been too hard on James, but she now felt that the consistency was important and that it showed Julia's concern for her son.

James's mother felt that his school behaviors mirrored her own as a young student, and she worried that his lack of participation was viewed by his teacher as a sign that he wasn't learning.

> I was like James is.... I can get my report cards out and they look just like his.... You know, there's nothing wrong with that, but Mrs. Davis feels that he needs to speak out more, and that kind of bothers me because—just because he's quiet doesn't mean he's not learning.

She viewed James's problem to be primarily one of low self-esteem: "He doesn't feel that he's good enough sometimes, and his teacher and I agree that, um, he just almost sets himself up as a failure." Julia wanted all of her students to see themselves as powerful people, whether or not they did well in school, and so when James wrote what she felt was an inappropriately gruesome story (modeled, in part, after the Jeffrey Dahmer case) that nonetheless demonstrated some effort and creativity, she was pleased that the whole class was "riveted" by the piece, and believed that this kind of validation "gave him identity."

James's status within the classroom community fluctuated throughout the semester but was often fairly low due to the climate of this classroom that placed value on school success. In collaborative groups, his ideas were usually not taken seriously, and he often played a slightly resistant (either angry or goofing off) but manageable role. This was a role that the girls were scornful or mildly tolerant of and the boys either tolerated or appreciated. During book groups, James often tried to incite others not to pay attention by kicking them under the table or encouraging them to engage in resistant behaviors. He spent independent work times off task. When James didn't complete his assignments, students would, at times, try to protect him by covering for his failure to complete work. At other times they drew attention to his failure to meet their standards for competence. A few of the sixth-grade girls, in particular, would tell him to write longer journal entries, reprimand him for not having come to group with his homework complete, or rebuke him for not having read the assigned chapter. James said that his role in book discussions was to listen.

Early in the year, he chose to be in a group that read *Where the Red Fern Grows* (Rawls, 1961) and expressed real interest in the book. After a few meetings, however, he fell behind in his reading and journaling, so Julia recommended that he consider moving to a group that read historical books at their own pace. James said he wanted to remain in *Red Fern*. His mother thought he wanted to stay because the group included more of his friends. She also mentioned that he seemed to love the book and enjoyed having her read it to him at night. When I observed this group, I noticed that even when James did complete a journal entry, albeit shorter than his peers' entries, one of the girls in the group would ask him why his entry wasn't longer or why he hadn't completed all the work that was assigned. When I mentioned this to Julia, she was pleased that he was being confronted with the standards of his peers, especially in light of the standards students must meet with little help once they graduate to junior high. Although I usually didn't offer an opinion at such moments, I did this time, explaining that although I understood the need for standards, I worried that if the little he did was not appreciated, he would stop working entirely. Julia struggled with how much to push James. She tried hard to apply the same rules about reading group to James as she did for all of her other students, but she found that at times the best course of action was to ignore his lapses.

Eventually, James couldn't keep up with the work in *Red Fern* and had to drop out of the group (the second book group he had to drop). He explained to me that he was so far behind in math class (for which he had another teacher) that he was unable to keep up with his work in reading. Once, when James didn't come prepared for reading group, Julia asked him if it was worth reading ahead doing the journal to be part of the group. When he nodded, she asked him what would happen if she allowed them not to do their work. James paused a long time, then said, "They'd [the group would] lose trust in you." When Julia asked if that mattered to him, he said no, yet his reference to trust signified an awareness of the interdependency Julia hoped would become a classroom norm. James did have serious problems keeping up with his work in math and by April had accumulated a debt of 55 recesses owed to his math teacher for work not completed. Julia, who was required to supervise this punishment, allowed him to "serve time" after school rather than missing out on his only time to play outside during the day, but his mother complained that the time after school was the only time she had available to spend with her son. They resolved the problem by having James come to school early in the morning before the school day began.

At various times during the year, Julia and James's mother would work closely together and, for a short time, James would keep up with his work. When she reentered a substance abuse program in the spring, James's work went downhill again. At one point, his mother told Julia that she couldn't help James because things were not going well at home. Julia told James that he was going to need to take extra responsibility for a while and really work hard to keep his life together, but this talk did not have a lasting effect. Julia felt that James needed constant monitoring, and she began to think that he would benefit from extra help with a special education teacher the following year. James eventually qualified for resource help in writing, which meant that a resource teacher would come to his classroom to work with him when he started sixth grade.

James saw himself as a good reader, although he couldn't tell me what that meant. He pointed out, though, that Julia always told him he was a good reader. His actions suggested a certain closeness with Julia—for instance, she was the one he first went to when David dropped him from his circle of friends—yet he saw her role as teacher in terms of the authority she held over him. He only talked during book groups "when the teacher [told] him to," and he pointed out that it was Julia's job to make sure that students did their homework. Along with David and many others in the classroom, he also believed that Julia favored girls, especially girls who did all their homework.

During our final interview, James's mother pointed out that James had "a lot of ups and downs with some boys in his room this year," a reference, I think, to the changing relationship between David and James that I mentioned earlier. James's social status in the classroom waxed and waned depending on the strength of his relationship with David, the male class leader. Julia felt that David was an important influence on James because he loved learning so much and could show James that it was "cool to be smart." Once, when Julia asked at the start of a small group discussion if anyone had any "burning questions" about the book thus far, James jumped in to say that he had one. Both Julia and I saw this as a positive development for James. During our March interview, Julia referred to the relationship between James and David and how she believed that it ignited James's interest in learning:

> I mean it was like watching this desert. What David said watered his [James's] soul. You know, he just needed to hear someone say those things. And he was enchanted. And then he just modeled those behaviors. I mean he just did what he saw David do.

Because of the benefits she saw in this relationship, Julia wanted to renew the bond between David and James. After asking James's permission, she invited David to help James with his work. David told her that he didn't like James and didn't want him around. He later told me that James was too interested in violence, complaining that all he says is "kill, kill." Once, David asked James how he would feel if his father got killed, to which he replied, "I wouldn't care.... He's not my father anyway. He's my stepfather." Julia explained to David that she wasn't asking him to be friends with James, just to provide academic assistance. David agreed and this led to the renewal of their friendship. David told me that he had decided to forgive James but the other boys in the group did not, adding that "no one else really likes James."

Julia had been convinced from the start that James loved learning, and she maintained this stance despite his efforts to prove her wrong. Early in the year, Julia told me that she had caught James engrossed in balancing cubes on the science scales during indoor recess. She said that she told him that she thought he loved to learn. "I hate school!" he replied. However, she wouldn't believe him, believing instead that until now he hadn't had positive experiences in school.

James's mother felt, in the end, that James had undergone positive changes at Emerson over the year. He now seemed more interested in school, having expressed to her a particular interest in science. She still had a hard time getting him to read, but pointed out that reading was not what she usually chose to do with her free time either. James, himself, felt that he had improved as a reader because he now read more pages of the books he began than he had at the start of the year. I noticed that James, who was free most days after school, volunteered to help with various school projects as the year progressed: He stayed late one day with two other boys to work on his coat of arms for the medieval feast, and he participated in a car wash meant to raise funds for a bird sanctuary. Overall, his mother saw this as a good year for James, whereas Julia saw it as a year filled with both successes and failures.

At the end of the year, each student wrote a list of often humorous awards that they felt characterized the "achievements" of their classmates. In addition, the sixth graders created "wills" proclaiming what they would leave to the fifth graders after they went on to junior high. Reading how James was characterized by other students in these writings provided me with a window into his multiple positions within the classroom community. One fifth-grade girl gave James an award for being "the person whose name won't erase off the blackboard," a reference to the section of the board where Julia wrote the names of students who had homework past due. A fifth-grade boy gave

James an award for being "friends with David," an accomplishment of high status among fifth-grade boys. Other achievements included "wearing the same shirt everyday," being the "most enthusiastic *Beavis and Butthead* fanatic," and, most poignantly, having "the power to survive anything." Finally, David willed James "the power of that one seat in the principal's office that I always sit in during recess." These representations of James serve as a kind of commentary on his life in the classroom. In that he found both status and stigma through his disengagement and mild resistance, it seemed possible that James might, indeed, "survive anything."

Nikki: "Stirring Up the Chickens"

Nikki, a fifth grader designated as middle-class and high-ability, was characterized by her mother as the member of her family who was always "stirring up the chickens." In some respects that phrase characterized her role at school as well. For Nikki, who dressed indifferently, shoulder-length blond hair often tied back in a ponytail, this was a year in flux. The making of one's identity is always in process, but for Nikki the manifestation of that process seemed almost palpable: She could be withdrawn and sullen, or giggly and animated; eager to please, or eager to irritate; engaged and curious, or bored and critical.

As I analyzed interview transcripts and field notes to find some way to represent who Nikki was during her year in Julia's classroom, I marveled at the range of descriptions I found:

- "Nikki's going to be the first woman president" (spoken by a student impressed with a report Nikki presented to the class).
- "Nikki's so poetic" (spoken by Julia when Nikki said the illustration on a book jacket made her think of emptiness).
- "Nikki's so cool" (spoken by several fifth-grade girls in response to Nikki's scorn for sixth-grade popular girls).
- "Nikki thinks life sucks" (spoken by the fifth-grade girl with whom Nikki left the school grounds one afternoon, causing utter pandemonium).
- "Nikki has no sense of her own power in the classroom" (spoken by Julia after Nikki left the school grounds, got caught, and seemed surprised by the state of emergency she had left behind).
- "She isolates herself" (spoken by Julia).

- "She really participates, would volunteer, likes to get involved" (spoken by her mother).

- "Leave it to Nikki to ask wonderful questions" (spoken by Julia in response to Nikki's journal question about why women weren't named in a book they were reading).

- "She's been a child that likes to be challenged" (spoken by her mother when asked to describe Nikki).

- "Stirring up the chickens" (the title of this section, spoken by her mother in reference to Nikki's role in the family).

At the start of the year, Nikki was rather unassertive, although she described herself as "opinionated" and "sensitive," and her mother referred to her as "argumentative in a positive way." Yet, after her participation in the first small group literature discussions of the year, Julia worried that "she'd say such important things and never get heard." Although I did feel that Nikki asserted herself in that group, I would agree that others had not yet characterized her as someone to take notice of in class. However, many of her classmates eventually saw her in this light. In David's end-of-the-year list of awards, for instance, he gave Nikki the award of "the daringest."

Nikki was perceived by her teacher, her parents, and her peers as a strong student. Her mother said that Nikki liked to engage with ideas and enjoyed being challenged. Other focal students pointed to her interesting responses to literature, and Julia commented on her perceptiveness: "Nikki is such, she's so perceptive.... I don't know anybody who could say about a book as hard as *April Morning*—'I think it is about choice.' Holy cow!... I have never known a kid who can do that."

Julia often demonstrated her support of Nikki's contributions to class discussions, and during our January interview, Nikki told me that she thought her teacher valued her comments. However, at the end of the year, when I asked her how the class viewed her as a reader, she said, "I'm not quite sure, but I guess as an average reader." Considering her academic status in the class, it's difficult to make sense of this response. Perhaps she was being careful not to appear arrogant because this interview came after she ran away from school and temporarily fell from grace (discussed later in this section). She did say that she viewed herself as a "pretty good" reader. When I asked how she knew this, she said that she was in the gifted program, and that the topics Julia brought up during literature discussions were topics Nikki thought of independently when she read the chapters.

When I asked Nikki what book group she chose to be in at the start of the historical novels unit, she said that she had chosen to be in a group that focused on reading easier historical literature with the purpose of helping a student from Guatemala who had recently come to the school. Nikki told me that Julia asked her to change to the group that would be reading *April Morning* (Fast, 1961), a complicated novel about the American Revolution. When I asked her why she thought Julia wanted her to change groups, she said that she supposed Mrs. Davis thought her reading level was too high for the group she had chosen.

Nikki can be characterized as a strong student, but also one who could be oppositional. Although her behavior was not generally disruptive, her interpretive stance frequently contested dominant cultural assumptions. Because her teacher associated this trait with Nikki's intelligence, and because Julia herself often made attempts to challenge dominant cultural norms (see chap. 5), she was at least sympathetic, if not attracted, to Nikki's opposition. Thus, when Nikki questioned why it is that people readily label Hitler evil without understanding the larger conditions that contributed to the Holocaust, Julia supported this line of inquiry; when Nikki had an epiphany about the cultural influences at work on what she had always thought of as boys' "natural" behavior, Julia celebrated the discovery.

However, as the semester continued and Nikki's comments leaned more toward criticism than tolerance or compassion, Julia became concerned that Nikki was not doing herself or her classmates any good. At the end of the semester, for instance, Julia and I took a group of students to see *Schindler's List*. During the next week's discussion led by Julia, Nikki announced that she wasn't particularly moved by the movie. Later in the discussion Nikki questioned the certainty with which students identified a main character in the movie—one who murdered many Jews—as completely evil. Julia, who had found this movie to be very powerful, also felt protective of the one Jewish girl who attended the film. Consequently, Nikki's comments irritated her and added to her growing concern that Nikki was isolating herself and "creating a stance for herself from which she either responds to or opposes others."

Julia expressed this concern to me in January when she told me the following story about a conversation she had with Nikki. Nikki had been standing alone looking out the window when Julia asked her if she was being "antigroupish" again, a reference to an earlier conversation between the two during which Nikki told Julia she could do anything better alone than she could with the help of other people. Nikki said that she wasn't being

antigroupish, but was just thinking how unfair it was that the students outside had a longer recess than did Julia's class. Julia responded by telling
Nikki that although she's bright she had to have goals and realize there were
more important things to do than to criticize. She added that Nikki ought to
think about what she could contribute and try to be more positive. Nikki
was "a brilliant girl," Julia told me, and like many "gifted kids," she had a
very developed ability for critical thinking. Julia believed, however, that
Nikki lacked academic goals and persistence.

Around the same time, Nikki and her good friend Lisa approached me
and asked, "What would you do if we told you that we were going to com-
mit suicide so that the world can be changed, so that it can be a better
place?" I emphasized that I thought the future of the world would be infi-
nitely better off with them in it. Nikki said that the reason for committing
suicide wouldn't be to escape, but to make clear their commitment to
change, that it would be a way of having people make the world a better
place in their honor. I asked them how they would like the world to change,
and they pointed primarily to environmental issues. One could read Nikki's
critical stance not as one borne of boredom or apathy, but as one borne of
adolescent despair, a willingness to advocate for change, but a sense of
powerlessness about how to do it. Such a reading is supported, I believe, in
the following excerpt, the first paragraph of a piece called "A Letter" that
Nikki wrote for the class literary journal.

> Dear Humans:
>
> I would like you to see the world through my eyes today. Now, you must
> know my age. This is very important: I am eleven. I have ears and I am old
> enough to understand what I hear. I can hear, but can I be heard? A pencil and
> paper is probably the best way for me to be heard. So please consider this:

The rest of the letter addressed issues of concern to Nikki—wars, hunger,
school, children, animals, and the environment—and ended with a plea to
adults not to ask her for solutions to the problems she addressed.

Julia talked with Nikki's parents about her concerns regarding Nikki's
attitude, and they agreed to help their daughter set a goal for each week related to some aspect of her life, academic or social. According to Julia, they
felt that their daughter was so bright that she was bored in school, a discourse about giftedness that Julia found very unproductive, even harmful.
She felt that such a view sanctioned Nikki's behavior and took the responsibility of social and academic engagement off of Nikki's shoulders, where
Julia felt it belonged.

In my two conversations with Nikki's parents, however, they never mentioned the possibility that Nikki might be bored with school because she was too bright. Instead, they stressed what a good year they thought this had been for her, and made light of Nikki's complaints. In November, her mother told me that Nikki had said "how much she loved the classroom this year," pointing to the fact that both Julia and Nikki love literature. During our final interview, she said that she thought "Mrs. Davis was a perfect match for Nikki."

> I mean there was just this kind of bonding.... I just think she really identified with Nikki.... She seemed to have this really pretty open, expansive way of interacting with [students], treating them pretty much adult-like.... She was kind of sarcastic and ironic and all these things that you do with more adult-like people.

Nikki had mentioned, as did all of the focal students, Julia's different treatment of boys and girls. As was true of most opinions Nikki held, her views on this issue fluctuated. One of her main complaints was that the sixth-grade girls, particularly Mackenzie and Brooke, received special privileges, pointing out that Julia too often made them leaders of literature discussions. Nikki strongly preferred unstructured literature discussions and resented Mackenzie's and Brooke's attempts to control the agenda. She thought that the boys who were disruptive might not behave as badly if they were given more power and felt included. On the other hand, she also complained that disruptive boys were given too much attention for their bad behavior.

Nikki's mother mentioned that at times her daughter complained to her about some of the boys goofing off during group work. From her perspective, however, the multiaged class was a positive experience for her daughter because Nikki "looks at Brooke and Mackenzie and I don't know who else—but I know those two—and she sees that they are the leaders, and I think she's looking at what they do." Although most of what I heard from Nikki about Brooke and Mackenzie was complaints, she certainly noticed many things about them—how they dressed, what they said, how they took control—and by March Nikki and her friend Kate were poised to take over as leaders for the next year. Nikki, in particular, began to dominate discussions and assert her opinions.

I did not anticipate, however, the departure of Nikki and Kate from school on a spring day in May. It was the day the class would have a good-bye party for a practicum student from the university. I wasn't in class that day, but later talked with Nikki, her mother, Kate, and Julia about the event. From all accounts, Nikki and Kate walked away from the schoolyard while outside during lunch recess. About 2 hours later, they were found downtown, approximately 2 miles away from school. Before they left, they told two friends they were leaving, and one of them, concerned about her friends' safety, told Julia, who then informed central administration. Staff and parents from the building, staff from central administration, and officers from the police department all searched for the girls until Kate's mother found them walking down the street. An initial rumor placed the girls at the public library, which intrigued me for its possible connections to literacy. Nikki told me that several boys, James included, told her she was "stupid" to spend her time at the library. She was annoyed with this response and decided not to deny being there for a while, so the rumor persisted for a day or two. Nikki didn't think that leaving school would engender the response it did. The girls were consigned to inside suspension for 2 days and were allowed no recesses for the last month of school. They ate lunch in the main office.

For Nikki, this event was a turning point. Throughout the year, she had become progressively more oppositional, usually about aspects of dominant culture (the culture's emphasis on money, popularity, etc.). Her views were often in opposition to those held by other students and she expressed irritation with peers during our interviews. Leaving school served as an act of rebellion that made visible to Nikki how important it was to her to be viewed as a good student and to be trusted by adults: "But I guess it was just really scary that, like, no one would trust me. But I knew I was trustworthy. But I wouldn't be trusted anyway because I made a mistake."

Whereas Nikki viewed the experience as a mistake, her friend Kate viewed their transgression as a badge of honor. During a field trip in late May, long after Nikki wanted to put this event behind her, Kate had a caricature drawn of her and requested that the artist write the words "May 5, 1995" across the top, in commemoration of the day she and Nikki left school. Nikki's mother felt that perhaps Kate had more rebellion to work out than did Nikki, but the difference in their attitudes toward this event created a rift between them. Nikki became more eager to please, and Kate became less so. During our last interview, Nikki was far more inclined to express values about the classroom and about literature discussions that matched her teacher's.

It was difficult to catch up with Nikki for interviews, so packed was her schedule. Her commitments to gymnastics, viola, piano, orchestra, and a paper route left her little after-school time for friends, let alone interviews with me. She still maintained a fairly active social life on the weekends. Her mother, who was completing a graduate degree, and her father, a health professional, spent much time talking with their three daughters, engaging in discussions about politics, relationships, books, work, and school. When I asked Julia how she would characterize Nikki's social class, she described the family's social class in terms of their values:

> The most interesting child from the viewpoint of class, I think is Nikki, whom I view as being quite obviously middle class in many ways, and yet, seeing herself as being a victimized group—that life has been unfair, that the values of the majority culture are unfair to people like her and like the family. I mean all the way from being very extreme about any reference to medicine, to life not being fair. And I think that refers to money.

Nikki was very close with both her parents and shared many of their opinions. She realized, however, the strong influence that they had on her life and wanted to leave open the possibility that she would see things differently someday:

> So I mean maybe I will grow up and say, "Hey, I love antibiotics. I am going to get them everyday, you know. I have that choice [According to Nikki, her father thought antibiotics were overused.] I guess I just try not to be too much on my parents strong opinions because I know that they are, like, my role model. Really I probably don't agree with them on lots of things that I think I do.

At the end of the year, Nikki, along with David and a few other students, was nominated by her classmates for the Presidential Academic Fitness Program. She told me in our final interview that she didn't expect to receive the award, but would like to. Julia ended up giving the award to another fifth-grade girl in the class, although she felt that Nikki deserved the award on academic grounds. Julia had explained to the students that she saw this as an award that rewarded effort and attitude as well as academic strength, and she shared with me that Nikki did not put forth enough effort. Julia did include Nikki, however, among the students she believed had grown the most over the year.

SOCIAL CLASS AND RACE AT EMERSON SCHOOL AND ITS SURROUNDING COMMUNITY

Making as clear as I can relations related to race and social class in the school community is critical in light of my argument that literary practices are enacted by readers who have been constructed through social codes that shape their relationship to peers and texts.

Previously, I explained that many people in the Emerson community believed that this community fostered good relationships among people of different socioeconomic status, and Julia herself described her class as "classless."[3] Although social class is a contested category, one aspect of schooling in which various indicators of social class converge is in degree and kind of parental involvement. According to sociologist Annette Lareau (1987), social class differences shape home–school relationships in that working-class parents possess less cultural capital (Bourdieu, 1977) than middle-class parents. In other words, working-class parents are sometimes seen by those with institutional power as lacking in the right kind of knowledge, dispositions, material possessions, and professional credentials. Moreover, the institutional model for family involvement, despite enormous changes in the reality of family structures, is that of a two-parent, economically self-sufficient, nuclear family (David, 1989).

In terms of parental involvement at Emerson, the school district's curriculum director, Emerson's literacy specialist, and Julia all noted that parental involvement often took the form of sharing knowledge or expertise, a role many Emerson parents were professionally positioned to accept. Parents volunteered to offer what they could rather than to monitor the school, according to the curriculum director, thus creating a more relaxed atmosphere compared to other schools in the district where she felt that parents made more demands.[4]

At Emerson, parents were generally supportive of the curriculum and the teachers. Julia mentioned that most Emerson families were concerned about "moral, ethical, and philosophical" purposes for learning rather than competitive ones. She felt comfortable asking her students to request assistance or information (about topics discussed in school) from their parents. Students whose parents worked in professional occupations and had expertise that dovetailed with the curriculum, and students whose parents were frequent visitors to the school, readily volunteered their parents' services: David's stepfather helped to direct a class play. Mackenzie's friend Brooke, an affluent sixth grader, volunteered her parents as drivers for an evening field trip without even checking with them first. Steven's father, a medical school resi-

---

[3]At the time of this study, 16.9% of Emerson's students were eligible for free and reduced-price lunch.

[4]It is interesting to note that the schools she referred to were schools at which the parents were of higher social and economic status than many of the teachers.

dent, directed the students for 3 consecutive days in the dissection of a pig. A total of 14 parents volunteered to help with the medieval feast. Julia expected that her students' parents would have knowledge about the subjects the class studied. When the class started a unit on the Middle Ages, for instance, she suggested that students ask their parents for information about this period. Whenever Julia asked whose parents might be willing to volunteer for a particular project—a question she often asked—many hands went up.

I don't remember ever seeing either James's or Jason's hands raised on these occasions. After interviewing both boys' mothers, it became clear to me that these mothers were very interested in their sons' experiences at school; yet my interviews with the boys reveal a separation between school and home that was rarely bridged. Referring to the assumption often made about parental involvement, David (1989) argued that "an identity of interests and needs is assumed … between families of divergent social class and economic positions" (p. 52).

This assumption of common interests and needs was visible in even the ordinary workings of classroom life. Once, for instance, Julia asked students in a literature discussion group if they found writing useful to help them understand what they read. One girl, who later won the Presidential Academic Achievement Award, noted that she used journaling to keep track of "the big idea" so that it wouldn't escape her. Julia then asked Jason how he used writing. First, Jason tried to just repeat what his successful classmate had said, but Julia recognized this game and asked him to think harder about how he used writing:

Julia: Is there any other case that you, Jason, would just use writing?

Jason: Never.

Julia: Never. I mean can you imagine a case in the future at or do you see any adults around you, your brother or your mother or dad using writing when they read?

Jason: No

Here, Julia assumed a particular disposition toward reading and writing, one that reflects the central position literacy practices hold in the lives of many middle-class professionals. Using writing to enhance one's reading is a very specialized practice, one that takes a good deal of time and may be most useful for work that requires much complicated reading. The girl who used writing to keep track of big ideas was the girl whose family "flew to

Europe at a moment's notice." She was constituted in particular social codes and practices that profoundly shaped her interactions with texts— how she positioned them in her life and how she was positioned by them. The same was true, of course, for Jason.

Some parents' comments pointed to differences among those parents who most shaped the school's social atmosphere and those who had little influence in this regard. Nikki's father talked of feeling like an outsider when he attended meetings organized by the school's Parent–Teacher Association. He was surprised to find that he wasn't comfortable at the meetings because he generally felt comfortable in schools, but it seemed to him that at these meetings an inner circle of parents (whom another parent described as affluent) determined an agenda about which he had little input.

Jason's mother also described herself as existing outside the inner circle. As I mentioned in my description of Jason, his family lived in a rural area that received bus service to the school. His mother noted that when her neighborhood was first included in the Emerson district, their families were welcomed with open arms, but that now living far from the school contributed to her sense of alienation.

I interviewed the mother of a sixth-grade girl I had intended to include in the study but was unable to observe in literature groups a sufficient number of times. The mother was concerned that her daughter's friends were extremely competitive about school, sports, and clothes, and felt frustrated to hear about the exclusive shops where some of the girls purchased the latest styles. This mother was particularly uncomfortable with the sixth-grade graduation party planned for the end of the year. She felt that the mothers who were most powerful in the community, those who were most affluent and able to spend much time in the schools, had planned a party that was more like a prom, a party that would cost too much money to attend and exclude siblings and extended families whom she felt should be included. The middle-class mothers she mentioned saw this as a time for their daughters to have a memorable experience with their friends, whereas this mother saw the celebration as one that should to bring families together to share food and company. She mentioned another mother, also from a working-class family, who shared her point of view.

I draw attention to these competing points of view because of the tensions regarding social class that they represent. The two main organizers of the graduation party were among the most powerful and affluent in their community, and their daughters were extremely popular. As a peripheral friend of these girls, my former focal student was easily hurt by them, and often felt as though she didn't quite belong. When I asked Julia about this student's SES, she said that there was not a whole lot of money in the family, but that they had good friends and were really "rooted in the neighborhood," emphasizing again the importance of time and intensity of neighborhood involvement in determining social status. Yet, even in this idealized community with its apparent acceptance of others and respect for difference, one can see that just below the surface there were hidden tensions regarding issues of social class.

As an outsider attending a meeting organized by the Emerson Neighborhood Association, I was struck by the homogeneity of the 60 to 70 people who gathered together. No one of color attended the meeting I visited, and only one parent brought a child. The people in attendance wore casual clothing that, despite its studied utilitarian appearance (e.g., Birkenstocks, heavy wool sweaters), was quite costly. The architectural history of the neighborhood was the subject on the night I attended, a subject of much importance to many who have cultural capital within the Emerson community.

During our first meeting, I asked Julia to describe race and ethnic relations within the school community. She told me that the children were not racist, but that there were race problems in the community. During the course of our year together, race came up on several occasions, and I witnessed some of Julia's attempts to confront issues of race with her students.

Julia did not romanticize historical moments in race relations for her students. For instance, when she talked with the children about the Selma bus strike, she told them that in the end it was a "bittersweet" victory because the bus company didn't acknowledge any wrongdoing; thus, she alluded to a larger systemic racism that must be overcome before real change can occur.

One day when I came to Julia's class, she was at the front of the room with both her own students and the students from a neighboring class gathered around her. Apparently, while at recess, a White student had made a racist remark to an African American student, an encounter that was then reported to Julia. When I arrived, discussion of the incident was well underway. Julia spoke directly to the issue of prejudice as she discussed with students the consequences such actions have on the community they had worked hard to establish together at Emerson. Woven into her comments were examples of prejudice in the news at the time: the civil war in Sarajevo and the defamation of a Jewish temple in a nearby city. After a talk about the specific consequences that should be brought on individuals who make racist comments, and about the ways in which the victim and other observers can take back the power in such situations, Julia took the discussion one step further: "We're not having this talk because a student's feelings were hurt. That happens all the time. We're having this talk because it hurts everybody. It lowers our expectations for civility. If that's the way Emerson is, I don't want to be here." This talk revealed Julia's willingness to confront race relations among students, not only by focusing on individual pain, but also on the more wide-ranging effects of racism. Because the student to whom the racism was directed was the sibling of one of Julia's students, the reality of individual pain was also part of the picture.

In Julia's relationship with Miriam, one of two African American teachers who taught in the building at the time, the raced conditions of their lives were central to their conversations and to their understanding of each other's pedagogy. Julia's friendship with Miriam was based on the passion for literature they shared rather than on shared beliefs about the teacher's role. Miriam was comfortable with the authority she carried as a teacher, according to Julia, whereas Julia herself was more comfortable establishing a collaborative role with her students. Julia respected Miriam's views on pedagogy, however, and shared this story with me to help me understand the dynamics of their relationship. Once when Miriam had doled out a punishment to some students who hadn't completed their work, Julia worried about how Miriam would fare in this town of rather liberal, child-centered parents, also acknowledging her own belief that Miriam was being overly punitive. In talking about the situation with Miriam, Julia tried to convey her misgivings, arguing that whether or not the students did well in social studies wouldn't matter much in the long run. "And she [Miriam] turned to me in a flash and said, 'You can say that because you're White.'" Thus, Miriam made it clear to Julia that even at Emerson, race is central—not only to Miriam's identity, but to Julia's as well.

Emerson enrolled 46 students of color (12.8% of the student population). Nineteen of these students were international students who received instruction in English as a second language (ESL). Flags of each of their countries—Brazil, Cambodia, China, Guatemala, Hungary, South Korea, Vietnam, and Zaire—created by the students were displayed around the double doors leading to the building's administrative office, and the signs on the restroom doors were printed in seven languages. The wall adjacent to the main entrance of the building held a fabric wall hanging entitled "Celebrate Friends," comprised entirely of children's faces, some brown, yellow, red, green, or multicolored.

Emerson had a Multicultural Club, formed and facilitated by Miriam. Attended by racially and ethnically diverse students, the club's goals included "an appreciation of our country's diversity, an appreciation of other cultures, and identifying ways to deal with conflict constructively." Staff memos written by the principal often included messages and quotes dealing with issues of diversity. One staff memo, for instance, included the following message to teachers: "If you snicker at racist or sexist jokes, so will [your children]." Other memos included quotations from Kozol's (1991) *Savage Inequalities* about the discrepancy between the education we offer rich as compared to poor children in this country. Despite these moves to foster a multicultural atmosphere, the only two African American teachers at the school were leaving at the end of the year to teach at another school in the district for reasons of which I am unaware.

The two material conditions of race and social class are important to this study. Although my focal students were not racially diverse, I attend to issues of race in the Emerson community because views about race shape the meaning of difference in classrooms, whatever the racial backgrounds of the students. As theories of deconstruction have taught us, discursive binaries (e.g., Black–White, Middle class–Working class) often serve to reify the two positions as they are defined in relation to each other.

Race and class are not distinct, of course, and in this classroom they intersected in uncommon ways. The three students of color in the classroom, two of them international students, were all middle-class to upper middle-class, and the working-class students were White. One student, Lisa, an African American student who had skipped a grade a year prior to this study, underscored the complexity of student identities through her explanation of the rigid memberships that governed seating privileges in the lunchroom. According to her scheme, later repeated by Nikki in a separate interview, the table where David sat held the popular sixth-grade boys; the table with Mackenzie and Brooke held the popular sixth-grade girls; the one where James sat held the fifth- and sixth-grade boys of average status; one table was reserved for unpopular fifth-grade girls; and another table was for popular fifth-grade boys; Lisa herself and Nikki sat at a table of "kind of popular" fifth-grade girls. Lisa, in limbo having skipped a grade, longed to sit with the sixth-grade girls, but was relegated to the fifth-grade table, ostensibly because she bought hot lunch, which was considered unacceptable at the sixth-grade table. Like most schools, Emerson's cafeteria marked boundaries related to status as defined by degree of popularity, which is often the way that children mark out difference (Eder, 1986). Gender, age, ability, popularity, social class, race—these identity markers intersect and compete to complicate life in school and create the social drama that shapes the local scene of the classroom.

LITERACY LEARNING IN THE DISTRICT AND SCHOOL

At the time of the study, Emerson School was one of 15 elementary schools in a district that included two junior high schools and three high schools (one alternative). The district mission statement boasted a "rigorous and creative" curriculum. Ties to the nearby university were strong. Teachers took classes and participated in research; university faculty presented workshops and provided consultation.

The elementary schools in the district began the shift to a holistic view of literacy learning in the 1980s by way of a grassroots movement of teachers. Teacher inquiry and experimentation initiated the movement and teacher testimonials and eventual staff development accounted for its adoption. In the district's literacy guidebook from 1986, teachers were encouraged to "integrate whole language into a basal framework," a framework that, by the time of this study, had been abandoned by most teachers at Emerson. Sections of the 1986 guide focused on novel units, literature discussions using Bloom's taxonomy, and observational assessment. Both Julia and the district's curriculum director reported the "basalization" of literature that characterized early attempts at thematic units that took the form of question packets, vocabulary study, and activities.

In 1992, 2 years before I conducted this study, the Language Arts Course Review Committee, consisting of administrators, literacy specialists, teachers, and parents, produced a new guidebook that made more explicit the whole language principles that were central to district practice. Drawing on such whole language educators as Holdaway (1979), Newman (1985), Calkins (1983), and Routman (1991), the guide offered teachers information on the theoretical underpinnings and practical applications of a holistic literacy program. Sections focused on language development, literacy models, reading and writing processes, and authentic assessment, along with sections delineating specific strategies and "minilessons" for literature discussions, reader's workshop, and writer's workshop, offered a comprehensive introduction to preferred practices in the district. These emphases remain in the newest rendition of the guidebook, distributed in 1997, but there are signs that the district is moving away from its philosophical roots in whole language.

Reading was a high priority in this district. Each building had a media specialist who, in addition to serving students, served as a resource to teachers with regard to literature for their thematic units. The curriculum director emphasized that reading for meaning was the "heart and core" of the reading program. She pointed out that teachers in the district had a great deal of flexibility to use their professional judgment in reading. New literacy initiatives were not mandated. Instead, staff development was offered and literacy specialists were available to help. Particular literature units were not required. Although copies of the thematic units that had been developed with district funds were centrally located, most teachers preferred to write their own or to collaborate with other teachers.

Emerson School's Language Arts Plan included a description of its reading program that reflected district philosophy. In kindergarten, children "participate in Shared Book Experiences"; the first- and second-grade unit had a "language-centered" reading program that added guided reading activities and skill work to choral and shared book experiences; the third- and fourth-grade unit continued to use a "language-centered" reading program that included novel units and an emphasis on "word identification and comprehension strategies"; the fifth- and sixth-grade unit used a "literature-based" program, focusing on novel units and self-selected books that were discussed in small groups and individual conferences.

Emerson's literacy specialist served Emerson and two other schools. Her responsibilities included developing the language arts building plan, providing consultation and resources to teachers as they implemented their reading and writing programs, working toward achieving consistency, and identifying students who had academic difficulties. According to both Julia and the curriculum director, the role of the literacy specialists varied, depending on the philosophy of the individual in the position, but in general, it was a powerful role in the district. The literacy specialists had teacher contracts and no formal evaluative power, but as Julia described it, they could make or break a teacher's reputation because they had access to a great many people in the district: "There are very few people that talk to a great number of other people in the district and on whose word your reputation rests." She went on to say that literacy specialists were among those few people. Because philosophies of the literacy specialists differed, and because there was no consensus about the meaning of whole language in the district, Julia felt that it was difficult for teachers to know what was expected of them: "I always feel like, oh wait a minute, this is a very silent system. This is a system, but it's really—we aren't articulating what it is we want."

The literacy specialist at Emerson was troubled by the lack of consistency in the building. She believed that each of her buildings needed to identify themes and core books at different ability levels for each grade. Her concern was that new, inexperienced teachers in the district and even experienced teachers who switched grade levels had no clear curriculum to fall back on. On the other hand, when I asked her what she thought most influenced the way the teachers in the building taught literature, she said that they were most influenced by their "sense of empowerment to make their own choices." She added that she was looking for "a balance of some structure and some freedom." In an effort to meet her goals, she enlisted the help of Emerson's principal who, despite his own inclination toward teacher choice, agreed that more consistency would clarify goals, help new teachers, and avoid duplication. Thus, several staff memos included messages about the need to coordinate themes and create a more cohesive program. Julia believed, however, that many teachers were more comfortable making their own decisions and would resist these moves toward consistency.

Emerson's principal was new to the building at the time of the study, having served as principal of a small-town school for the 2 years prior. He believed that his 18 years of experience as a fourth-grade teacher made him a credible advocate for teachers. Having been integrally involved in the state's Writing Project since 1979, as both instructor and participant, he spoke of the "profound impact" this experience had on his work as a teacher and administrator. In his view, the Writing Project worked because it changed people rather than practices, thereby empowering teachers to change their own practices, and he hoped to enact this model for change at Emerson. He was pleased to be in a district that he identified as both "kid-centered" in the classroom and "teacher-oriented" in the district, and noted that his beliefs about teaching and learning literacy were fairly consistent with district philosophy.

The principal felt that he could best communicate his beliefs about language learning to his staff by living them: He loved storytelling, often sharing stories in the classrooms and at staff meetings; he talked about books with students and staff and included memorable quotations in his staff memos; and, most of all, he hoped to give teachers a chance to discover what worked for them, a process he had valued as a teacher.

One question that I asked of the building principal, the curriculum director, and the literacy specialist brought a similar response from all three: I asked each to tell me what they hoped the students would get out of reading literature in school. All three initially emphasized the importance of enjoying literature, then went on to elaborate in different ways. The curriculum director said that literature is more engaging for kids to read, that they "naturally gravitate toward stories" both in their own writing and in their reading. The literacy specialist said that fiction is easiest for children to read and that there are many good books to choose from, in contrast to what she saw as a scarcity of good nonfiction. She added that it is easier to identify with the characters in narrative writing and that such writing lends itself to "heartfelt discussions." The building principal reported that he would like students to "get a taste for the richness of literature" and become "lifelong readers." He hoped that students would have an opportunity to discuss books with each other in the way that adults do when they chat informally about books. Teachers "go to great extremes" to control book conversations and keep them focused, he pointed out, thus missing the chance to help kids see that a discussion group is an opportunity to learn by making personal connections to texts and associative connections to others' responses. When I asked him about the possible effects of student diversity on peer-led book discussions, he said that he thought diversity would broaden everybody's perspectives. He then read me a quotation attributed to Sitting Bull about the innocence in the hearts of children of all colors that adults, to our collective detriment, have lost.

This description of teaching and learning literacy in the district and building depicts an environment steeped in the discourse of whole language. From "developmental practice" to "lifelong readers," from "childhood innocence" to "teacher empowerment," and from "heartfelt response" to "authentic conversation," the philosophical underpinnings of the curriculum were clear. As in any institution, this district philosophy is articulated as true and natural—what Foucault (1980) called a "regime of truth" (p. 31)—rather than as discursively constituted and regulated practice.

The practice of literacy in Julia's classroom was in some ways regulated by this regime of truth; that is, it matched the descriptions offered by the administrators, specialists, and district documents. Her students spent most of their reading time in small groups, each discussing a book that bore some thematic connection to those read by the other groups. These small group discussions did not begin until late September, however, because of Julia's commitment to starting each year's reading program exclusively with a daily read-aloud (a practice fully described in chap. 3) and whole-class discussion. The other literature practice that occurred in addition to the read-aloud at the start of the year was independent reading, during which students read books of their own choosing with no formal discussion. Students were occasionally asked to write in reading journals or engage in other activities related to the read-aloud book or their independent books. They kept a "tension chart," for instance, to track and explicate the fluctuating tension produced by the plot of the first read-aloud.

In October, the class began the first of the thematic units. The first theme—medieval times—was integrated with a social studies unit on the Middle Ages, culminating in the medieval feast for students and their families described earlier. Other themes were less cohesive, with little if any whole-class focus due to lack of time or need, centering instead on the small group experience. Once during the year, Julia was unable to get much consensus from the students about themes and books they would like to pursue, so she asked the five focal students, along with other interested students, to meet to discuss their different texts of choice.

In all of these groups, students could expect to read one or two chapters per day (to be negotiated among members of the group) and to write journal entries that regularly asked them to respond rather than summarize, ask questions about sections that confused or intrigued them, and jot down tricky or interesting vocabulary. At times, Julia would ask them to think about a specific issue or question related to the chapters. When they met as a group, students would read their journal entries (or key sections) and comment. The discussions were meant to work associatively, with students piggy-backing off of the comments of others and answering each other's questions and issues of interest. How this actually played out in the various groups is discussed in subsequent chapters.

Starting in October, then, the class shifted from two to the following four literary practices:

1. Whole-class read-alouds: Julia read aloud four novels and many shorter books during the year. One text, *My Brother Sam Is Dead* (Collier, 1974), was read during social studies. The first was by far the most important due to its symbolic weight as an enactment of classroom culture.

2. Teacher-led small group literature discussions: This was the most prevalent practice connected to the thematic units. Although Julia felt the best descriptor for these groups was "teacher-led" rather than "teacher–participant," we both agreed that they were not teacher-led in the traditional sense of teacher control.

3.   Peer-led small-group literature discussions: This practice occurred
     most frequently among the higher ability book groups that were
     part of the thematic units. Although the groups were formed ac-
     cording to student choice of text, students were encouraged to
     choose books not only of interest to them, but also within their
     range of ability.

4.   Independent reading: Students were given time for independent
     reading almost every day. In addition, in January, two book groups
     finished their books before the third group, thus leaving time for the
     two groups to engage in independent reading and optional discus-
     sions during regular reading time. During the last month of class,
     students again read independently during reading time, but held
     fairly regular, although technically optional, discussion groups
     along gender lines.

Although these practices and procedures appear to be in keeping with the
district design for its reading program, what occurred in Julia's class on a
deeper level, a level related more to meanings than procedures, challenges
some of the assumptions about teaching and learning literacy I have described. As the next chapter reveals, Julia's beliefs about what it means to
read and discuss literature both matched and differed from those of her colleagues, thus creating a context-specific set of expectations in the classroom. The production of meaning in her class was shaped by both the local
scene she and her students created through classroom ritual and discourse
and broader district, community, and institutional contexts.

II

Literary Practices

3

Enacting Classroom Culture Through the Ritual of Read-Aloud: What Do We Have in Common?

Since ritual is a good form for conveying a message as if it were unquestionable, it often is used to communicate those very things which are most in doubt. (Moore & Myerhoff, 1977, p. 24)

This chapter frames a slice of life in Julia's classroom—the first read-aloud of the year— to represent the classroom culture that Julia and her students enacted. To understand this slice of life, I must first introduce Julia, whose very comments about the read-aloud practice she initiates at the start of every year underscore its ritual power. When I asked Julia what she did to form a community in her classroom, she gave a lengthy and thoughtful response. (The book she refers to here is the one she read aloud at the start of the year, *The Brothers Lionheart* [Lindgren, 1985].)

Julia: I think the central, the most important thing I do at the beginning of the year is I read to them ... and I think that's the strongest message I give them of what life is going to be like—that we all have something to say, that there are no right and wrong answers, that, that I don't know everything, that I use some strategies to put things together in my head and it might be different from the way you do and I want you to share what you do with me and I'll share what I do with you.... I always read a hero tale. I would always choose a white hats/black hats book.

Cynthia:	[after turning over the audiocassette] You were talking about why you always choose a hero book, and you were saying you like the line in *The Brothers Lionheart* that says /
Julia:	In *The Brothers Lionheart* that said, if I didn't do this [save an enemy from certain death], I would be a speck of dirt. That there are choices that we make in life that articulate who we are.... Sometime in these two years, they *all* test authority in these ways. They have that first glimmer of beginning to internalize the moral system that's been imposed on them, and saying, "What can I—what will I—take away?" The world, my culture, my family, have given me these feelings, most of which are unconscious about the way the world ought to be ... somewhere in this fifth and sixth grade you can almost see it happen to most kids—that for the very first time they say "What happens if I don't?" which is the beginning of "What will I take as mine, and what will I discard?" And I think ... we cannot have a culture without it. I mean we have to do that, and nobody does it perfectly....
Cynthia:	But do you relate that not only to who they will become, but to the class context for the year?
Julia:	Well, that *we* become.... It's our one piece of common background. It's the one piece, the one referent in terms of a tale that I know we all have in common.... We have this story in common and it binds us together.... There's something about that curling up on the floor together, get a pillow, take your shoes off, and I never say that, I just *allow* it.... That's Emerson, that's Emerson, that's the building, that's the neighborhood, that's we're-all-in-this-together, that's, you know, years of shared history—I remember when your garage burned down, and I remember when.... This is our shared experience ... it's much more than modeling the reading process. Really what I'm about with that first experience is seduction into this community. This will be—especially it worked beautifully for James—this is a place in which you will be safe. This is a place in which you will be at least part of the time intrigued because of *the quality of the question,* not because the teacher wants you to be, and not because it's where you ought to be, and not because this is your task in life at this time, but because aren't stories wonderful.

Julia's comments made explicit the meaning she gave to the read-aloud practice and the context she hoped to create with her students. Understanding the ritual function of the read-aloud was no mystery. Julia signified this function through the language she used to talk about read-aloud: culture, common stories, community bonds, shared history, first experience, safe place, seduction. When she talked to the children about the purpose of her reading aloud to them, she focused on the modeling of reading processes—thinking aloud, visualizing, posing problems. However, it was the ritual experience that was most important to her, for it transcended these academic skills. Indeed Julia believed that participating in rituals at school was particularly important for these students, who she felt had little ritual in their lives outside of school: "There is very little of that ritualized anything for most kids, especially Emerson kids ... not being religious, not having extended family, and not being ritualized sort of people." Thus, ritual in Julia's class was meant to "convey a message as though it were unquestionable"—a message of what this culture of the classroom could become.

To understand the kind of culture Julia hoped to create with her students, one must know something about Julia, her background, and her beliefs about teaching and literature. As with any teacher, Julia's background and beliefs played a role in shaping the expectations for social and interpretive competence in this class. I am defining *social expectations* as those related to the beliefs, codes, and norms for action and interaction promoted within the classroom. *Interpretive expectations* are those related to the reading, understanding, and discussion of literature. Although it is important that I draw distinctions between these two sets of expectations for the sake of clarity, the literature events depicted throughout this book show that the social and interpretive are intertwined. As I stated in chapter 1, readers are constructed through social codes and practices that shape their relationships to texts, including literary texts and how such texts might be defined.

THE CLASSROOM CULTURE: SOCIAL AND INTERPRETIVE EXPECTATIONS

The social expectations that Julia promoted were shaped, in part, by the social conditions of her own life. Julia grew up in a Western state where, in her view, individualism was prized and social expectations were not as codified as they are in the Midwest. The premium placed on being self-expressive back home caused her to care less than she felt she should about how others viewed her. Although she wanted to be seen as a team player in her school, she was willing to make her opinions known and did not want to adopt a set of procedures or beliefs that would force her to compromise those that worked for her and her students. Julia was confident of her opinions. Once, for instance, when the class was studying Columbus, I suggested that she might want to read aloud the picture book *Encounter* (Yolen, 1992), which depicts the arrival of Columbus and his men from the point of view of the Taino people. Julia said that she found the book reductive, taking sides without considering the complexity involved. Religion was as much to blame as Columbus was, she argued, and one cannot judge past actions without fully understanding the worldview at the time. She feared that kids would be too quick to say "Oh, how terrible," without fully understanding that history has context, that disease killed more Tainos than slavery, and that one shouldn't trust "White folks" to speak as though they were Tainos. This highly charged response, which took place in the space of a few moments before the children burst into the room, was typical of the strong, well-articulated opinions Julia held. Thus, I was not surprised when Julia told me that she wanted her students to learn to "talk back" and "question authority."

Julia explained that her own education in Catholic schools, where "everyone knew who was smart and who was stupid," convinced her that "collective learning skills are vital—more important than being able to take the test." She believed strongly that her students benefitted when they were allowed to learn from each other. In an effort to facilitate this shared learning, signs hung from the ceiling, each labeled with a color to represent the cooperative learning teams that students formed at various times during the day, most often during social studies. Collaborative learning occurred informally as well. On the first day of school, Julia asked the students if they understood a particular concept. When few raised their hands, she asked them to talk with their neighbors and told them to get some ideas from each other. "We're all learning together and we'll all have opportunities to teach," she told them. She also emphasized on the first day of class the students' responsibility both to help and learn from a boy who had just come to Emerson School from Guatemala.

Julia wanted students to share with her the responsibilities of forming a classroom community. "Hopefully, more and more of the talk will be talk that you do," she told them during the first week of school. I can think of countless examples when Julia asked students their preferences for the day's agenda or future events. What activities did they want to plan for the class party for the practicum student, she would ask them. What book unit did they want to do next? What were their specific book preferences? Class rules were formulated through a group process of brainstorming and prioritizing: Behave safely, respect yourself and others, and participate in everything you can. Time spent on read-alouds and in reading groups was negotiated; students were taught to view their classmates as experts. Julia kept a journal along with her students for a book she hadn't read before. Students participated in assessing their own growth because, as Julia told them, "I see you from the outside," but "you see from the inside." Throughout the year she shared power with her students in many ways, although she wielded power as well.

Julia felt comfortable making her expectations known. She usually included a reason for the expectation and tried to relate the reason to the communal need for safety and respect. When Julia talked about vandalism that had occurred in the bathroom the prior year, forcing monitors to accompany students to the restroom, she told the class, "All of society pays the cost of one person's wrongdoing. It is symbolic of what happens in society." Once, in a section Julia read from a book about the American Revolution, the author wrote that a man's head bounced off his body. The children laughed and whooped. Julia stared at them in silence, then spoke softly. This was not Wiley Coyote, she told them, but human life. Forming a community was important to her, but it had to be the kind of community in which she would want to live.

The kind of community Julia wanted to live in was one where people took an interest in what others thought. The students kept a spiral notebook of their language skills work, but for those students who wanted more communication with Julia, the spiral notebook also served as an optional dialogue journal that Julia would read and respond to on a weekly basis. One girl, Lisa, loved to read and frequently used the journal to discuss books with Julia. When Lisa read *The Andromeda Strain* (Crichton, 1969), she wrote that she was put off by the scientific "macho" language of the book. Julia wrote back that Lisa's classmate, Mark, liked the book for the very things that Lisa disliked. "I'm interested in your perspective on the macho language," she wrote. "Ask Mark what his feelings were at the same point in the book."

Julia also wanted to live in a community that had a historical ethos on which to draw. She often extended the community beyond the classroom or even the particular historical moment, referring to those in the "Emerson community" who had since left, again demonstrating the importance of being rooted in this neighborhood over time, of knowing the people and the terrain. In the same dialogue journal, for instance, Julia told Lisa that *The Trumpeter of Krakow* (Kelly, 1928), which Lisa had been reading, was the favorite book of a former student whom she mentioned by name. At other times, she mentioned remembering a particular book according to the way a former student had responded to it:

> I remember books by the people who were touched by it. The questions the book raised for them … like I can't teach *Where the Red Fern Grows* [Rawls, 1961] without talking about Billy being sexist … because [a student from the past] raised it.

As I mentioned in chapter 1, Turner (1969, 1982) suggested that the breeches that occur within a culture, the unravelings, can lead to either cultural change or affirmation of existing norms. Such affirmation occurred when Nikki left school and repented. One can read, in the discourse of Julia's initial irritation with Nikki, the meaning of social competence in this class: to be social rather than isolated; to value learning from others; to think critically, yet set goals and work toward positive action; to appreciate human connection and collective history. This was the social community in which Julia wanted to live and it was the social community she promoted. Many students worked in consort with her to promote this notion of community. During our last interview, Julia shared with me an image she held from the last day of class for the year, a day I was unable to attend. Julia had asked her students what they cared about that happened during the year, what they would take with them. After a few initial comments, Brooke said, "We all loved each other." They found a song that they all knew on the radio "and they spontaneously got into this huge circle with their arms around each other and started dancing." I do not include this image to suggest that everyone felt as though they were equal members of this community, or even to suggest that everyone felt loved; rather, I include it to underscore the value Julia placed on having this living evidence of the culture she hoped to create, this proof that at least for some students, and Brooke was one of the most influential, the enactment of a certain kind of culture had been complete.

In addition to these expectations for social competence, Julia's beliefs about what it meant to read and discuss literature also created a set of interpretive expectations in the classroom. Julia held high expectations for student engagement with texts. Toward this end, she regularly modeled her own engagement, talking casually with the class about books she had enjoyed, for instance, and making connections among her experiences, her readings, and the life of her classroom. When a student noted that evil in *A Wrinkle in Time* (L'Engle, 1962) was like smog, Julia referred to St. Paul's phrase "to see through a glass darkly." When Julia couldn't understand why a character behaved in a particular fashion, she would express her confusion to the class, take them through some of her thinking, and ask them for help in figuring out the dilemma. She showed them what it meant to be intellectually curious and to engage in critical thinking, often asking questions that focused on what was left out of the texts they read and the films they saw. Once, for instance, she demonstrated how she might come up with a topic to pursue for the medieval project by explaining her interest in what happened to Jewish people during the Middle Ages and in what life was like at that time in the countries that are now Japan and the Americas.

Meaningful inquiry was important in Julia's class. She frequently asked students if they had burning questions at the end of a literature discussion, journal entries were to include intriguing questions, and book choices should be made with questions in mind. "There ought to be some questions that you're going to have about the book. Otherwise, it won't be worth your time," she told students as they began to choose their first books for small group discussions.

To extend this academic engagement, Julia was willing to spend much time with her students outside of school. As already mentioned, she invited all interested students to stay after school to help her, to chat, and to have a can of pop. Although the invitation was open, it was primarily the sixth-grade girls who felt comfortable accepting the offer. Julia also spent time after school and on weekends participating in school activities or taking students on field trips related to a unit of study. She occasionally called Kate (Nikki's friend mentioned in chap. 2) to attend concerts with her because they shared an interest in classical music. One Monday in the spring, Julia told me that the past weekend had been the first in 6 years of teaching during which she had not come to school at all. Julia's desire to extend the academic community she hoped to create was perhaps most evident in her commitment to "Friday School," a program she developed for any fifth or sixth grader who wanted to visit places of educational interest—museums, historical collections, laboratories, and such—after school on Fridays.

Julia placed much value on reading in her class. On the first day of class, she told her students, "Pick your favorite spiral and label it reading." She told me that she had sympathy for the student who sat with a book in his or her lap ignoring the teacher because she had once been that kid. When it came time to assign chapters for the next day's discussion, Julia never limited the amount a student could read as many teachers do because it disturbs their plans to use prediction as an instructional strategy. Instead, she told students they could read as far into the book as they wanted to, but they needed to be prepared to discuss the chapter the group had agreed on, and they must never tell others what would happen later in the book. Once a student raised his hand during read-aloud, announced that someone in another room had told him what would happen, and started to tell what he had learned. Julia, who had made her feelings about this well known, interrupted him: "Nothing makes me angrier than when someone's mean enough to steal the pleasure of a good book." During an interview with David, he told me that he knew that reading was important to Julia because "She acts different. Like if it's reading homework [that has not been completed] it's out of the group forever, you know. And if it's science homework, it's a recess in." Indeed, students who came to literature discussion groups without having read the chapter or written a journal were given one warning and then expelled from the group.

Julia expressed confidence to me about her own reading and writing experiences. When she was in high school, one of her teachers submitted to a national writing contest a paper she had written about a friend's death, and she won first place. That experience made her cautious about usurping ownership of her own students' writings because her winning paper had been very personal, and she hadn't wanted it submitted. Although Julia was confident about her writing, she didn't often find time to write, but reading was an important part of her daily life. She owed this, in part, to having had much exposure to literature as a child both at school and at home. She attended Catholic school, where her teachers were nuns who were "very well educated." Underscoring their impact on her life, she added, "I think they sent them [out west] for humility, I really do. I mean these were *strong* women." Her father was an attorney and her mother a "strong-willed" woman, both of whom used an extensive vocabulary at home that Julia learned to understand in context. In addition, much conflict was aired at home, creating in Julia a reason to go off and read, but also exposing her to language and concepts that she strove to understand.

Now, as a teacher, she was sometimes accused of speaking over her students' heads, and she was occasionally teased by her colleagues for using somewhat esoteric vocabulary. Her former principal thought that she presumed that the students knew too much. She agreed to some extent, but she also expressed confidence in her students. Julia told me about a read-aloud literature discussion I had missed, during which she told her students she had struggled with a question related to a character's action "all day, into the night, and the next morning." She went on to explain that she decided that the character's action was "not other directed but inner directed—something to do with who the character was, with his essential core, with his personhood."

Although she worried that "this may be a question only an adult could formulate," she asked the students to think about something that would be essential to their core sense of personhood. To my surprise, given the difficult nature of that question, Julia believed that the ensuing discussion was very rich, with "everyone" contributing, especially once the students modified the direction of the conversation by focusing on what they would be willing to die for. "When I aim too high for them, they can almost always do it," Julia told me, and as excerpts from my interviews with David's and Nikki's mothers reported in chapter 2 make clear, they would agree.

Julia attended a small, Catholic, liberal arts college, graduating with a double major in theology and philosophy. The "quality of the question" was something that Julia had thought about related to her own life as well. She had decided not to accept a fellowship to attend graduate school for philosophy because she was tired of "unanswerable questions" and decided instead that "living the unanswerable question is a lot more interesting than trying to answer them."

Julia always seemed to me an odd combination of someone at once elitist and egalitarian regarding educational issues. On the one hand, she valued the early exposure she had to Shakespeare and the Brontë sisters, the Latin masses with the "language that washed over [her]," and the experience of skipping a grade in school, which she thought worked very well for her and many other girls. On the other hand, she did not believe that success at school had much to do with success in life, and although she talked often about how her bright students could almost teach themselves, she also believed that the two subjects she valued most, science and language arts, "are so intrinsically important to anyone who is human that there isn't anyone, given the opportunity, who would not love them." She found her own education too competitive and believed that children learn best in a cooperative environment that affords them a good deal of control. She had been influenced by Atwell (1987), Graves (1983), Calkins (1983), and the state Writing Project, and she believed that students needed to use their experiences as a basis for extending their knowledge. Although she understood that her students' lives often included a love for popular culture, she remained steadfastly out of the loop (a stance that is more fully developed in chap. 6).

Julia's beliefs had been shaped by a range of experiences, some in conflict with others, resulting in a multivocal view of the world, of teaching, and of learning. An awareness of the voices that shaped Julia's teaching underscored for me the complexity of classroom context and the myriad lives that all the members of the classroom carry with them.

Julia came to teaching after a 2-year stint as a social worker right after college and many years at home with her children. When she came to Emerson, she told her principal that she wanted to try using literature rather than basals for reading instruction. She started out by reading novels aloud and, finding that she could plan activities around the novels, decided to try literature units for small groups. Julia preferred groups that were mixed in terms of gender, ability, and grade level, but acknowledged that the reality didn't always match the ideal. More important to her was that students in the unit were reading the book that they most wanted to read and discuss. (Group formation is discussed more fully in the next chapter.)

When the students chose book groups for the first time, Julia compared choosing a book to having a houseguest for a month and stressed the need to find a "comfortable fit." The seriousness with which Julia approached the topic seemed to rub off on her students. Few, if any, chose their first books based on friendships. As the year progressed, students could anticipate which of their friends would most likely choose particular books, but they did not claim, nor did I observe, friendship to be their primary influence as they chose books for literature discussion groups. However, as discussed in subsequent chapters, peer status relations did play a role in book choice.

Most often each group discussed a common book to make for the more substantive book conversations Julia valued. She found that students who came to her class after having been in a class where all the students read individual books of choice (using a reader's workshop approach) were good at "empty chatter about books" but didn't read closely or talk about anything substantive. Reading closely was a priority for Julia, and interpretive competence in her class meant, in part, that a reader must refer to text in the process of supporting claims or working through difficult sections. When discussing *The Brothers Lionheart* (Lindgren, 1985), for instance, Julia asked students, "What exact words did [Lindgren] write to make us all decide Hubert is a traitor?" When Julia asked about another character in the book, one student suggested that maybe the character was somehow connected to magic. Julia replied, "What's in the book that you're putting in the box in your head labeled magic?" The way that Julia approached close reading was quite literary. That is, close reading was most often connected to a real question that she or a student had about a literary element of the text. Once she asked students, "Do you know enough about Park to know what he's going to do when he sees Jonathan?" focusing on the connection between character development and plot. Close reading of texts was so important to Julia that its absence in an Emerson teachers' book club that had been formed 2 years earlier made the group unappealing to her. She had tried it early on and found that the books they read were not of interest to her and the conversations focused too much on personal experience and too little on issues connected to the text.

The entries students wrote in their journals were also shaped by the boundaries of interpretive competence. When Julia first discussed journal entries, Lisa, a high-achieving sixth grader, raised her hand and said, "Here's a hint to fifth graders. Don't say 'This character did this and then he walked.' Tell us what you *think* about it." Julia, affirming Lisa's comment, told the class, "Yes, we all have read the book, so we know what happened. We need to know what you *think*." A fifth-grade girl who often did not meet class standards for competence once wrote a plot summary in her journal. Because she knew that Julia would call her on it, she prefaced her reading of the entry with "I wrote what happened." Julia asked her if this was what she was supposed to do. After an exchange of "no" and "why not," the student replied "because everybody knows [what happened]."

Up to now, the approaches to teaching literature I have described mesh fairly well with the district's philosophy as described in chapter 2, with the exception, perhaps, of more emphasis on close reading of text in Julia's class. However, the significant difference between what I learned from other district personnel and what I learned from Julia was in the meanings each gave to the reading and discussion of literature. The emphasis on the part of other district personnel was on enjoyment and motivation. Julia, as her words demonstrate, had a highly developed belief system about why literature is important in the lives of young people. I asked Julia on several different occasions what she wanted students to get out of the reading and discussion of literature at school, and although her answers differed somewhat each time, they worked together to establish a cohesive philosophy about literary practice, a philosophy that was at the core of everything that happened involving the use of literature in her classroom, one that shaped the meaning of interpretive competence as it was embodied in the classroom. During an interview that took place in November, Julia had this to say about the subject:

> Mostly that—we all own books in different ways depending on where we are and the life we've lived … and I want kids to know there is no right interpretation, even about nonfiction. I want them to read with a little bit of doubt in their minds about anything they read … *a little skepticism, a little distance from it*. At the same time that I want them to own it, I want them to say, "Oh yeah, this is, this is one way of reading this right now."

In June, she added the following comments: "Imagining yourself having other lives gives you, it seems to me, more power over the kind of life you *do* lead."

To Julia, then, reading literature involved entering into the text world, resisting text worlds, and examining one's immediate world. When Julia commented on the meaning that particular students gave to the reading of literature, she alluded to one or more of these purposes:

> Liliana [who was from Brazil] read all of *Ronia* [Lindgren, 1983] to find out whether her worldview—which is that family, your own family is the most important thing—was borne out in this book. Or was this going to be challenged and was she gonna have to, to take this character in a book that she's loved and fit in her brain another way of doing things that was supposed to be acceptable.... That's what I want. I want them to be having a dialogue with the book.

Liliana, in Julia's view, was using the text to resist the text world and probe her immediate world. She expressed a similar view in talking about a Vietnamese student she had in class the prior year:

> I really feel most successful as a teacher if I can bring the kids and the book together in that way—where either the book will illuminate their life that they hadn't really looked at before, or whether their life illuminates the book … because this Vietnamese [boy] who read *Dog Song* could appreciate the animistic feeling in the book. I mean he knew what it was to believe that animals had spirits … and that made him appreciate his heritage for the first time in a long time, because he had been trying to overcome it in some way.

Again, there is an element of entering the text world involved in her description of how this boy used *Dog Song* (Paulsen, 1985), there is also the notion that somehow reading this book caused the boy to rethink his immediate world.

In this and subsequent chapters, it becomes clear that David, Mackenzie, and Nikki gave meaning to the reading of literature in much the way Julia did, whereas James and Jason did not. The standard for interpretive competence, these chapters suggest, is discursively produced and regulated through the rituals of classroom life. I turn now to the collective dimension of the read-aloud ritual.

CLAIMING COMMUNITY: THE COLLECTIVE DIMENSION

It is most often the dramatic but peripheral school activities that are viewed through the lens of ritual, activities with obvious coherence functions such as homecoming, pep assemblies, and the like. In an article about the uses of ritual theory in educational research, Quantz (1999) argued that educational researchers would do well to examine the daily rituals that establish cultural meaning in school—a teacher's lecture, for example, or classroom patterns of interaction. School ethnographers should examine how students and teachers "perform their identities and their politics" (p. 509) in the seemingly mundane ritualized activities that make up school life. As Quantz pointed out, "[It is] in the smaller, daily rituals, we are likely to find the real stuff of cultural politics. It is there that we are able to see how power is skillfully applied and just as skillfully resisted" (p. 509).

Those of us who agree with Quantz's argument must still determine what, if any, are the boundaries of ritual—how, for instance, one knows when a daily event has enough significance to be viewed for its ritualized elements. In exploring these boundaries, I have found ritual theorist Bell's (1992) position most useful:

> Rather than impose categories of what is or is not ritual, it may be more useful to look at how human activities establish and manipulate their own differentiation and purposes—in the very doing of the act within the context of other ways of acting. (p. 74)

In keeping with Bell's suggestion, this book examines the four reading practices as they have been established and differentiated through human activity in situated context. The functions these practices serve can be understood through their differentiated meanings as represented and enacted by participants. Julia's own description of the significance of read-aloud, quoted earlier, makes clear the ritualized function this practice serves. In their work on analysis of ritual, Moore and Myerhoff (1977) described formal properties of collective ritual that are useful in analyzing what occurred during read-aloud. These properties— repetition, order, acting and evocative presentational style, special behavior or stylization, and the collective dimension—were enacted by both Julia and her students in ways that drew attention to both cohesion and contradiction.

Repetition and Order

Both repetition and order were evident in the read-aloud setting. At the beginning of the year, read-aloud occurred daily at a prescribed time. Julia sat at the front of the room on a chair. The girls and a few of the boys gathered around her on the floor. Two or three boys regularly sat on the floor, outside the cluster of girls. Most often seven or eight boys chose to sit at desks surrounding the read-aloud area. The girls clustered together, some sitting, some sprawled out on the floor. Several brought pillows. The room was quiet except when Julia or a student interrupted the reading to ask a question or make a response. Spontaneity occurred at prescribed times such as when Julia expected students to feel excited enough to shout out, and she paused, waiting for their response. Nearly every day, many students moaned and begged for more read-aloud time at the end of the session.

Acting and Evocative Presentational Style

Julia always read in a soft and soothing tone, with little variation except to make slight changes for different characters. The lights were often dimmed. Students were allowed to bring pillows and sit where they chose. Julia stopped at exciting points to ask for predictions. At the end of a day's reading, she often asked for "burning questions." For instance, one time at the end of a book, just before the recess bell rang, Julia asked, "The book's going to end now. What question would you like to have answered for you as it ends?" She frequently extended beyond the time allotted, which suggested to students that they might be able to convince her to read even longer. Julia would purposely think aloud between sections of text, making visible her reading processes.

The inner circle of girls who sat close to Julia and each other performed the role of engagement: laughing at funny parts of the story, asking and answering questions at appropriate times, and wanting more. Students who were often disengaged (mostly boys) performed expected roles as well: distancing themselves from Julia and others, not making eye contact (heads on desks), talking with other students or playing with objects, and shrugging their shoulders when asked a question. To provide a clearer picture of disengagement, I include this excerpt from a field note written in September:

> Adam is turned with his back to Julia as she reads aloud. He's facing Sam and Mark, who is lying on the floor. When Julia asked Sam to move away from the other boys, he chose to sit at his own desk. Later, Julia asked him to move up if he'd like to, but Sam stayed put. "You needed to move your seat, but it didn't need to be that far away," she told him.

Special Behavior or Stylization

Most of the special behaviors were related to comfort: One fifth-grade boy usually sucked his thumb (a behavior not acceptable to peers during other school or social events); students brought pillows and often took off their shoes; the girls gathered on the floor clustered together, leaning on each other's shoulders or resting in each other's laps. They often changed places and bonded with another girl nearby.

The central symbol of special behavior and stylization was the hairbrush. Read-aloud time was seen as a time for the girls to brush and braid each other's hair. Julia did not challenge this behavior, although she sometimes asked questions to see if girls who seemed to be immersed in preening one another were actually listening as well. At times two girls brushed one girl's hair. This work was not casual; it was carefully executed and involved intricate styling. For most of the year, sixth graders styled the hair of other sixth graders and some fifth graders, but not the other way around. Fifth graders did style the hair of other fifth graders. In the spring, several confident fifth-grade girls, preparing to assume their roles as leaders, began to initiate the exchange. Two girls with very curly hair, one a White fifth grader and one an African American sixth grader who was a class leader, did not receive styling, although they gave it. The girls often traded places. Despite this continuous bonding behavior, the girls appeared to be listening closely to the story and actively participating in discussions.

As Julia read aloud, she stopped at exciting points to ask for predictions, seeking responses from most students before returning to the book. She also shared personal experiences, talked about what she visualized as she read, engaged in musing about the text, asked herself questions, compared what she read to other books and characters, and, in general, modeled reading processes she hoped would become part of her students' repertoires.

The Collective Dimension

Commitment to a collective experience was evident in Julia's description of what she saw as the meaning of this kind of literary practice—enacting a classroom culture. Through this ritualistic display, Julia and her students worked in tandem to enact a community ethos, one that suggested acceptable academic and social performances, including intellectual engagement and social allegiance. Rhetorical theorist Reynolds (1993) defined ethos as "a complex set of characteristics constructed by a group, sanctioned by that group, and more readily recognizable to others who belong or who share similar values or experiences" (p. 327). The ritual of read-aloud served as an enactment of ethos as it was defined within the culture of this classroom.

During discussions, the underlying question was one related to Julia's desire to enact a culture: What do we have in common? This underlying question was present from the first day of class when Julia asked students "Where do you want to travel this year? What do you want to accomplish?" and then added, "We're coming from different experiences to come together as a group." Thus, Julia's words, actions, and behaviors right from the start worked to produce a common culture, one that acknowledged differences but emphasized commonalities.

The following excerpt from a discussion of *The Brothers Lionheart,* the first read-aloud of the year, serves as an illustration of this emphasis on common concerns. The book is a fantasy about two brothers who are devoted to one another. They die in the first chapter and end up in a land called Nagiyala where their purpose is to fight evil. It was late September and Julia had just completed reading aloud the last chapter of the book. In this chapter, Jonathan, the elder brother, is paralyzed by a dragon's flame. Not wanting to continue living, he asks his brother to carry him on his back and jump off a cliff to another death and another land called Nagalima.

Nikki:	It seems like this book's trying to say you couldn't die, cause, I mean, maybe you have a life and maybe your life's not as good as the first one, then you go to Nagiyala.
Lisa:	Yeah, maybe the book's trying to say it's okay to die—that you don't have to be scared to die.
Julia:	How many of you think it is normal, natural, right and just, that there will come a time when you do not exist in any way? How many of you find it an easy thought that you will at some point not be? [No hands go up.] ... How many of you think that in some way some part of you will exist forever and ever and ever and ever? [Most hands go up.] Tyler, you don't?
Tyler:	Well, I do ... that I will live for a long time.
Julia:	For a long time, but not forever?
Tyler	... but when I die, it's like I'm still going to be living but somewhere else.
Julia:	Okay, so you *do* think that you'll exist but in another place.
David:	I think that when I die that my soul, like the Dragonwing's, will go somewhere else [referring to *Dragonwings,* a novel by Yep, 1975].

Lisa: Oh yeah, that thing.

David: And if my life was good, I'll become a dragon, and if it was poor, I'll become a softskin.

Lisa: Yeah, but what will happen, what will happen when the earth blows up? Where will you go then?

David: Well, then I'll go back in time, and I'll become something completely different.

Julia: David, for the fifth graders who haven't got a clue what David's talking about, he's talking about a book that we read last year called *Dragonwings* in which a man who is of Chinese heritage explains to us some ideas that have been existing in China for a very long time—and other civilizations have thought about this, have written about this, have art that is on the subject of what happens after this. What do we think? ... Okay, if we know we're going to die, and maybe going to change a lot before we die, do you have anything that you really do believe about what will happen in some future life?

...

David: I think that for the reincarnation thing, that if you're reincarnated your soul just goes alone, but I think that your talents go [with your soul].

Julia: Your what?

David: Your talent, like that story I wrote. I think that's how it goes. [David is referring to a story he had written the year before, as a fifth grader in Julia's class.]

Julia: I think you had something to add Jane. [Jane smiles and shakes her head no.] Have you ever thought about it? [Jane again shakes her head.]

Lisa: I have a question. Would this really be their first life because they talk about remembering their other life before that—would you really remember that?

Julia: Do you remember another life before this?

Lisa: No.

Julia: Nikki?

(Nikki speculated about what she might have been in another life.)

Mackenzie: I think that reincarnation—that's what all my family thinks, so I think that now—that you were some other person before or some other thing.

Julia: Jamie, how about you?

Jamie: I think that once you're dead, you're dead.

Julia: Okay [laughs].

Julia asked James what he thought. He shrugged his shoulders. She asked him if he'd ever thought about it and he smiled and shook his head to say no. Julia then asked Jason to contribute. Jason said he didn't have anything to add. Julia then asked Sam and Andy for a response and got the same reply. (All these boys were sitting at desks rather than on the floor with the others.) Others talked more about their conception of Nagiyala.

Julia: In some ways that hooks up very comfortably with the Christian notion of heaven which is that you're yourself, only *perfect*, and for some people that sounds wonderful, especially those of us whose favorite part of this book is when they very first came [to Nagiyala] and it was all heaven. But for some of us it was really *boring* [laughter].

Jane: They keep saying that a little bit of time on Nagiyala is like a long time on earth, so it's been ... wouldn't their mom have come there by now?

Julia: Would you put that in the end of the book if you were writing the end of the book?

Evident in this discussion is what Julia meant when she mentioned, in the interview excerpt at the start of this chapter, that she hoped students would be intrigued by "the quality of the question." She led a discussion of beliefs about death and afterlife in an effort not only to help students make personal connections to the text, but also to claim a particular kind of classroom culture through the exploration of a subject that she knew would be meaningful to many students. The collective dimension of this ritual is evident both in terms of the subject of the discussion—death and afterlife is a common interest and concern to many early adolescents, despite cultural, religious, and familial differences—and in terms of the dynamics of the discussion—particular interpretive and communicative norms are coconstructed in this excerpt.

Sociolinguistic research emphasizes the interdependent nature of social and academic structures in classrooms (Erickson, 1982; Green & Weade, 1986; Gutierrez, Rymes, & Larson, 1995; Hymes, 1972).To be a successful student, one must demonstrate knowledge of standards for participation as well as knowledge of the academic content relevant to the moment (Cazden, 1988). In this way, academic content is shaped by participants through social interaction. Teachers and students together must negotiate norms and standards to understand each other's meanings and create an interactional context (Cook-Gumperz & Gumperz, 1982; Gutierrez, 1995; Puro & Bloome, 1987). Bloome and Bailey (1992) noted the intertextual, historical nature of this competence, suggesting that students who do not develop such competence are excluded from other related events in academic settings.

Of the focal students, David and Nikki were most comfortable participating in the read-aloud setting. David, in particular, was an active participant in this discussion, fulfilling the social norms that were important to Julia and to his own desire for engaged conversations about literature, which he demonstrated in all four settings. In this *The Brothers Lionheart* discussion, he contributed his interpretations with interest without being called on, thus helping achieve Julia's wish for authentic conversation instead of routinized responses. His responses were built on by other students, leaving openings for collaborative meaning making. He spoke of texts and contexts that made visible the shared history of the classroom community. As a sixth grader interested in literature, he knew that Julia's questions were not merely rhetorical—that is, she expected analysis, dissension, and argument. Thus, the social and academic contexts can indeed be seen as interdependent, and David embodied a literary habitus—a set of dispositions—much like Julia's.

David demonstrated his interpretive competence repeatedly in this segment and in most discussions of read-aloud books. In this discussion, it is clear that the question of afterlife was one he had thought about, and he conveyed his beliefs in a remarkably literary manner, making comparisons to *Dragonwings* and to one of his own stories. These references are not only intertextual, but also what Floriani (1994) called "intercontextual" (pp. 256–257). That is, David not only made the literary comparisons across texts that mark his interpretive competence, but he also helped Julia to enact a classroom culture by drawing attention to what the class had in common—a common history of readings and stories. Of course, the fifth graders were not yet a part of that common history, but here David served to initiate them into that history, a move that Julia extended by explaining the *Dragonwings* reference to the fifth graders. Recall that Julia talked about the ritual function of read-aloud using phrases that could also be used to describe the function of David's contributions: "common stories," "shared history," and "seduction into this community."

During other discussions, David compared this book to *Redwall* (Jacques, 1987), suggesting that they were both sagas—a term Julia had previously introduced—and announced that Olympus is perfect, kind of like Nagiyala. Again, David demonstrated his interpretive competence, making intertextual references and noting genre. Even when David's responses were personal, they made literary or philosophical connections—referring to one's talents being reincarnated with one's soul, for instance. These responses were a good match for Julia's sense of interpretive competence in that they included textual connections, philosophical thinking, and a questioning stance.

Even religion was not sacrosanct in Julia's classroom, despite her own religious convictions. She taught in a rather liberal community where one could safely challenge dogma, and she regularly brought up topics that invited students to do so. In this case, afterlife was viewed as a construct that could be examined and responded to intellectually and personally rather than an unquestionable aspect of one's faith. Yet, as Heath (1983) and others have shown, not all readers are constructed through social codes and practices that would allow for such a relationship to texts. Here, again, the social dynamic and the academic (or interpretive) were interdependent. David, Nikki, and Mackenzie, among the focal students, were comfortable challenging authoritative texts, both the religious "text" of the afterlife, and the institutional text (the novel that is part of the school curriculum). Their ways of reading texts easily aligned with their teacher's, enabling them to work together with their teacher and others to create and sustain a classroom ethos, including a set of social and interpretive norms—in short, what became the collective dimension.

Evident in this discussion excerpt about afterlife, and in other discussions of *The Brothers Lionheart,* are some of the features that characterized the discussions Julia led during read-aloud times and in the small group, teacher-led setting (see chap. 5). I include next examples of four categories of teacher moves that reveal more specific information about the interpretive norms that Julia hoped to promote. The following four categories point to Julia's tendency to underscore the text as construct (as opposed to a reflection of real life) and to explore cultural norms and symbols within a reader response framework.

Text as Construct.   Julia talked about both student-generated texts and professionally authored texts as constructions. "The point is to begin constructing our lives as if it were a story that made sense," she told me once when describing her students' writing in terms of its literary qualities. The same sense of constructedness came through in the way she talked about literature: "We have to change course. The author threw us a loop—Jossi is the traitor—and we have to change course. In the next chapter, I want you to ask yourself if the new information meshes with what you already know." Here she makes visible the author's role in positioning readers to believe that someone else, other than Jossi, was the traitor. Thus, she asks students to stand back for a moment, to resist the pull of the story to understand how the text has created a particular response in them.

Another way that Julia made visible the constructedness of texts was to ask students how they would write the story differently if they were the authors. "Would you put that in the end of the book if you were writing the end of the book?" she asked a student who wondered why the ending of *The Brothers Lionheart* didn't include the boys' mother. "So if David were writing the story, Hubert would return," she told the class, after David predicted that this character was important enough for the author to bring him back into the story. In a similar vein, she asked students for written responses in which they considered how the story would change if written from another point of view, as in the following request for a "diary entry from Jonathan's point of view": "We see the story from Karl's point of view. Would the story be different if Jonathan were to tell it? How would Jonathan put things? You decide."

Experiential and Subjunctive.   Julia often asked students to relate what they read to their own experiences. For instance, she asked her students to place the feelings they had related to their own fears into the story to help them understand Jonathan and Karl's fears. Often, these questions were followed with a "what if" question leading students to use subjunctive mood to imagine themselves in the lives of the characters. For instance, after reading a section of the book in which the main character feels responsible for saving and caring for an enemy who might otherwise kill him, Julia asked students if they ever felt "they really ought to take a stand." Continuing, she asked, "What would you do if you were Karl?" Another time, she told students "Okay, here's your chance.... There you are in the woods with these older men. What would you say?"

Personal to Cultural.   At times, Julia related her personal experience to the text, but then made visible the culturally constructed nature
of that experience. For instance, one student asked why Lindgren, the
author, decided to refer to day and night although Nagiyala is supposed
to be timeless. Julia explained that when her own son died at age 4, it
seemed like a very long time before she would be with him again, so she
took comfort in reading Einstein. Julia pointed out that according to
contemporary physics the farther away you are from anything, the faster
time goes. "Most cultural conceptions of afterlife are timeless, so I think
Astrid Lindgren is connecting to these ideas of afterlife being timeless,
yet knows we're comforted by night and day so has them go to bed at
night." When she referred to her personal experience in class, she almost
always did so for the purpose of sharing with students what it means to
connect oneself to larger systems of meaning.

Cultural.   Frequently, Julia's responses served to culturally situate
the text or probe the cultural assumptions students brought to the text. At
the end of the class reading of *The Brothers Lionheart,* for instance, Julia
was very uncomfortable with what students might think about the
book's representation of the main character's suicide. She explained to
the students that Scandinavia (Lindgren's home) has the world's highest
suicide rate. She suggested that many of them probably substituted their
Christian notions of heaven onto Nagiyala, but that other cultures have
different conceptions of the afterlife. (This category of response is highlighted in chap. 5.)

The collective dimension—the move toward coherence of class
ethos—can be found in the enactment of social and interpretive norms and
in their interdependence. When David referred to prior texts from the previous year, he fulfilled both social and interpretive expectations. The interpretations that were built on—by the teacher and by other students—met
social expectations that then shaped the boundaries of what was likely to receive attention in a text and what was likely to be understood.

CONTRADICTING COMMUNITY:
BOYS ON THE MARGINS

McLaren's (1993) book on ritual performance in education describes the
functions of ritual as gleaned from works by leading scholars of ritual theory. Ritual, his work suggests, can serve three seemingly contradictory
functions: reifying the social order, subverting dominant norms, and trans-

forming participant statuses. A closer look at James's participation in read-aloud reveals all three functions at work.

James sat in a desk outside the inner circle. He was a fifth-grade boy in a class where the central power was mainly in the hands of sixth-grade girls. Although James did not participate during the discussion about afterlife, he often appeared to be engrossed in this first read-aloud book of the year, offering his predictions and getting caught up in the excitement of the story. Once, sitting at a desk between David and another classmate, he seemed particularly involved, his hand raised every few minutes. During the course of that day's discussion he announced proudly that David had told him something that was going to happen in the book. Julia saw this as a good sign and made the assumption that "James has never had an experience in school before where it was okay to work together and piggy-back off each other." Once when Julia asked students a related question, James jumped in and asked, "Can I share what Hubert's job might be?" Thus, she felt that Read-Aloud worked especially well for James and, indeed, for many discussions of this book, he seemed caught up in the classroom ethos.

At other times during the reading of *The Brothers Lionheart,* James responded much as he did in the conversation I discussed earlier in this chapter; that is, he shrugged and said he had nothing to add. On a day when Julia asked the students to talk about their favorite thing to do—something that brought them joy (related to a section in the book)—one student talked about sitting in a first-class seat on an airplane and looking out a dark window, Lisa talked about reading by the fire, and James said he didn't know. Another time James was able to answer a question Julia asked about an important character, Hubert, making another appearance in the book because "David told me." David, slightly embarrassed, added, "Yeah, because he was such an important character early in the story, and usually authors bring important characters back." The juxtaposition of their responses made the contrast in their degrees of interpretive competence in this setting all too clear.

The contrast was clear, also, in James's frequent references to violence during literature discussions, even when the storyline didn't necessarily warrant these references. This interpretive difference was constituted in the social codes and practices familiar to James, practices that included the regular consumption of popular media, particularly horror movies and *Beavis and Butthead.* "They'll blow up everything and go to Nagalima. Then they'll get another bomb," he said after eagerly jumping into the conversation once. In another class, this kind of response might have engendered enthusiasm from male peers in particular, but such was not the case in this class at read-aloud time. This ritual served to reify the social order by the collective reinforcement of the classroom ethos, even as it allowed for certain acts—such as preening, pillows, and overlapping talk—that transgressed the social order of traditional school behavior.

After James's initial sporadic involvement, he had trouble existing within the community as it had been coconstructed by Julia and his fellow students. For James, a first-class seat on an airplane and quiet time reading by the fire were far from his social reality. At the time, things were not going well at home, and eventually he was expelled from two literature discussion groups for not completing his journal for two consecutive days. As mentioned in chapter 2, the sixth-grade girls frequently reprimanded him for not writing long enough journal entries.

These breaches aside, James held authority in the classroom to varying degrees. Julia was particularly fond of him—a fact he pointed out to me in an interview. He thought of himself as a good reader (at least compared to his other school subjects), and he was, at times, the closest classroom friend of David. As Julia told me, "James has got a lot of acceptance, but the people from whom he seeks acceptance accept him because he is naughty." David was attracted to James's resistance to school until it threatened his own school identity, but as the year progressed, he again embraced James as his friend. There was power in James's performance as a resistant student, power that was complicated and intensified because of his closeness to Julia. (For instance, he turned to Julia when he wanted to talk about David's having dropped him as a friend.) James, like all of the students, had multiple and sometimes contradictory identities within the culture of this classroom.

Because read-aloud was clearly enjoyable to many students (those who begged Julia to keep reading), I asked Julia during our final interview if any of the students mentioned read-aloud as something they liked about their time in her class that year. This was her reply:

> You know some of them, you know some of them would say they hate that ... the ones who sit at their desks. And, you know, "You can't get me. Boy, I'm not going to be involved in this." [Julia named four boys, among them James and Jason, who sat at desks and generally seemed disengaged.]

Clearly, Julia was well aware of the dynamic. She felt the boys' resistance to read-aloud as collective ritual, and when one of the boys asked her if students could draw at their desks while she read to them, she told him no—that she herself was unable to do two things at once. In light of the sanctioned hair styling, this might not have seemed the most convincing argument to the boy who asked. Although I did not ask her, I suspect Julia was responding to the boys' resistance to enacting the classroom culture she sought to create. Given the social expectation to connect with others in the class, Julia might have viewed drawing as an activity that focuses on the individual in isolation, whereas hair styling involved bonding with others, and thus served to reinforce the communal ethos of the read-aloud practice.

The cultural geographer Soja (1989) argued that the use of space in social life defines social relationships, thus embodying tensions and contradictions related to power and status. Such tensions and contradictions were visible in the practice of read-aloud, particularly in the clearly embodied contrast between the girls and boys in relation to the teacher, to the text, and to each other. Luke (1992, 1994) described the ways in which literacy is learned through one's body and gender, regulated through institutional practices that position bodies in particular ways to perform literate tasks. Certainly, the boys' embodied rejection of read-aloud can be interpreted as a rejection of literacy as a feminized practice (R. Gilbert & Gilbert, 1998). During read-aloud, in particular, the feminine was accentuated, through the voice and body of the teacher, the ritualized and exaggerated display of female bonding among the girls, and the social and interpretive norms associated with girls' presentations of self in relation to texts. Although the social hierarchy may seem clear—powerful and engaged girls gathered around the teacher, bonding with each other and with her, while the disengaged boys sat at their desks outside the inner circle—this view is overly simplistic. Where did David fit in, for instance? He and three other sixth-grade boys often sat on the floor, closer to the teacher than the other boys, but on the outer edges of the inner circle. This physical position reflected his shifting allegiances as described in Chapter 2: good student and bad boy; engaged learner and disgruntled adolescent. Despite David's stellar performance in the afterlife discussion, he was fully capable of clashing with Julia. As his sixth-grade year slouched toward junior high, David's interest in being an engaged student waned. His status with Julia diminished as his status among the boys who often got into trouble rose.

Despite what may seem like rigidly defined boundaries, with girls in the center of the action and particular boys on the margins, these dynamics can be viewed dialogically. In positioning themselves as outsiders to the social and intellectual project of read-aloud, the boys took up insider positions relative to their own social and power relationships. Moreover, as Stallybrass and White (1986) pointed out, "what is socially peripheral is so frequently *symbolically central*" (cited in Hall, 1993, p. 113). In the deconstructive sense, the boys' presence on the margins actually defined what it meant to be central. What was central, in this case, was a performance that was hardly life as usual at school. The girls' almost carnivalesque (Bakhtin, 1984) transgression of the school-regulated body (i.e., sit straight, eyes on teacher, hands to oneself, feet on the floor) was clearly endearing to Julia, as her own description of read-aloud makes clear. Yet, this performance of the feminine left some of the boys, those who had more at stake in giving up their normative male stances, little choice but to reject the entire enterprise, and see it as yet more evidence that girls were physically and metaphorically at the center of this classroom.

PERFORMING READ-ALOUD: WHAT DO WE HAVE IN COMMON?

What does it mean for Julia's class to enact a culture? It means that there will be collective and disharmonious dimensions of that culture, the dialogical tension that Turner (1974) referred to as communitas. The boys who sat outside the inner circle during read-aloud, often as nonparticipants, manipulated the social codes available to them within this context to resist the expectations of others. One can claim that they were excluded from the inner circle or that they performed roles that drew attention to the margins. Although the read-aloud practice, in its display of collective ritual, was not an open space for much negotiation from the margins, the next chapter shows that the peer-led practice in the classroom resulted in more space for such negotiations.

This chapter focuses on the meanings that Julia gave to the reading and discussion of literature and the ways that social and interpretive competence were coconstructed through the read-aloud ritual. The underlying question, "What do we have in common?" was ever-present in read-aloud discussions. In many ways, this ritual served much the same function that literature served from Julia's point of view. It was a way of constructing classroom life "as if it were a story that made some sense." However, as Julia told me during another conversation, she also believed in "the power of narrative to prevent premature closure—that if the story isn't over, you don't shut your mind yet." Thus the ritual of read-aloud involved continuing stories and was itself a continuing story, an attempt to enact a cohesive culture in the face of, as Moore and Myerhoff (1977) put it, "those very things which are most in doubt" (p. 24).

4

Negotiating Classroom Culture in Peer-Led Literature Discussions: What Are Our Social Roles?

Ritualization cannot turn a group of individuals into a community if they have no other relationships or interests in common.... Ritualization can, however, take arbitrary or necessary common interests and ground them in an understanding of hegemonic order; it can empower agents in limited and highly negotiated ways. (Bell, 1992, pp. 221–222)

In this chapter, I turn again to ritual and performance theory to help me understand what it means to enact a classroom culture in the face of that which is most in doubt, the precarious sense of community to which Bell referred in the epigraph that begins this chapter. Here, my central focus is the peer-led practice in Julia's classroom, the time when students discussed literature in small groups without Julia's physical participation. As the literature events depicted throughout this chapter underscore, much negotiation of social roles and identities took place in peer-led groups, but these negotiations both sustained and contested normative and hierarchical elements of the local culture of classroom and community. As Bell pointed out, ritualization exposes "hegemonic order," and my examination of peer-led discussion groups bears this out. Although, as she suggested, this form of empowerment is limited, it led to important interruptions of power that allowed for at least temporary transformations in participant status.

In the last chapter, I focused on the enactment of ethos as it was defined within the temporary culture of the classroom, and began to address some of the ways in which class norms for action and interaction were complicated or "contradicted," as I emphasized in my discussion of James. Luke (1995) pointed out that the social practice of reading is constituted in "interpretive rules and events constructed and learned in institutions like schools and churches, families and workplaces" (p. 97). Given that the rules shift from institution to institution, however, many students find that they must negotiate conflicting sets of rules and events. In this classroom, the most obvious conflicting norms were those associated with social class. Middle-class students possessed social and interpretive aptitudes and dispositions that matched those of the classroom, whereas working-class students possessed aptitudes and dispositions suited to their families and communities. Recall, for instance, Julia's discourse about Jason's family and what they wanted Jason to be, or James's marginal status during read-aloud. Although the shaping influence of social class was obvious in the data from interviews and observations, it was not spoken about as directly as differences related to perceived ability, age, and gender. Yet, the literature events included in this chapter continue to show that the working-class students were not as successful academically or socially as the middle-class students, suggesting that social class differences intersected with other social conditions in ways that shaped classroom context and interactions with texts. I begin with a description of the three complicating conditions of perceived ability, age, and gender that were important to the classroom context and its relation to the discussion of literature.

DIFFERENTIAL STATUS AND POWER WITHIN THE CLASSROOM CULTURE

These three conditions, *ability*, *age*, and *gender*, surfaced repeatedly in the data, representing a challenge to the enactment of classroom culture and making visible differential status and power within the classroom, and, consequently, within peer-led literature discussions. In the last chapter, the shaping effects of these conditions were evident in my analysis of read-aloud, particularly in terms of gender. In this chapter, readers see all the conditions at work as they shape literature events in peer-led groups. Before moving to the peer-led literature events, however, I describe in isolation what in actuality were dynamic and intersecting conditions of classroom life.

Perceived Ability

I begin this section with a discussion of perceived ability and the tensions it produced within the classroom culture. This section includes a discussion of how book selection was related to the discursive construction of ability in this class. When I asked the teacher and Mackenzie what they saw as the difference between the large group and small group discussions, their answers, on separate occasions, centered on issues of ability.

Julia: The large group is to show us that we are all the same, that we're not high kids, medium kids, and low kids—that we all have something to contribute.

Mackenzie: It's kind of hard for me to discuss whole group because I'll get it, you know. I'll understand what is happening, but she'll have to stop and explain it for everyone else and it just kind of gets annoying sometimes.

In another interview, Mackenzie mentioned that during whole-class discussions she didn't like having to listen to students who speak because the teacher asked them to rather than because they care about the book. Mackenzie added that she preferred being in groups with sixth-grade girls because "they are at my speed." She felt that there should be a test at the beginning of the year to set up groups "of people that can and can't process certain things." When I asked her if she meant something like a high, middle, and low group, she rejected the language I used.

Mackenzie: No, it wouldn't be like that ... it would be like people that can process things among people that can't process things and people that just need a little boost. Yeah, that's it.

Cynthia: Isn't that like high, middle, and low?

Mackenzie: No.

Cynthia: How is it different?

Mackenzie: High, middle, and low are separating that this is better ... it really isn't better. It's just different. High, middle, and low are saying the high is best and low is worst. This is different.

Cynthia: Like how? Tell me about this difference?

Mackenzie: Um, you wouldn't have journals in the high one, because you wouldn't need to do that. And you would have group less … and for the people who have trouble processing, you would have group a lot, and you would journal and stuff, just so you could get your mind rolling. You would probably have a teacher and that kind of thing.

Journal writing, to Mackenzie, is an activity suited to those who "have trouble processing." She made very clear the cognitive differences she saw in students, and although she insisted that one kind of cognitive functioning is not better than the other, her preference would be to join a group that functioned the way she did.

Nikki expressed similar sentiments about read-aloud discussions:

I mean, I've tried like just sitting there and listening, but I really cannot do it. I just can't be in school if I don't contribute. So I try to contribute, which I like doing and because they [the teachers] want to call on all the people who haven't been contributing, and then I start to get bored. And then I start goofing off while they are trying to make the other people not goof off.

These comments suggest that whereas Julia yearned for a collective experience, Mackenzie and Nikki interpreted the whole-class context as one constituted in difference.

Perceived ability was implicit in procedures related to book selection for small group literature discussions as well. Although Julia admitted to encouraging students whom she perceived to have chosen unwisely (the book was too easy or too difficult for them) to switch books, she hoped she never forced them to do so. Nikki and several other students, however, reported having changed from their first choice to another book at Julia's strong urging. The process that Julia used to determine book groups left room for her to make decisions based on ability. When it was time to start a new unit, Julia introduced the unit and gave "book talks" about each book (at this point more books than would actually be used for the unit). Students then were given an hour or so to skim the books and record their top two choices along with an explanation for each choice. Julia would review all of these preferences and choose the three books most often listed in first and second place. From that list, she tried to place students in books of their choosing, but reserved the right to choose a student's second choice over his or her first choice if she thought that book would be a better match for the student's ability. When I asked Mackenzie how she thought Julia formed the different book groups, she began with the most obvious factor—the student's choice.

Mackenzie: Well, probably your first choice.

Cynthia: But you've talked about the book groups, like the high book groups.

Mackenzie: Well, that's probably, it's probably not all choice. It's probably, um, choice and what she thinks is their level of reading. I mean if she thinks people can keep up, she might try them to see if they can and if they can't then /

Cynthia: Does that ever cause problems for people, do you think?

Mackenzie: I think so. Cause maybe if your first choice is something way below you, but yet you really really want to read it and sometimes she won't put you in that group because it was below you.

Julia rarely chose groups based on her perception of how allegiances would play out or in an effort to create gender balance. More often than not, the groups could be classified as high, middle, and low, in terms of ability range, with high and middle almost indistinguishable from one another. Mackenzie noted this phenomenon in the following excerpt from an interview:

Cynthia: Now that you have finished the book, the *Alanna* [*Alanna: The First Adventure*; Pierce, 1983] book, what can you tell me about the difference between what the three groups were doing? How would you characterize the three groups?

Mackenzie: Well, I think that *Minstrel* [*Minstrel in the Tower*; Skurzynski, 1988] is for people that like easier books and don't like much challenge, or even for people like fifth graders—that [book] might be a challenge for them. Um, *Ronia* [*Ronia, the Robber's Daughter*; Lindgren, 1983] is kind of about the same as *Alanna*, except *Alanna* has harder print and smaller print and kind of things like that.

Nikki also pointed out that the *Alanna* group did more activities independent of the teacher and speculated that this might be because "this group was probably a little higher, so, more of the sixth graders were—like Mackenzie and Brooke and those guys that are really leaders—were in that group, so that helped out lots."

One of the book choices in the historical unit, *April Morning* (Fast, 1961), was a book about the American Revolution that had much difficult vocabulary. Julia worried that many of the boys who were unable to read at that level would choose the book because they would expect it to be an action-packed war story. She counteracted this effect when she introduced the book by reading a difficult treaty scene that would cause the boys to choose an easier book. Often, though, a student or two whom Julia perceived as less able would find their way into the high or middle group.

The illusion of choice that I describe here is one that Walkerdine (1985, 1990) argued is a hallmark of what have come to be known as "student-centered" or "progressive" classrooms. Such approaches, she argued, position students as individuals who can determine their paths through exploration and choice, when, in fact, schools operate within a set of available discourses that regulate what it means to be a "good" student. Although none of this is explicit, because it is institutionalized rather than promoted by individual teachers, students are quick to "read" the discourse and position themselves within it. Consequently, students who are not thought to be good readers learn quickly to listen for the books that are coded by the teacher as "long," "containing difficult vocabulary," or "a challenge," and avoid them. By the same token, students who have been successful know to choose those very books. To some degree, then, the students work with the teacher to group themselves according to ability (Davies, 1997; Laws & Davies, 2000).

Age

Age was another complicating factor in terms of the classroom collective: The fifth graders often felt as though they were outsiders in relation to the insider status of the sixth graders, nearly all of whom were now in their second year with Julia. For instance, Anne, a fifth grader, complained about the sixth-grade girls: "We want to be friends with the sixth-grade girls, but they don't want to be friends with us. They're not nice to us." Kate called the sixth-grade girls "The Stretch Pants Club," repeating a mockery of their well-matched outfits I had heard before. All agreed that only Jane, a fifth grader who had been friends with a popular sixth grader since early childhood, was allowed to associate with the sixth graders.

Even Nikki, who generally wasn't afraid to speak her mind and characterized herself as "opinionated," felt intimidated being the only fifth-grade girl in one of her book groups. Another time she mentioned that it bothered her that Julia chose only sixth graders for leadership positions. She always knew that either Brooke or Mackenzie would be chosen to lead book groups, for instance, and felt that there were responsible fifth graders who could handle the job as well. "They just don't get recognized, of course." Jason, too, explained that "In the *Alanna* group, like most of them were sixth graders, and so I'd kind of get left out a little bit, but I was kind of scared to get in 'cause they were older." He added that the sixth-grade girls didn't invite him to speak until everything he wanted to say had already been said. This was an important issue for Jason. Repeatedly, he told me that he preferred to be in groups with only fifth graders. Jason made it clear to me how he saw the relationship between age and power in the classroom when I asked him who made most of the choices in the class: "Mrs. Davis and some sixth graders," he told me.

Corroborating Jason's perception, Mackenzie discussed the power of sixth graders in this class when I asked her if she felt she had an opportunity to make choices.

> Mackenzie: Lots. Tons. I mean especially since—more than if I was in fifth grade. I think sixth graders kind of gear the fifth graders towards certain things and stuff.
>
> Cynthia: Mrs. Davis gives the sixth graders more choices?
>
> Mackenzie: Mrs. Davis doesn't. It is just kind of like the sixth graders say something and the fifth graders kind of think, "Well the sixth graders think that, and … I want them [the sixth graders] to think so and so about me, so I better do that book too."

Mackenzie made the important point here that the power the sixth graders held did not emanate solely from the teacher, but was produced by students as well.

Gender

Gender also contributed to differential status and power in this classroom. Julia was well aware of her reputation, among students and parents, as a teacher who favored girls and she discussed the issue with me during several of our interviews.

> Oh, yeah. My reputation is I just like girls.… But I simply don't have as much of a reference for boys. I don't do baseball. I don't play ball of any kind. So I just think I have more in common with the girls … because I have a lot of daughters, and they [the girls in her class] are in a lot of things with my daughters. So we have a lot of common bonds.[1]

---

[1]Earlier analyses of some literature events included in this chapter are published in Lewis (1997) and Lewis (1998a).

During this interview, I also asked Julia why she thought girls were so powerful in her class—even, I admitted, at times controlling. Her response was quick and forceful: "Oh, I don't think it's possible for a woman to be—I really don't. I mean I think you have to be focused or you end up being patted on the head." She talked to me about her concern that the temptation to play the "pretty girl role" is too inviting for some girls who will respond by making unreflective choices. Thus, she purposely acted against the socialization of girls to be overly concerned with image. Julia explained that she was "blunt to the point of brutal with girls." When I asked her if she was more brutal with girls than boys, she replied that she was as direct with boys but that it was not "politically popular" to tell girls "No, that won't do." She relayed a conversation she had had with Kay, a sixth-grade girl who was particularly interested in boys. During a field trip, Kay ignored an adult who tried to talk to her to sustain her conversation with a boy. According to Julia, she told her, "Your body language, everything about you said my social life is far more important than any content here. If that becomes a pattern, you have closed a huge door."

Three out of five focal students (David, James, and Nikki) initiated conversations with me about girls being privileged members of the class. Here's what David had to say on the subject:

David: Mrs. Davis doesn't realize it, but she's really sexist, I think.

Cynthia: You mean nicer to the girls?

David: … I remember one time one of the girls that had never been up on the board before got her name up there. And she cried, and she didn't have to stay in [for recesses].

When I asked David if he felt he was able to make choices in the classroom and pointed to the seating arrangement as one possible choice he was often able to make, he argued that it was the girls who helped Julia determine the seating arrangement so that they could sit next to their friends. David mentioned—and I also observed—that it was most often boys who had their names up on the chalkboard (for incomplete assignments) and girls who "act like teachers even if the teacher is not there." When I asked James to tell me whom the teacher thinks is a good student, he immediately mentioned Brooke "because she is a girl, and that she always does her work good."

Mackenzie had a dissenting view about Julia's alleged favoritism toward girls. She pointed out that she and many other girls had gotten their names up on the board many times when they were in fifth grade, but because Julia never let them off the hook, they learned to turn in their work.

Some parents perceived a bias toward girls that they mentioned either to me or to Julia. Several boys' parents told Julia, "You just don't like boys," when she offered critical comments about their sons. Nikki's mother, on the other hand, thought Julia was especially good for Nikki because Julia was a teacher who had a special connection to girls: "I think there are certain kinds of personalities, teacher-wise, that I think, that this, is a good match. Mrs. Davis likes girls. For example, I think she understands girls—and gifted girls." When I asked her what gave her this impression, she replied:

> Mrs. Davis mentioned that she identified with Nikki being gifted and verbal and all that, and that's how I picked up on it. I mean there was just this kind of bonding, and she made several comments about [how] this is the way it is for gifted girls.

During my first interview with Julia before school started, I was struck by the way she described her class to me. In trying to characterize the class in one broad sweep, she told me about the wonderful girls, returning as sixth graders, who valued education and reading, and the immature boys, "Nintendo freaks," some bright but not productive in school. Perhaps an excerpt from a journal entry I wrote in May best expresses my ambivalence about Julia's response to gender difference:

> In the short time I was there [five minutes to drop something off], I had this wonderful feeling about the room. It's a very comfortable feeling, yet I noticed again that in the five minutes I was there, Julia was interacting [with], hugging … several girls—Lisa and Brooke come to mind right away—and I always wonder how the boys feel in the class. The girls have so much in common with what Julia's interests are. Brooke was reading a book of poems that Julia had suggested to her and was crying over one of them and Julia was touched by this.

The students brought to their classroom the complex conditions of their lives, as did Julia herself, whose strong beliefs about the lack of power girls too often experience surfaced repeatedly during our conversations. Julia assigned the sixth-grade girls leadership roles (particularly in literature discussion groups), but it was understood that when acting as leaders, the girls would follow through with their teacher's agenda. In this way, girls were often positioned as mothers and teachers whose job it was to regulate the behavior of boys (Walkerdine, 1990).

As described in the last chapter, however, gendered behaviors are complicated both by the local culture and the larger culture, with the two sometimes working at odds. Alloway and Gilbert (1997) discussed several reasons boys may either passively or actively resist school literacy practices, given dominant definitions of masculinity outside of school. They argued that literacy practices require students to be regulated emotionally due to the emphasis in many progressive language arts programs on "processes of self-disclosure, introspection, and empathic response" (p. 55). These emotional processes, commonly coded as female outside of school settings, become the standard for what it means to be a good reader, writer, and interpreter of literature (Simpson, 1996).

Alloway and Gilbert (1997) also argued that texts marketed for children "tacitly endorse dominant standards of morality as well as sensitivity and aestheticism" (p. 55), thus promoting a moral self-regulation that opposes hegemonic masculinity outside the school setting—that which often depends on showing one's physical strength and hiding one's emotional sensitivity. These opposing expectations may well be difficult for boys to negotiate. To laugh, for example, when a man's head rolled off his body in *April Morning* (see chap. 3), can both empower and disempower a male reader in a school setting. Such would be the expected response among boys watching a similar scene on television together (Buckingham, 1993), yet in Julia's class, as in the classrooms of many teachers, laughing at bodily harm was seen as a rejection of the class ethos. At the same time, of course, it was potentially a response that would position a boy unambiguously within the discourse of masculinity as it matters most—in relation to other boys in his social world.

Resisting regulation, in the form of the female teacher and authorized female students, then, may be a necessary performance, one that comes with its own sense of self-righteous indignation, as we shall see in the literature events included here. I should point out, however, that the need for such performances differs based not only on individual differences but especially on complicated group identifications, including social class. For some groups of boys more than others, family and community expectations related to literacy are closer to those of the school, particularly when literacy is associated with economic power and an open opportunity structure (Alloway & Gilbert, 1997; R. Gilbert & Gilbert, 1998). Thus we see David, in chapter 3, positioned to accept school literacy practices much of the time, and James and Jason not so positioned. "Much of the time" is a key phrase here, however, because as we saw in the last chapter, David did not always engage with literacy practices in the classroom and James did not always disengage. Moreover, chapter 5 on teacher-led literature groups shows Julia expanding the nature of acceptable literary response with James and other typically disengaged boys and chapter 6 on independent reading illustrates James's engagement in literary genres in the classroom that allow him to express and question dominant forms of masculinity.

All of these factors—Julia's feminist stance and personal knowledge of girls, institutionalized conceptions of literacy, progressivist and student-centered district approaches, social class and achievement status of the students, and conceptions of dominant masculinity—played a role in how gender was enacted and interpreted in this classroom.

PEER-LED DISCUSSIONS

In examining how literary understanding is shaped by different talk structures, researchers have begun to study peer-led literature discussions in elementary classrooms, which have been found to provide increased opportunities for participants to construct knowledge collaboratively (Almasi, 1995; Langer, 1993, 1995; McMahon, 1992; Wiencek & O'Flahavan, 1994). Peer-led groups are not without their complications, however, and recent studies suggest that taking the teacher out of text-based discussions does not necessarily result in equitable relations (Alvermann, 1996; Evans, 1996). The remainder of this chapter takes a close look at peer-led literature discussions to underscore the critical role of the peer dynamic and make visible the status and power negotiations that were most salient. Because social and interpretive power are thematic references throughout this chapter, it is important that I clarify my use of the term *power*. In analyzing the literature events in this chapter, I follow many other educational researchers of the last decade who use power in Foucauldian terms. As such, power emanates not from one dominant source, but from disparate points at all levels of social systems and hierarchies. Power relations are dynamic and shifting, produced through available and often competing discourses that inscribe particular rationalized forms of action and interaction (Foucault, 1978/1990, 1980).

It was most often the group that included students whom Julia perceived to be strong readers that had the chance to engage in peer-led discussions. Several times, Julia mentioned that strong readers would be fine on their own, whereas the weaker readers needed more guidance. The students were well aware that those groups characterized as higher ability had more opportunities to work independently. Nikki, for instance, pointed out that "lots of people who were capable picked that book [referring to a book in the sea unit] ... so, she always has them do the independent stuff." In allowing for more independent work among students she perceived to be high ability, Julia was basing her instruction on her knowledge of her students. She had observed that students who had less confidence and interest in reading, students who defined her participation as authoritarian during small group discussions, were students who sometimes didn't complete the reading, often didn't complete the journal assignments, and might not be interested enough to follow up on the comments of their peers. Therefore, she saw her input as important to their development as readers and responders. Her focus was on improving instruction, rather than on transforming social relations in the classroom, but she did not take lightly decisions regarding grouping patterns.

In helping students learn to work together collaboratively, Julia tried a variety of approaches, some that she used only when she first taught group dynamics near the start of the year. For instance, during the first peer-led discussion, students started with three poker chips each and placed one in the center of the circle whenever they contributed to the discussion. She also discussed how to make connections between one's own comments and those of others as in the following instance when she tried to explain how students could form relations among the three different novels they were reading:

> When you share your journals today, what I'd like you to do is listen very hard to other people's journal entries to see if there is anything that you either wrote down already in your journal or any thought that you have that is somehow connected to what they're saying. This requires that you listen very hard and very actively to what they're saying and see if you can connect it to the book you're reading.

In addition to learning to take equitable turns and learning to build on each other's responses, Julia occasionally requested that students write a discussion agenda. Each student in a group was expected to write an agenda item (question, concern, or interest) related to the book under discussion. These items would then become the agenda for discussion. In this way, something that each member of the group thought was important was sure to be discussed. Julia explained to her class that she came up with this idea after listening in on a group and finding that important things were said with no follow-up.

I now turn to a depiction of peer-led literature discussions in Julia's classroom. The theme I discuss in this chapter, performing social roles, focuses on social competence and negotiation in peer-led groups and considers how interpretive competence shaped social power within the groups. The key and illustrative events depicted reveal two patterns related to the performance of social roles based on data from peer-led literature discussions: (a) achieving social and interpretive power, and (b) interrupting social and interpretive power. I begin with an anecdote important to understanding the patterns that follow. I asked each of my focal students to tell me who controlled the talk during peer-led discussions. David answered without hesitation, "Whoever's got the clipboard." Julia would ask one student in each peer-led group to keep a clipboard that held a form to be used for documenting group processes. When I asked Nikki the same question, she thought a moment before replying, "Well, Mrs. Davis writes it down. And then the person with the clipboard—it's like the congress and the president, they make the laws. But then the police keep them enforced." I asked if the congress and president were Mrs. Davis, and the police were Mackenzie and Brooke, as Nikki often complained about the authority these students held in the classroom. She responded, "Yeah, I guess. And then ... but, you know, they can take one subject [for discussion] that they like more and enforce it more."

Two students in Julia's class regularly held the clipboard: Mackenzie and her good friend Brooke, both viewed by their teacher and peers as competent and responsible. There were no stated procedures for selecting the person for this position; Julia simply chose someone, usually a sixth grader whom she thought would responsibly handle the job. This anecdote serves to underscore the issues of power relevant to the two patterns discussed in the following and to situate Nikki, David, Mackenzie, and Brooke, who figure prominently in the literature events.

Achieving Social and Interpretive Power

In peer-led groups, talk was often used as a way of achieving social and interpretive power. Revisiting the relation between the social and academic in this classroom reminds us that to have social and interpretive power in this culture meant taking learning seriously and accepting an ethos that centered on inquiry and achievement. To achieve such power, students vied for it, creating solidarities and boundaries between themselves and others in the process. Achieving social and interpretive power often meant making visible its absence in others.

During peer-led discussions, whether one performed or was accepted as an insider or an outsider had much to do with one's social and interpretive power. Even when the girls weren't designated as leaders by their teacher, they would take it upon themselves to direct the discussion. Nikki pointed out that "if they [Mackenzie and Brooke] get told they are a teacher, they have a feeling that they have to do everything teacher-like, you know." One reason for Mackenzie's "teacherly" role in discussion groups may have been that she was uncomfortable when discussions did not meet her need for order. She felt that with Julia as part of the group, students were more attentive, there were fewer incidents of misbehavior, and "Mrs. Davis help[ed] them get their point across." When I mentioned that other students I talked to felt that the teacher would sometimes recast their ideas in ways they didn't understand or felt alienated from, she told me, "What you need is confidence enough to be able to say 'No, that's not what I was thinking. I was thinking this.'" She explained that this was easy for her to do with her teacher because Julia didn't mind when students disagreed with her point of view.

In fact, Mackenzie thought that it was easier for her to express what she really believed about a book when her teacher was present. She gave as an example a discussion I missed in which the group had discussed whether it was right for a character to plot revenge. Mackenzie felt that she had to say she thought it was right to plot revenge because everyone else in the group thought so, many of whom were her friends. However, when Julia asked her what she thought, she found herself saying that it was wrong because, "That's really what I thought." I asked her if having Julia there had anything to do with her decision to say what she believed: "Probably. I mean, knowing that Mrs. Davis was definitely gonna, I knew before she said it that she was gonna agree with me." The meaning that Mackenzie gave to the reading and discussion of literature matched well that of her teacher, whose views are discussed in chapter 3, and Mackenzie regularly performed that match. When I asked Mackenzie why she thought her teacher asked her to read literature in school, she replied:

> To expand your mind. To make you think about things differently.... Different from your own lives. Different from what you think of things. Different from what your parents grasp.... I think it's important to learn about things that aren't close to you.

Given that Julia thought it was important to retain some distance, some skepticism, as readers, it should come as no surprise that Mackenzie, who also valued a critical stance, was a student who helped to shape and sustain interpretive and social competence within this classroom culture. When Mackenzie had trouble keeping up with her work, her social class and social acceptance in the classroom enabled her to forcefully state her case, as in the following example that took place when members of her literature discussion group wanted her to read more chapters over the weekend than she was willing to read:

> Today, I go home. I have piano. Then I come home at 5:30. I have to go to the dance 'cause I have to set up. Then on Saturday, I have to clean the house, then go to my grandma's to color eggs. Then on Sunday at eleven, I go to one grandma and at about five I go to the other grandma. Then it's Monday already. Just so you know.

Her peers accepted this explanation, I suspect, because Mackenzie's life as she described it seemed entirely natural to them. Such was not the case for James. When James's life got in the way of his school work, his home culture, social class, and lack of academic status marked his difference from the others and made visible his failure to perform social and interpretive competence. He did not proudly announce his reasons for not having his work done, as Mackenzie did. In fact, he often tried to hide the fact. Because his home life did not meet the acceptable pattern other students had in mind, his incomplete work was viewed differently than Mackenzie's, and he eventually had to leave the group reading *Red Fern*. Even David reprimanded James at times, although at other times, he would cover for him when the teacher, who represented an authority to be resisted, was present.

Once, near the end of James's participation in the *Red Fern* discussions, at a point when he was barely hanging on, he came to group with a short journal entry. After he read his entry, two girls asked him if that was all that he had written. He said "Yes," but looked down as he spoke. One of Mackenzie's friends, Tara, asked, "Didn't you do chapter eight?" James shrugged his shoulders. David told him, "You were supposed to do chapter eight." The students were to look for examples of the way that the main character exaggerates. James had no examples and did not contribute to the discussion that followed.

This was a common occurrence for James. Even at the end of the year, when he had read *A Wrinkle in Time* (L'Engle, 1962), his role in the peer-led group combined resistance with silence. In the following scene, the students had finished their respective books and Mackenzie's job was to direct a discussion of advantages and disadvantages of each society represented. When she asked James about the advantages of living on the planet Comazotz from *Wrinkle,* he initially had nothing to add. Later, James said that the disadvantage was that "The black thing's gonna take over all the planets in the world," and added at this point that the advantage was "The Dark Thing's cool," but no one responded.

After this point, James starting repeating, again and again, the words "no fear" a phrase that had come up in the discussion, Mackenzie, hoping to include James in the discussion, asked, "But is there fear in *Wrinkle*?" James told her he didn't know, and she replied, "There isn't, is there" (spoken as a statement rather than a question), and continued:

> Mackenzie: Think of a situation where there was [fear].
>
> James: When that person got pulled into that black hole.
>
> Lisa: I know, *teacher* Mackenzie. I know one.

Although Lisa used a sarcastic tone in addressing Mackenzie as "teacher" in this example, she was willing to play the game. Later in the discussion, Mackenzie asked James about the lesson of *Wrinkle.*

> James: In what? In the book? [He had been busy making airplane noises when she interrupted him.]
>
> Mackenzie: Yeah, what do you think the message is?

James didn't answer. Here James played the "bad boy" role (making noises, not meeting expectations for social and interpretive competence) and the girls attempted to regulate his behavior. When James offered an example of fear on the planet, no one followed up on his comment, underscoring his outsider status despite Mackenzie's teacherly attempts to include him. It should be remembered, however, that terms such as insider and outsider, are relational, despite their usefulness in describing students' positions relative to the official classroom ethos. For example, as James defined himself as an outsider to the classroom ethos, he may have defined himself as an insider to the ethos of some of his peers. During the first peer-led literature discussion of the year—a 1-day practice discussion related to the first read-aloud book—James joined a group of three other boys. James and another boy were not concerned about pleasing adults, and despite the fact that I was taping the discussion for the first time, they playfully whispered into the microphone and rolled around on the floor, connecting with each other as they resisted the nascent literary culture of the classroom to engage out of interest in the text.

Achieving social and interpretive power in the classroom also depended, in part, on allegiances formed in and out of school. These allegiances among students, often based on long-term friendships within the community, played a part in determining what was said during peer-led discussions and who was empowered to say it. One vivid example occurred during a discussion of *Red Fern* that included 7 students: 5 sixth graders—4 of them good friends—and 3 fifth graders—none of them close friends. When Mackenzie read the following sentence from her journal, "Billy's living his grandfather's dream," a conversation ensued about the students' grandfathers, a conversation that included only the 4 sixth-grade insiders, all girls, and 1 fifth grader, Kate. This led them back to fruitful comparisons between their own grandfathers and the grandfather in the book, a conversation in which, again, only the insiders participated. When Brooke brought up that the dogs in the book yelped with every step they made, an animated discussion took place with Kay, a popular sixth grader, jumping in to explain what the whole scene must have looked like:

> But then they're running so fast, I don't think it would be able to come out of their mouth that fast … 'cause you know when, when dogs run, because they, they like move like their front and their back foot and they go like this and like that and like that [gesturing to demonstrate].

At this point a fifth-grade girl, Tina, who rarely met class expectations for social or interpretive competence and whose friends were not in this group, tried to jump into the conversation.

Tina:	So, my dog, my dog, my dog /
Kay:	[talking over Tina] then move this one and then they move like that one and then /
Tina:	My dog, my dog runs /

Brooke and Kay carried on, talking over Tina. Tina continued to say "My dog …" and Kate finally softly told others to let Tina talk. Tina tried again:

| Tina: | But, but my dog, my dog's front feet, when my dog runs / |

The sixth-grade girls continue to talk over her. Finally, Tina finally stood up and tried again:

Tina: When my dog runs, his two front feet run like this [demon-
                 strates] but his two back feet jump. He looks like a bunny rabbit
                 … [The girls continue to ignore her throughout.]

Finally there was a pause in the sixth-grade girls' conversation and Tina told them quickly about her dog, giggling nervously at the end of her sentence. No one followed up on what she had contributed. Instead the sixth-grade girls' allegiances to one another came into play again as Kay addressed her next comment to Brooke, referring to Brooke's dog by name:

Oh my gosh, Brooke, when we came to do that thing with [Brooke's dog], remember we came to your door for the money for your parents, well your dog
… she came up and she stood where—these are the bushes right here, she
stood there and she goes and then she started jumping up and down like
this, like she wanted to get out.

Mackenzie picked up this conversation because she knew Brooke's house and dog, too, and the conversation continued among the three good friends until the session was over.

When students were comfortable with one another, the act of interpretation was fostered by the affirming and conflicting comments of others. Affirmation from peers contributed to David's unusually comfortable position in literature discussion groups. When I asked him at what times he most felt like an insider during literature discussions, he told me that he felt like an insider most of the time because his peers often tell him, "Yeah, yeah, that's right. That's what I think, too." He valued group discussions and made a surprising announcement to that effect in the middle of a particularly animated peer-led discussion about *Alanna*:

I like how in group, you know, when you're reading by yourself you have to
think everything for yourself, but when you're reading in group you get to
take time to think about the whole chapter and stuff, and you get everyone
else's idea, so instead of solo thinking, it's [all of our] thinking.

This confession, met with a sarcastic round of applause, positioned David as one willing to chance potential ridicule, from which he was generally shielded due to his high status among his peers. Indeed the discussion during which David made this comment was one that included much engaged talk.

Both Mackenzie and Nikki talked about the value of consensus as well. Nikki, for instance, often talked about the strong connection she felt to Lisa and her ideas. She enjoyed being in groups with Lisa because they were so much alike: "Because she is just like me. It is like we are half of like the same person and we got cut in half or something, you know." Nikki went on to explain that they thought so much alike that they could build on each other's comments. In the same vein, Mackenzie discussed her special relationship with Brooke. One of her favorite book groups had been one that included only Brooke and herself in a discussion of *The Diary of a Young Girl* (Frank, 1993). Mackenzie liked the discussion because she and Brooke knew each other so well and "think the same things ... so we knew what not to talk about with that certain person [each other], to not offend them." In an earlier interview, she said that her friends didn't put her down during book discussions: "They won't say 'Well, not really. There's no text supporting it,' " a comment that demonstrated both the power of allegiances and the power of interpretive competence as defined in this class.

Social and interpretive power were sometimes achieved by drawing attention to those who lacked such power. This dynamic was evident in peer-led discussions of *Alanna: The First Adventure* (Pierce, 1983) that included many high-achieving students. During an interview, Julia described the *Alanna* group this way:

> But the *Alanna* group, now here is an issue we care about.... I mean, it has all the hooks. Besides which, they are a passionate bunch. *They are vying for power, social power with each other.* A lot of them are trying on adolescent wings to see how they fit. (emphasis added)

Of the 4 focal students who were part of the *Alanna* group—Mackenzie, Jason, Nikki, and David—the latter 2 loved both the book and the discussions, particularly those that were peer led. Nikki and David both valued the lack of structure in the discussions, the way that students sometimes ignored the journals entirely, focusing instead on intriguing questions or sections of the book. They loved that their teacher had very little input into many of these discussions, unlike the *Red Fern* group, which was more controlled procedurally. Neither minded that at times everyone would talk at once or engage in separate conversations in pairs or triads. Both Mackenzie, also in the group, and Nikki mentioned that "the loudest voice gets heard," but only Mackenzie was bothered by this.

Jason enjoyed the book but was intimidated by the group and felt uncomfortable during the discussions. As described in chapter 2, Julia described

Jason's family as working class, close knit, but not particularly interested in education. She saw Jason as a student who had trouble with reading comprehension and who often chose books, including *Alanna*, that were too difficult for him. Jason's mother, on the other hand, thought that Jason didn't participate for fear that he would be put down by other students. He and another student, Sam, were indeed the center of much discussion during *Alanna*. During one peer-led discussion, Julia noticed that Jason and Sam were not included and insisted that the group had to arrive at a plan to make the discussions more democratic. The students argued with her, expressing, in the course of the conversation, the following comments, which I selected because they represent the dominant theme of this conversation. Jason and Sam were present when the comments were made.

Nikki:	Why can't they talk to somebody else?
Brooke:	Why don't they open their mouths and start talking?
Kay:	We like it this way.
Lisa:	We aren't talking to our friends. We're just talking to everybody.
Steven	We're just talking whenever we have a good idea to say about the subject.
Brooke:	You think that we're not all hearing it but we are. We hear.

Julia told them to write in their journals about solutions to the problem. When she left, the students expressed more indignation, including the following comments:

Brooke:	Everybody write, "I want to keep it the way it is."
Mark:	He [Jason] gets as much out of this as we do.
Lisa:	Yeah, because he listens and we talk and he gets a whole bunch of ideas.
Jane:	And, I mean, if you don't want to talk, then that's fine.
Steven:	Do you like it the way it is Sam?
Sam:	Yeah, I don't want to talk.

Lisa: You like to listen, right?

Brooke: You get to listen to everyone's ideas.

Nikki: They just don't have as strong as opinions.... If Jason doesn't
             want to talk, he gets to listen.

Eventually, Julia returned and told the students that if they wanted to break into small groups with people they enjoyed talking to, she could arrange for that at times. However, other times would be spent talking equitably in the designated group. Although the issue never again came up directly, the remainder of the group discussions included references to Jason's and Sam's contributions or lack thereof with solicitous attempts made to include them.

Interrupting Social and Interpretive Power

Conquergood (1989) proposed that researchers need to look for spaces where performances interrupt authority because those are the open spaces where social conditions and power relations can be transformed. Interruption of social and interpretive power occurred during literature discussions, with one example taking place during a discussion of *Red Fern* that became a key event in that participants characterized it as significant.

There were 10 members of a group, gathered to discuss the first four chapters of *Red Fern*. Attached to the clipboard, which Brooke held on this day, was a list of questions written by Julia to be used as a springboard for discussion. It was unusual for her to provide such a list, but because the class would be having a substitute, she wanted to provide a bit more structure than usual. She left a message with the substitute, as well as on the list of questions itself, stating that the questions were meant to initiate discussion, not to limit it, and that they need not all be answered. Other group members in this scene included Lisa and Steven, a fifth grader new to the school that year who had been home-schooled for several years prior and often appeared passive or uninterested during literature discussions. What follows is a brief transcript of the *Red Fern* discussion, just after the students had finished reading and commenting on their journal entries.

Brooke: O.K. How does the family make a living? Steven, How does the
             family make a living? Let's not draw pictures.

Steven: Uh ...

Brooke:	Set down your pencil. No more drawing. And I don't think you should be drawing.

...

Brooke:	What ... how did the family, Billy's family, make a living? What did they do to make a living? Are they, are they accountants? Are they bankers?
Lisa:	Steven, where ... Steven, you should know this. Don't look in the book.
Steven:	*I don't know!*
Brooke:	Steven, see, what did they *do* ... where do they live, and what did the common ( ) do in the country?
Steven:	*Farm!*
Brooke:	They are farmers. They have chickens. Did you read that part where they had the chicken head soup?
Steven:	Yeah, and then he caught the chicken in the trap.
Lisa:	They had mules. You should know ... Steven, if you can't understand what the job they're doing, then you need to read over it and talk about it to yourself and maybe with another person before you come to group because you can't just sit there and go, "Duh, I don't know."
Brooke:	O.K. you guys. So how does Billy's father make a living? *By farming!*

Clearly, Brooke and Lisa had strong beliefs about what it meant to participate in a literature discussion group, but their beliefs did not match Steven's or those of their teacher, who often emphasized the importance of everyone's contribution and the value of working collaboratively to answer each other's questions. Still, the girls felt empowered to insist that Steven follow their agenda. Note, however, the contrasts between Lisa's and Brooke's discourse. Lisa expected book group members to come prepared to talk. She would have wanted Steven to know the answers to the questions, but she also believed that through dialogue with himself or others he could deepen his understanding. For Brooke, on the other hand, competence meant responding correctly. There were right answers and wrong ones, and she was going to nudge Steven to answer correctly by giving him whatever clues it took. She wanted to get the job done with as little resistance as possible. Lisa's social and interpretive competence was much more in keeping with Julia's sense of how one should act (talk, think, and be) during literature discussions; yet Brooke was so able to carry the authority of a teacher that she frequently was given or took up the role.

Within a performance perspective, context is not static. The norms and expectations evolve through negotiation among participants—what Bauman and Briggs (1990) called "the emergence of texts in contexts" (p. 66). They argued that for a researcher to ascribe static features to a context is to ignore the ways in which ongoing performances continually shape and reshape context. The text of Brooke, Lisa, and Steven's interaction emerged as part of a complex context, one that included the teacher's expressed wish for a democratic discussion as well as her habitual designations of power. The text created that day by the students played some small part in reshaping classroom context. Brooke, who appeared to set the standard for competent communication at points in the discussion, was unable to sustain her position at other points. The meaning of communicative competence during literature discussions did not hold stable throughout the discussion, thus complicating the norms for competent communication.

Within this classroom, Brooke was a girl everyone talked about. Every time I asked a student to describe the role of another book group member, if Brooke was in the group, she would be the one described. Social relations extend beyond the classroom as well, shaping social codes within the classroom. When I asked David why he thought Brooke had been so upset with him and his friend at another point during the discussion—she had, in fact, been very upset with what she saw as their misbehavior—David replied, "She always thinks of me as a bad person ... cause we really hated each other last year." Indeed, Julia had mentioned earlier a serious fight the two had the previous year, during which David had misunderstood something Brooke said and kicked her very hard in the back. In Julia's words, Brooke "realized for the first time how hurt a woman who is misunderstood could get, fast, and she was scared, really really scared." Brooke's lack of power in this gendered and violent conflict with David contrasts sharply with her more privileged role in the classroom.

These are the conflicts that Turner (1982) referred to as social dramas that represent the dynamic nature of rituals and their meanings. The daily ritual of literature discussion groups in this class took on different meanings for different students. For Brooke, such discussions were sites in which she felt empowered to lead and obligated to enact the role of "teacher." Lisa also felt empowered to lead, but for her the discussion ritual took on a different meaning—that discussions were for deepening one's understanding. For Steven, who had less power in the class by virtue of his newness to the community, his lack of familiarity with what counted as a "good" literature discussion in this classroom, and his status as a fifth grader in a class that included many high-achieving sixth graders, discussions served to situate him as an outsider.

Lisa's responses to literature were always intellectually and personally engaged regardless of group makeup, teacher participation, or the nature of the book. It was almost as though entering a text world came as naturally to her as living in the actual world. When the time for group discussions of *Alanna* was over each day, for instance, Lisa would often form another self-selected group to continue the conversation. Once, after visualizing the characters with Brooke, Nikki, and another fifth-grade girl, she eagerly looked forward to the next day's discussion and drew Nikki into her excitement:

Lisa: You know what we can do tomorrow for an activity? We can draw each person. I picture [Alanna] as /

Nikki: We could go to the library and check out some books on magic and we could try a spell....

By contrast, Brooke always seemed to be regulating others through the voice of Julia that she carried in her mind. She was particularly teacherly with boys, often telling them not to draw, make paper airplanes, rough house with each other, or make silly noises. Her first inclination in any literature discussion group was always to legitimize the group process. Mackenzie had this to say about Brooke's stance on literature discussions:

Mackenzie: Brooke pretends she likes to [discuss books].

Cynthia: You don't think she likes to?

Mackenzie: Brooke's a good actress. She's told me she doesn't. She has told me she hates discussing books.

Later in the conversation, I asked Mackenzie if she knew why Brooke felt this way, and she replied:

She hates sharing her experiences, because she is afraid the teacher is going to say, "Oh now, that's wrong. That's not what you are supposed to think," you know. That kind of embarrasses her—that she could be thinking something totally different.

As seen through the eyes of her close friend, Brooke was not interested in entering, examining, or resisting texts through discussion. Rather, Mackenzie saw her friend as one who performed competently because she understood how to speak and act in this context.

An interruption in Brooke's discourse occurred when another sixth grader in the group had just read her journal entry. Brooke wanted to move on to her next question, but before she could, Lisa asserted her very different notion of interpretive competence during book discussions:

Lisa: Does anybody have any /

Brooke: Okay. [She wants to move on.]

Lisa: Wait. Before you go on, before you go on, does anybody have any questions, I mean /

Brooke: about the chapters.

Lisa: or, or things to talk about that they have any ideas about.

Brooke: We have to answer the questions.

Brooke regained control, but her discourse had been interrupted. An open—or liminal—space existed in the moment, and the meaning of communicative competence had temporarily shifted, thus reshaping context and, potentially, future interactions. When Brooke's control of the meaning of literature discussions wavered, an alternative view surfaced. Lisa pointed to the value of asking questions of personal significance and talking about ideas, a view much like her teacher's. The students also read their journal entries for discussion that day. After Brooke read her entry, another student, Kay, accused Brooke of rehashing the plot in her journal instead of sharing her thoughts or interpretations. Here again Brooke's notion of interpretive competence was called into question. Therefore, although Brooke was, in many ways, inscribed with power in this class, although she was from an affluent family, was achievement oriented, followed all the rules, and spoke with confidence, although she was "going to deliver the goods every single day" as Julia once said of her, these factors alone did not result in her unwavering power. In fact, not only did students point out her lapses in the area of interpretive competence as it was defined in this classroom, but several resisted her version of social-communicative competence. Two of the boys in the *Red Fern* group consistently undermined her leadership, keeping up a consistent hum as she spoke, and questioning her authority in attempting to discipline others when she herself at times talked to her friends.

This book discussion, which lasted 50 minutes, eventually dissolved into disparate chatter, causing Brooke to panic at the loss of control and request that I turn off the tape recorder. She was very upset that she was unable to complete the questions Julia had given her, and primarily blamed the boys for the group's demise. When Julia returned the next day and learned of Brooke's distress, she rewarded her for her efforts, but reminded her as well that the questions weren't meant to limit the discussion as they seemed to have. The moment of Brooke's unraveling took on folkloric proportions for the three focal students who were there. Their voices were mixed with sympathy and resentment as they discussed Brooke's role with me. "She didn't mean to," they told me. "She thought she was doing her job." "But she is *so* bossy." As is true of the continuing thread related to gender issues throughout this book, the way gendered relations were enacted within the classroom is clearly shaped by the way they are inscribed in the larger patriarchal culture. Consequently, the power that Brooke had in the classroom, and the ways in which she may, indeed, be rightfully depicted as "bossy," must be read through the lens of gender norms beyond the classroom, norms that often place females in regulatory positions and then label them "bossy" for keeping order.

The roles performed by the key players in this discussion sustain certain structures of privilege and power based on factors such as social class, gender, age, perceived ability, and peer status, but they also interrupt the influence of those very conditions. It is noteworthy that this interruption occurs, in part, through Lisa's enactment of interpretive and social competence according to Julia. Therefore, although Brooke's power had been interrupted, the teacher's interpretive authority remained intact.

A vivid example of a student's interruption of interpretive power occurred among a group of 8 students during a discussion of *Number the Stars* (Lowry, 1989), a book about the Nazi takeover of Denmark. The students included three focal students, Jason, Nikki, and David. This illustrative event begins with one comment that Jason read from his journal.

Jason: [reading from his journal] Lise died when she was just a few days from marriage which was pretty sad since she was so close to getting married. There was also a king named Christian and then her little story was over.

Nikki: I have a question. Why is it so sad that she got—died just before she got married?

Jason: Well 'cause/

Lisa: Because she was getting married and then all of a sudden she
              died.

Kate: *Duh.*

Nikki: But I don't get why that means sad because like it'd be sad if
              she just got married and died, I think.

David: It'd be *sadder*. It's always sad when someone *dies*.

[laughter]

Kate: Not to Nikki. It's like, oh great a person's *gone. Yes!*

Nikki: What's it matter if she died before she got married. [Others are
              talking over her, teasing her.] I mean, marriage isn't that big of
              a deal.

Several   OOOOH!
Students:

The students continued along these lines, contesting Nikki's critique of Jason's journal entry for another 27 turns, ending with Kate apologizing to Jason because "Nikki had to make such a big deal." Jason was absent from the
entire event after his initial quietly spoken "Well 'cause."

During an interview, Jason told me that he didn't like discussing big issues because it was too hard and too slow. His favorite literature group was
an optional all-boys group that discussed independent reading at the end of
the year (see chap. 6). This group consisted mostly of fifth graders who, according to Jason, talked about "what's happening, how we like the book,
what we like about it." Although Jason told me that the gender makeup of
the group didn't matter to him, just the grade levels, it is interesting to note
that his favorite group was an all-boys group. In keeping with research findings on the relation between reading preferences and gender (Cherland,
1994; Sarland, 1991), it was a group where the boys focused on plot and action rather than on character relationships. Although the *Number* discussion was one time when Jason attempted to meet the expectations of an
audience that valued talk about characters, he still functioned as a silent
member of the group. Having already described Jason's performance in literature groups and some of the sociocultural conditions that may have
shaped that performance, I turn to Nikki, whose role is central to this event.

It is important to remember what constituted interpretive competence in this classroom as it was constructed by Julia and like-minded students. Julia talked about the importance of distancing oneself from texts and gaining power over one's own life by envisioning the lives of others. Implicit in her view of literature is the sense that literature pushes us in new directions. Like David and Mackenzie, whose comments about reading literature I referred to in chapter 3, Nikki also viewed literature much as her teacher did. Nikki was a reader who often read against the grain of the text, a role very much in keeping with Julia's vision of what good readers sometimes do. The meaning that these students and their teacher gave to the reading and discussion of literature contrasted sharply with that of Jason, who looked for opportunities to talk about a book's plot and felt intimidated by the kind of talk Nikki and others frequently engaged in—talk that probed institutional or cultural knowledge, the kind of talk Nikki initiated when she challenged Jason's response to Lise's death before her marriage.

Nikki was considered an oppositional thinker by her peers and her teacher. The discussion about marriage and death was not the only time that Nikki's performative role served the function of critique. Often, during both peer-led and teacher-led discussions, Nikki challenged the status quo, insisting that she wanted to read books from alternative points of view. When a group of students read *April Morning* (Fast, 1961), a book about the American Revolution narrated by a young boy whose brother was a Committeeman, Nikki brought up an alternative point of view:

> I notice how everyone's like "Oh those Redcoats are horrible," but like we don't really know that because—that's just our point of view. But the literature that we have here is all written from someone who's thinking of our point of view. But, you know, everyone who fights a war thinks they're right and thinks the other person's a bad guy.

Other students who used literature largely to probe dominant cultural assumptions identified with Nikki. For instance, as she spoke about the need for a British point of view, David, another sixth grader in the group, expressed agreement, saying, "I was just thinking that." In my final interview with David, I asked him if when he thinks about literature discussions anyone's comments particularly stand out for him. He told me that Nikki's did:

> She always thinks like, for some books that are from the American side of view, like *April Morning,* she'll try and think of what the, what the British soldiers are thinking, you know. And that's exactly what I was thinking, so she says a lot of the same things as me.

Nikki was a reader who often read against the grain of the text, a role very much in keeping with Julia's vision of what good readers do. For instance, Nikki believed that money was the cause of most of our contemporary social problems. During a book discussion of *Alanna,* she expressed her preference for cultures that barter over those that exchange money:

> I mean, if everybody just shared then nobody would be poor and everybody would be the same and there would be no such thing as poor and rich because it would be one thing, and everybody would share, and if you were, like, really good at hunting then you could, like, share your meat with everybody; then you trade it for clothing.

Despite Nikki's interest in ideas, early in the year, Julia was concerned that Nikki wasn't getting heard during literature discussions:

> What worries me about her is she would say such important things and not get heard ... and in that position when they are all vying for social power and they are all wanting to be the run of the show, it might be the kiss of death for the teacher to, for them to become teacher's pet, so I'm always hesitant about underscoring that.

My field notes indicate that Julia did indeed demonstrate her approval of Nikki's ideas, patting her shoulder, hugging her, telling her, "I can always count on you in a crunch!" However, by midyear, when Julia was concerned that Nikki used her intelligence only to critique rather than for the purpose of positive action, she worried that Nikki didn't think she had anything to learn from others. At times, then, Julia showed appreciation for Nikki's insights during literature discussions, yet at other times she expressed irritation with Nikki's penchant for critique and argument. Nikki told me why she preferred peer-led discussions:

> The teachers ... really have their own questions to hand out, you know, about blah, blah, blah. And then someone says something. You get this really big question in your head and she's like, I mean, you know, she's like finishing her questions and she has just enough time. And then, you know, it's music time and you have this humongous question [but] you never got to ask it or share your comments.

Whereas Jason felt intimidated by sixth graders, Nikki, also a fifth grader, felt challenged by their presence in her book groups. She joined the other fifth-grade girls in their public disdain for the sixth-grade girls, whom they felt were snobby and exclusive, but privately enjoyed what she felt the sixth graders could offer her.

Sometimes I feel like when I get around the fifth graders and—tell me if this
sounds right, it might sound really snobby or something—but I just get annoyed because they sound, they are just, they talk about things I haven't
even considered talking about. I am just not interested, and they are just kind
of immature sometimes.... And so sometimes it's fun to get in a group with a
tough, meaty group, and a group of more mature people.

Later, Nikki said that she liked being in literature discussion groups with
people who "are into deep thinking and they like sharing their ideas."

From a performance perspective, Nikki's interpretation of Lise's death
before her marriage both met and resisted audience expectations. Pineau
(1994), writing about the potential that performance studies holds for educational researchers, noted that performance studies "acknowledges that
identities are always multiple, overlapping ensembles of real and possible
selves who enact themselves in direct relation to the context and communities in which they perform" (p. 15). These multiple selves are everywhere in
Nikki's performance, given what we know about her position in relation to
her peers, her family, and her teacher. In challenging the notion that one
ought to be sadder if someone dies before marriage, she questioned the importance we place, within the dominant culture, on the institution of marriage, suggesting that perhaps marriage isn't "such a big deal." In doing so,
Nikki resisted the version of reality promoted by the text as well (Patterson,
Mellor, & O'Neill, 1994). We are formed as readers not only through the
cultural and historical conditions of our own lives, but through the construction of the text as well (Beach, 1993; Bennett, 1979). A particular
reading formation is clearly promoted in the following passage from *Number* telling of Lise's death:

It was Lise who was not [alive]. It was her tall beautiful sister who had died
in an accident two weeks before her wedding. In the blue carved trunk in the
corner of this bedroom—Annemarie could see its shape even in the
dark—were folded Lise's pillowcases with their crocheted edges, her wedding dress with its hand-embroidered neckline, unworn, and the yellow
dress that she had worn and danced in, with its full skirt flying, at the party
celebrating her engagement to Peter. (Lowry, 1989, pp. 16–17)

Thus, the text is constructed to produce a particular kind of response, the
one that it had produced in Jason. As readers, our emotional response to
Lise's death is meant to be connected with her impending marriage. The
reading formation produced by this text is powerful when combined with
that produced by our cultural reverence for marriage. Nikki's response resisted both, and her peers attempted to censor her for having done so. One

could say that Jason, although he had given the more conventional interpretation, was censored socially. His low status as a social and interpretive performer in the classroom kept him out of the discussion, unable to provide support for his original journal entry or claim a space in the quick-paced interaction that followed his reading.

Despite her critique, which brought a round of "ooohs," Nikki was uncomfortable setting herself apart from her peers and contesting the expected response, especially for females, to place importance on marriage; thus, when she added that she liked to make a big deal out of marriage, she opened the way for Kate to suggest that her comments about Lise's marriage worked against her own beliefs. Although Nikki resisted the interpretive expectations of both the text and her audience of peers, the latter unwilling to join her in questioning the cultural reverence for marriage, she did meet her audience's social expectations by performing as Nikki was expected to perform: staging a critique and offering an alternative point of view.

Although the teacher was absent from this scene, she was always a presence in the classroom. As Bakhtin (1981) would have it, speakers are aware of other voices in or around the interactional context. Nikki's performative role worked on two levels in relation to her teacher: on the level of interpretation, with Nikki performing in ways consistent with the meaning she and her teacher gave to the reading and discussion of literature, and on the level of social dynamics, with Nikki manipulating the discussion so that it sustained debate, and so resisting her teacher's expectation for how a literature discussion should unfold. Nikki's performance interrupted the power of the text and its social currency, yet this interruption should not be viewed apart from the social conditions that surround it. As this discussion excerpt demonstrates, interpretation itself is a performative act embedded in social contexts.

The next day when Julia met with the group she commented on the audiotape of the discussion she had listened to. She told the students that she wanted them to think about whether or not their turn taking was equitable and went on to model a different kind of conversation they might have had about Jason's journal. She started by modeling how Nikki might have expressed her point of view, then moved on to Jason's perspective:

> I think it would be tragic that she died. Whether she died before she got married or after she got married was really irrelevant in relation to the enormity of dying. It doesn't seem to me that it made any difference whether she died before or after she got married.... Your feelings and your thoughts would be on the table and then Jason could take them and consider them and say, "Gee, you know I hadn't thought of it that way. But, oh, I understand what you mean, but, but I think it is almost sadder that she died before she even got to be

married because that is one of those, you know, life moments when you sort of have made a major choice. And she didn't even get a chance to do that."

Julia's response focused more on group processes than interpretation, but it also legitimized and extended both Nikki's and Jason's interpretations of the text. It inferred possible reasons for their responses, reasons that never got voiced during the peer-led discussion. Although Nikki's critique had been "on the table," the debate centered more on the social nature of Nikki's performance (as in, isn't it just like Nikki to object to something everyone else takes for granted) rather than on the substance of her interpretation and the way in which it challenged cultural assumptions. Whether or not Jason would have responded, had he felt comfortable doing so, with an interpretation akin to the one Julia ascribed to his position, I can't say. However, she quite literally gave voice to an interpretation that one might attribute to Jason's comment and in so doing she legitimized his contribution.

PERFORMING PEER-LED LITERATURE DISCUSSIONS: WHAT ARE OUR SOCIAL ROLES?

Within the culture of a classroom, as Erickson (1986) noted, meanings shaped by social and cultural conditions beyond the classroom are sustained through interaction. As the events I included in this chapter reveal, such conditions of meaning are not only critical elements of the classroom culture, but they are also critical dimensions of literature discussions.

The achievement and interruption of social and interpretive power were the most salient features of peer-led literature discussions in this classroom. These discussions often sustained, but sometimes interrupted, status and power relations as they existed in the local scene of classroom and community. Some peer-led discourse—Brooke's, for instance—would be considered more authoritative (in Bakhtin's terms) than others. Rather than decentering power in the absence of a teacher as they are meant to do, these peer-led discussions often gave dominant students a position of power. Just as context shapes performance, however, ongoing performances continually shape and reshape classroom context, such as when Brooke was in charge of the *Red Fern* discussion only to have her interpretive competence called into question. In this case, Lisa's performance interrupted Brooke's authority, creating an open space for cultural change. Another liminal space occurred when Nikki challenged dominant assumptions about marriage during the discussion of *Number the Stars*. In doing so, she had to juggle the roles she played and the selves they represented: oppositional student, strong critical thinker, antisocial learner, fifth grader primed to be a leader next year, and young girl wanting to fit in. The roles and social networks are intertwined and knotty, leaving students with much to negotiate, not only in terms of how discussions proceed, but also in terms of how texts are understood.

Students used peer-led discussions to comment, directly or indirectly, on the constraining and enabling features of social and interpretive competence as they were constituted in this classroom culture. Many of the key and illustrative events described in this chapter include such moments. Although these comments did not inevitably lead to transformation, they did, at times, lead to a metaknowledge of classroom interaction and structure through which multiple voices came into contact with and changed one another. The social drama that existed in this classroom surfaced often during peer-led discussions creating situations in which students negotiated social positions and engaged in metadiscourse about the meaning of social and interpretive competence. The ritual of peer-led literature groups brought to the foreground the "understanding of hegemonic order" discussed in the epigraph of this chapter, an understanding that can "empower agents in limited and highly-negotiated ways" (Bell, 1992, pp. 221–222).

Bakhtin (1981) used the term *heteroglossia* to refer to the social languages that intersect and sometimes collide when we speak, the ways in which one social language is embedded within our utterances as well as our interactions with others. Peer-led groups functioned as spaces where social languages within the classroom came into contact with one another, bringing to the surface the competing identities students must address within themselves and others. These competing identities were evident linguistically as well as socially, with peer-led groups borrowing from the culture of the classroom as well as from youth culture. At times, when Julia listened to her own audiotapes of peer-led literature discussions, she marveled at students' uses of linguistic constructions and interpretive norms appropriate to both spheres. She described the range of registers as moving from "in your face" to "as profound a statement as you would read in *New York Times* book reviews." This range of registers and topics is evident even in a quick look at such conversations as David's confession about the value of book discussions, Mackenzie's teacherly questions directed at James, the sixth-grade girls' animated turns relating a book to their lives outside of school, and numerous discussions peppered with "duh" and other lexical markers of youth culture.

Although the classroom teacher and like-minded students will inevitably have more power in regulating classroom discourse (in its broadest sense), they are not the only shaping influences. All members of the classroom perform roles through interaction that reshape the classroom culture and thus the ways that literature can be read and discussed within the culture. When students read literature, they must find a position from which to speak in the midst of the many voices they confront within the texts they read, the classrooms they create, and the worlds they inhabit.

5

Probing Cultural Norms in Teacher-Led Literature Discussions: Why Do We Believe What We Believe?

Literacy takes part of its meaning from its association with the critical transmutation of experience ... and much of its power from the struggle to liberate oneself from the institutions and immediate realities of one's culture. (Phelps, 1988, p. 122)

This chapter highlights small group literature discussions in which Julia participated to show the particular kind of dialogue she invited her students to take up—one that often invited students to become aware of, if not liberated from, "the institutions and immediate realities of one's culture."[1] For several reasons, less attention is paid in this chapter to the sociocultural conditions that shape interpretation: First, these conditions have been thoroughly described in previous chapters, and here I assume a base of knowledge about the research participants; second, as the literature events that follow reveal, performances during teacher-led discussions focused more on interpretation than the negotiation of social roles. This is not to suggest that the two are disconnected. As the previous chapter made clear, and as the events depicted in this chapter reinforce, I see interpretation itself as constituted in social codes, conditions, and identities. However, when Julia led a group, she held the locus of power, so that although students occasion-

---

[1]Lewis (1999) includes an earlier version of parts of this chapter.

ally contested her authority, they spent less time contesting each other's. Particular students still had more interpretive and social power than others, but conflict and negotiation tended to go underground as students performed the interpretation of text.

Julia felt strongly about her role as an active member of literature discussion groups and defined these groups as teacher led despite reservations about her degree of involvement. Although she believed that children need time to construct knowledge together without the interference and control adults often impose, she also felt strongly that, as adults, teachers must offer children their knowledge and guidance. This view of the teacher's role stood in opposition to some of what she had learned in university classes, in educational journals, and from district philosophy. Often, she felt, these sources promoted a "hands-off" approach that did not make sense to her. When Julia was part of the discussion group, she often moved the discussions from the personal to the critical. Through the personal, students learned to immerse themselves in texts, whereas through the critical they began to distance themselves. Occasionally, the discussions took on the interactional pattern of more traditional teacher-led talk, but the nature of the talk, I believe, was something quite different in that it invited readers to take up a critical stance toward texts, one that led to the probing of cultural norms and textual ideologies.

As established in chapter 3, for Julia reading literature involved entering into the text world, resisting text worlds, and examining one's immediate world. Considering Julia's beliefs about the meaning of literature, her interest in adopting a critical stance is not surprising. When readers enter a text, they make connections between life and text, and when they resist the text or examine the immediate world, they must push against textual ideology and probe cultural assumptions. I don't mean to suggest that these probes always emerged from a radical perspective. Instead, what Julia was after was a certain habit of mind, a way of reading that included in its repertoire the ability to achieve in engaged distance from the text, as she herself does in the following example.

When responding to the book *Alanna: The First Adventure* (Pierce, 1983), a novel set in medieval times about a girl who disguises herself as a boy to become a knight, Julia resisted the position she felt the text promoted, one that equated feminism with traditional male roles. At one point in the book, the main character, Alanna, worries that she will never be as good as even the least able male. Julia told the students that this genuinely troubled her, that she could not understand why Alanna would have so little self-worth. Nikki responded that this was a time when women were not viewed as positively as even an average man and therefore Alanna could not feel she was as good as a man. Julia invited Nikki to examine the immediate world in relation to the text world:

> Okay, you're living in a time when the average male will make roughly twice as much at what they do than the average female. Even though things have changed, there are things that are still fairly unequal today. Does that make you doubt your self-worth?

My initial response to Julia's comment was to want to push against it, to suggest that indeed a systematic lack of economic power does cause women, and others of oppressed economic classes, to question their self-worth. Often, in my conversations with Julia and in her conversations with her students, she represented the power of the individual as precariously balanced against the socially constructed conditions that shape the individual. Later in this chapter, I include an exchange in which she questioned her own desire to accent the individual. In this case, although her response did not key into the effects of systematic inequality on self-worth, it did lead to a discussion about the ways in which medieval women may have had more financial stability, at least through marriage and inheritance, than women today. Thus, the students challenged prevailing assumptions about the current status of women and resisted the reading position promoted by the text.

In analyzing similar literature discussions in Julia's class, I use the language of cultural theory as it has been applied to the teaching of English. According to P. Gilbert (1987), discussions should focus on "how 'personal experiences' are culturally constructed" (p. 249) and on why particular subject positions get validated in texts over others. Patterson et al. (1994) argued that reader-oriented approaches view literature as a reflection of life, whereas the cultural perspective holds that "texts promote interested versions of reality" (p. 67). Furthermore, rather than viewing texts as sites where "readers bring their personal experience ... and make their own meanings," the authors claimed that from a perspective based in cultural theory "readers are constructed as meaning-makers by the readings available to them" (p. 67). These suggestions call for an approach that sees texts as sites for "cultural conversations' (Graff, 1987, p. 257). Such conversations would address the ways in which texts are culturally, historically, and politically constituted; they would include discussions of how one can make sense of the competing voices within a text (Bakhtin, 1981) and consider how one might find a place to stand within these competing subject positions. All of the aforementioned authors argued that a cultural approach to literary response in the classroom will engage students in critical awareness of the interests promoted by the text and the dominant culture.

Julia's own literary background did not include specific training in current theories about response to literature (either reader response theories or cultural studies and critical theories), but she was influenced by them nonetheless. Reader-oriented approaches were encouraged in the language arts and reading journals she read, the writing projects she took, and the district's language arts guidebooks. Responding to texts through one's personal experiences was promoted as what teachers and students should aspire to in a student-centered classroom, and it was, indeed, one way that Julia encouraged students to respond to texts as discussed in chapter 3. However other conditions in Julia's life—her educational background in philosophy, her family background, and her own reading experiences, for instance—predisposed her toward viewing literature from a more culturally oriented or critical position. Thus, Julia encouraged students to probe and, at times, resist the ways in which certain cultural assumptions and textual ideologies shaped their readings of texts and experience.

The next two sections focus on how two reading positions—cultural critique and resistant reading—take shape in the discussion setting. The emphasis, as it has been in previous chapters, is on the ways in which these reading positions of cultural critique and resistance take shape in the discussion setting and how they are embraced and contested through moment-to-moment interaction.

CULTURAL CRITIQUE

> You know I thought about it, and I think the day that somebody says to me, "Okay, your job is just to get these books and give them to the kids, and you just quantify the time, and you just analyze their … reading and writing samples," that's the day I will say I don't want to do that.… And it's not because I think that I—this role I serve—is so important; it's because of this feeling that … *asking questions that you wouldn't automatically think of yourself is important.* (italics added)

In the following two excerpts from discussions of *War Comes to Willy Freeman* (Collier & Collier, 1983), Julia pursued a question suggested by one student's comment, one that most students in the group would not automatically think of as important. The main character of the book is Willy, an African American girl who witnesses her father's death at the hands of the

British during the American Revolution. Her mother is taken prisoner and Willy disguises herself as a boy to go search for her. The book group consisted of James, Tyler, Andy, and Sam (although Sam was absent for the two discussions from which these excerpts were taken), all of whom were perceived by Julia to be low- to middle-ability students. James, Tyler, and Sam often didn't complete their work, and Andy lacked confidence and the willingness to take risks. *War,* one of the books read during a historical fiction unit, appealed to these students in part because other books in the themed unit were longer and contained more difficult vocabulary (see chap. 4 for discussion of self-selection according to ability). The discussion that follows is about a section of the book, quoted here, during which Willy questions whether it really matters if she supports the Americans or the British:

> And then I began to wonder: Why was I on the Americans' side, anyway? What had the Americans ever done for me, except keep me at the bottom of the pile? ... There was Captain Ivers trying to put me back in slavery again, and nobody teaching me how to read or do sums, so's I couldn't even tell what town I was in without asking. And knowing I would have to take orders so long as I lived. Maybe in heaven black folks gave orders to white folks and women gave orders to men. (Collier & Collier, 1983, pp. 71–72)

Willy decides that it doesn't really matter what side she's on, but nonetheless she considers herself American and would therefore support the colonists' cause. That passage from the text is the subject of the following discussion exchange.

Julia:	Do you have any sense that Willy is on one side or another, James?
James:	I think she is on the right side.
Julia:	Okay, why?
James:	Because that her dad fought for the army, that the American side freed her.
Julia:	Okay. Let's skip ahead to the end of the book. Pretty soon, you know, sooner or later we are going to finish this book. When we finish this book somebody is going to have won this war. What difference do you think that will have made to Willy's life?
James:	I don't know.

Julia:	Now she says before, because she is female and because she is Black, she is going to be at the bottom … and people are going to be ruling no matter what. They are going to be White males. The men who are White and have land are going to be the ones who are calling the shots. If the British win, what do you think might happen to Willy?
James:	She might think that her mom died. I don't know.
Julia:	Do you think her mom might die if the British win?
James:	Uh.
Tyler:	They'll be slaves together.
Julia:	Okay, they could be slaves again; her mom might die. Andy, what do you think?
Andy:	Well, I don't think they would be slaves again because all of the Americans might, like, be dead.
Julia:	Okay, they might be dead. If they're not slaves, they could be dead. Okay what if the Americans win? What do you think's going to happen to Willy?
James:	All the slaves are going to be free?
Julia:	Okay, you think if, if we win this war all the slaves in the country are going to be free?
Tyler:	No because, uh, I mean they're still Black. I don't think that they'll free 'em. They'll still be slaves even after the war. Some of 'em will.
Julia:	Okay, James says the slaves will be free. And Tyler says there will still be slavery.
Tyler:	Even after the war. And then Martin Luther King will come /
Julia:	And then he will free the slaves?
Tyler:	Yeah.
Julia:	Martin Luther King will come and free the slaves.
Tyler:	Yeah.

Julia: How about you, Andy?

Andy: I think they will, um, keep 'em as slaves because like the war is
                over and it doesn't really matter when, if they … if they win the
                war, it will probably get … well … I mean you fought for us and
                we won so you are going to be a slave again or something.

Julia: Okay, so you think that the people like Colonel Ledyard, who
                are in charge of the American side, are going to just use the ser-
                vices of the slaves in the war to fight and then the minute the
                war is over, they are going to go back to saying "Okay, too bad.
                You be slaves." Do we have any evidence for any of these in the
                book so far? Is there anything to make us think what you think?
                Is there any character, any event in the book so far, that makes
                you say "Yeah, that's what's going to happen, all right?"

In this exchange, Julia makes several moves characteristic of her performances during literature discussions. Shortly into the exchange, she asks
students what difference the war's end will make on Willy's life, a question
students wouldn't "automatically" ask on their own. She draws James out,
and although he doesn't pick up on her efforts to complicate his rather
dualistic thinking (e.g., "I think she's on the right side" and "All the slaves
are going to be free"), he does remain a participant. Julia attempts to push
students to think about the social and historical complexity of Willy's position, and Andy and Tyler eventually join in, despite the ahistorical reference to Martin Luther King to which Julia responds with some surprise, but
chooses not to challenge.

One week later, the following exchange about *War* took place. Tyler
started by predicting that Willy would be free if she could get the legal papers that proclaim her freedom.

Julia: Okay, so even in this situation … Tyler, you still believe in those
                papers' power? …

Tyler: [Tyler asked Julia to help him identify a character's name.]
                Yeah, Colonel Ledyard. Captain Ivers, um, he said that he
                bought her before, um Colonel Ledyard died. So, and, I don't
                know if he could, because don't, does, Colonel Ledyard still,
                um, own her, even after they made her free?

Julia: Hmm. Okay. So you are asking, what I hear you asking is what
                does it mean to be a freed slave?

Tyler: Um hmm.

Julia:	Um. From what, uh, from what you have read in the book, what do you think it means to be a freed slave?

Here, Julia underscored Tyler's comments, presenting them in the form of a question she would like the group to consider. During our March interview, Julia explained to me why she didn't think she'd have the *War* group discuss the book on their own:

> Partly it's the feeling that maybe in ... both in *April Morning* (Fast, 1961) and *War,* there are issues there that aren't kid's issues.... I mean when Tyler said, if Tyler had said, "What does it mean to be a freed slave," at least I heard that question. Nobody else would have heard that question.... So in some ways maybe I'm talking myself into that I serve more of a purpose than I perceive myself as having served.

Julia saw her role both in terms of asking questions students wouldn't automatically ask on their own and hearing the questions of students that otherwise wouldn't be heard. The term *question,* for Julia, referred to that which is intriguing, confusing, or challenging. She lost patience with students who treated her questions as routine and authoritative, yet she used her authority to let them know that she expected more of a commitment. What follows is a continuation of the previous discussion (after a break of several turns):

Julia:	Now what does it mean to be a freed slave? Now let's think about this.... Mrs. Ledyard and Mrs. Ivers are free women. Willy and her mom were not free and have now been freed. They are freed slaves. When you say it means that they are free, are they exactly the same as Mrs. Ivers and Mrs. Ledyard now?
Andy:	Not really as powerful /
Julia:	Okay. So ... there is some difference between them and other free women. What difference do you see besides power? Or what makes the other free women powerful?
Andy:	They, maybe they were, like, born not to be slaves.
Julia:	Okay. They had been free all their lives. Do you think that would change the way you were? Stop. [James was being reprimanded.] Are you interested in, not interested in, this question? [spoken to James] Because that's what I hear you saying by distracting Tyler. What do *you* think? Do you know what the question is? Okay, go ahead and restate your question for James so maybe he'll be as interested in it as Andy and I are.

Tyler:	Um. What does it mean to be free?
Julia:	If Willy is free, what does that really mean?
James:	That she can do whatever she wants.
Julia:	Does it mean she can do whatever she wants?
James:	No.
Julia:	Why don't, why did you say no?
James:	I don't know. I just /
Julia:	It was just an answer? Okay, if Willy is a free person, what are the kinds of things she is going to be able to do that she can't do as a slave? Let's do that first.
James:	Go somewhere when she wants to.
Julia:	Exactly. She is not free. She can't change where she is if she is a slave....

Julia began by reviewing the characters and their roles, moving quickly to a question that asked students to consider the meaning of freedom from the perspectives of different characters. She wanted them to understand that the concept of freedom is not black and white, that what most of us ordinarily believe about freedom is overly simplistic and in need of examination. Andy was beginning to understand something about the relation between power and race. James was learning that when the teacher was part of the group, even his friends bought into the classroom ethos.

The discussion continued under Julia's direction in an attempt to historically situate events in the text, yet point to the persistence of racism today.

Julia:	Are the circumstances of their lives [the women's lives] different? Is there a difference? Even if you are all free, are some people more free than other people? Andy, you said you thought so. What do you see as the difference? You saw Colonel Ledyard and Mrs. Ivers as being a lot more powerful. Do you know why?
Andy:	Because they are White.
Julia:	They are White. Um, what difference do you think that makes?

Andy: Maybe because he is a Captain.

Julia: Maybe because he is a Captain.

James: They make more money.

Julia: They have more money. He is a Captain. And you are right.
           Some of the status the women have is a result of their hus-
           bands' status. So some of the power they have is if they marry a
           powerful man they have more money and they are White.
           What other differences do you think being White makes? Let's
           say Colonel Ledyard's wife walks into a store. She wants to buy
           something. She doesn't have enough money to buy it and she
           says "Oh, hold on to it for a minute, and I will go get some
           money." Do you think the store owner is going to do that?

Andy: Maybe.

Julia: Okay. Willy comes into the store. Do you think the store owner
           is just as likely to do that?

They established that the store owner might have responded differently to
Willy, and Julia asked Tyler to read from his journal. Julia made a few comments on the journal before she was interrupted by Andy who had a question:

Andy: Um, if the store owner was Black, would that /?

Julia: Make a difference? What do you think?

He thought that it probably wouldn't make much of a difference, but
sounded unsure. Julia helped him to visualize the scene, first with a White
customer, then with a Black one, and Andy decided that the Black store
owner would still trust that the White person could pay but would probably
trust the Black customer more than the White store owner did. Julia tried to
explain why this might occur.

> Just common experience. Just this is a person who is in some way similar to
> me. I mean these are huge generalizations. It would obviously depend on the
> people.... But one of the constraints of the time was that it was very difficult
> for Black people to own anything. That is why Sam Francis [to whom the
> book refers] is so, is such a, a, character that you hear a lot about, because he
> was a very famous man and owned a very famous location during this war.

Julia's role in this discussion was to move students toward an examination of the relation between power and race and the relative meanings of

freedom. In addition, she historically situated the position of African Americans with regard to ownership before the American Revolution. Although I believe that Julia's probes and responses during literature discussions worked to develop in students a critical awareness, I did find myself wanting to enter this discussion to comment on the systemic nature of inequality, to point out that it is not just "common experience" but racism that keeps White store owners from serving Black customers. However, Julia's comment came after an extended exchange about race issues, and she may have felt that to further extend the discussion would have served her needs more than the needs of her students. Such is the problematic nature of discussions that highlight critical positions. Teachers must determine when to provide information and when to listen, when to probe further and when to let go.

It is clear that Julia took more turns in these *War* discussions than did her students, and her turns were lengthier. Furthermore, contrary to much that is written in educational literature about good discussion practices, the student responses volleyed back to her rather than building on one another. "I'm happiest when they just go off [building on each other's comments], but they don't do it very much when I am there," Julia explained. She recognized and accepted responsibility for her power in teacher-led groups, but wanted to find ways to make the talk more equitable: "I get to say when we start. I get to say when we finish. I mean, I'm the one who calls time." She attempted to decenter her own power by providing students with choices: They played a role in choosing the texts they would read in groups, decided as a group how many pages to read per night, and often kept a group agenda for discussion. Students also kept response journals that served as the starting point for the day's discussion. This strategy kept Julia from monopolizing and focusing on her questions and her agenda. In addition, there were opportunities for students to discuss books in peer-led groups without her participation. Julia felt that the historical novels unit required more direction from her in terms of culturally and historically situating the texts, yet speculated that if she were to listen to the audiotapes of herself, she would be "horrified at the number of questions [she] asked."

Although she had reservations regarding her degree of involvement in literature groups, Julia had as many reservations about repeatedly leaving students to discuss on their own:

> What [teachers] say is terribly powerful with others. And I think all adults abdicate that role. I mean most of the adults in their life abdicate that role and say, "You decide." Well, decide over or against what? And most cultures de-

liver with something for them to decide over or against by the time they are in sixth grade. And in our culture something has happened.

Despite her suggestion that contemporary U.S. culture does not "deliver" what she believes to be important values, she was not naive about how her students were positioned within the larger culture. She purposely avoided reading a book by the series author R. L. Stine, for instance, although her female students loved Stine's books and repeatedly asked her to read one (not to the class but on her own).

> I kept promising I would read one of them, and I never did.... They are doing whatever task they need to do with that book all by themselves, and I suspect it's into aspects of the culture I don't want to support. And so I could maybe raise questions about those tasks.

Julia recognized, here, that she could bring popular texts into the curriculum to make visible their discourses—naturalized views of violence and sexism, for instance:

> But I think adults serve that role of saying, "This is beautiful." Especially those subjective judgments. "This is good. This is beautiful. This is just there...." We give meaning to kids for those terms by what we do and by what we model. And so I don't think we can lightly not do that.

At the end of another unit that focused on issues of individuality and conformity, the students' talk turned to despair over the state of the world. Each of the 8 students in the group had read books in which conformity leads to evil and fascism. After a conversation about abuses of power, Mackenzie said that she thought "everybody human should die." Julia's reply is of interest in light of her vision of her role:

> It [this view] seems to abdicate the power that you have to change things, and I just have too much data that humans can make a powerful difference toward good—that we aren't always going to win. It's going to be messy, just as you've all decided that messy societies are perhaps preferable for their messiness ... but if you are not going to be a player because you think you are going to fail, I am scared to death for the rest of us ... I mean, I want you to think ... it may not be possible for me to know at this point what the cost will be in human terms, but I want you to engage. I want you to be a player.

The ensuing discussion was long and philosophical, with the 5 girls contributing more than the 3 boys in the group. Julia addressed this gender issue, telling the group, "We cannot allow just fifty percent of the human beings to be concerned about this stuff." Lisa argued that David was concerned and that he had been talking: "You just really haven't listened because I hear him," she insisted. Julia told about a work of art she liked that showed a little boy looking vulnerable wearing his pajamas that had the word "hulk" written across his chest. "I'm worried that that is what we do to males. We keep dressing them in these green hulk pajamas.... We tell them that they have to consider themselves to be powerful or not to exist," she added. Lisa said that males were like "frightened little kittens" now that females have more control. At one point, Julia specifically addressed James:

> James, you are not saying anything. You think guys are more powerful than females? Females are more powerful than males? Does it matter? [James shrugs and says nothing.] That is not a response ...

A few turns later, Nikki, entered the conversation:

> I just never ... realized why boys always act tough and we're never like that. I always just thought they were stupid or [others laughed].... All of a sudden, I realize it's just maybe how they were, how they were supposed to be in this society. I never, I never got that.

Julia took a turn to talk about the value of studying gender relations in other cultures. She talked about Margaret Mead and suggested that students might want to read *National Geographic* to learn more about that subject. Another student, Kate, entered the conversation next:

> Men are supposed to be powerful in our society. But then when they *do* do crimes like raping, I mean, then we look down on them. But we're sort of, our society is sort of encouraging that behavior. I mean, not like we are telling them to, but /

In this classroom, as described in chapters 3 and 4, a handful of sixth-grade girls and two fifth-grade girls controlled the direction the conversation took in most of the book discussions in which they took part. Julia often tried to include others in the group, as in the previous scenario. However, it is not hard to imagine what it would be like for a fifth-grade boy like James to assert himself in such a group—a boy who lacked experience with such discussions, who had not read the amount and kind of literature the girls had read, who was new to the school, who had many conditions that marked him as an outsider, and who was only beginning to understand the standards for interpretive and social competence in this classroom. Clearly, he could not do so without jeopardizing the power he did have; that is, the power to be mildly disruptive and to resist group norms.

It is hard to ignore the fact that many girls in this group were making interesting, thought-provoking comments that would sweep many teachers away—into the girls' minds and their worlds—and that also, because of the frequently existential content of their talk, required the kind of guidance that Julia felt obligated to give them. Thus, the girls' contributions were, in various ways, affirmed and addressed.

Whereas David often participated in such discussions, he was not an active participant in this one, perhaps because it was nearing the end of the year (late April) and he was distancing himself from sixth grade. Indeed, his participation patterns shifted dramatically starting in April. When I mentioned this observation to him during our final interview, he acknowledged that he was tired of elementary school and looked forward to junior high. Jason participated once or twice in this long discussion, most notably when he talked about his grandmother's views on children and how they should have more power in the world, a contribution that Julia quickly picked up and reinforced. As a whole, however, he said very little during the discussion.

Julia worked to include students like Jason who found it difficult to enter discussions with students who were highly verbal and willing to compete for the floor. At one point Jason read a journal entry about Alanna in which he mentioned that she was good in most of her subjects at school. Julia responded by saying that she thought Jason's comment was important in that he focused on Alanna's capabilities, whereas most everyone else in the group had focused on how overwhelmed and frustrated she felt. Julia "revoiced" Jason's comment so that others in the group would listen to it rather than simply hear it. O'Connor and Michaels (1993) observed teachers using strategies that initiated students into participant roles that assigned them social identities as valued members of the classroom. Specifically, the teachers used student response as the basis for a teacher inference called "revoicing" (p. 327), thus lending authority to the contributions of students who lacked classroom status. For Jason, a quiet student who rarely offered unsolicited responses to texts, the revoicing strategy worked to legitimize his contributions.

She also tried to include Jason by asking him to imagine himself in a character's position, and then revoicing to lend authority to his response:

Julia: Jason, if you put yourself in the position of one of these children [Jewish children whose homes were invaded by Nazis in

Number], what happened to you over these two chapters in time? How have you felt, and what are you thinking as a kid?

Jason: I feel, like, mad that they are here and ruining our stuff, and I don't know, sad that it is going to be a lot harder to live here now.

Julia: Okay. So the shoes and the cracked button seem like minor inconveniences to us but they are really symbolic of a much larger problem—that it is becoming difficult to live....

During teacher-led discussions, Jason and James fared better in groups such as *War* that included students (in that case all boys) who were similarly competent in terms of social and interpretive expectations. In these groups, Julia still spoke to students in the adult way that Nikki's and David's mothers noted was characteristic of her style. She still posed intriguing questions and followed up on theirs, moving often from the personal to the cultural. The difference was that the students in those groups, as Jason made very clear to me, felt more comfortable contributing when the very confident and verbal sixth-grade girls were not present, saying all there was to be said before inviting others to speak, as Jason had noted. The earlier illustration from the *War* discussion is typical of the interaction that occurred in such groups, and although James's competence was inconsistent, he remained a player. He never disappeared.

Students, with the exception of Mackenzie, had many complaints about the constraints of teacher-led groups, yet there was an air of intimacy in small groups like *War*. The students leaned in close, instead of slouching back in their seats as they did when they felt unable or unwilling to compete in other groups. Julia often patted a shoulder or ruffled hair, and spoke softly or smiled at them. This behavior was not reserved for small groups of boys perceived to be of low ability; in fact, Julia often used eye contact and touch in the larger, more heterogeneous groups as well. However, boys like James would pull away or look embarrassed when receiving her attention in the heterogeneous groups, although they never seemed to mind the attention in the smaller, more homogeneous groups.

When Julia participated in literature discussions, she continually pushed in the direction of cultural critique. Clearly, she saw her role in her students' lives as important, and literature discussions were times when she could have an effect on the way students viewed significant issues in their lives—a time when, in her words, "the quality of the question" mattered.

Sometimes the questions were ones that Julia asked herself and invited the students to help her answer. At the start of a discussion of *April Morning*, a book about the American Revolution narrated by a young boy whose brother was a Committeeman, Julia presented the students with a section that gave her trouble. The *April Morning* group included 6 students perceived to be of middle to high ability. Julia referred to a section of the book in which some of the men are talking about being more afraid of women than they are of God, and Julia asked the group to help her understand how this could be true in a culture as sexist as this one was. Two girls made brief forays into the topic, with Nikki suggesting that women are feared because they are not really known. Mackenzie then built on Nikki's statement with a cultural critique.

> Mackenzie: I think they don't know anything about women and so ... that is why they are scared of them. And it's like ... in *Witch* group [*The Witch on Blackbird Pond*; Speare, 1958] how they are saying ... if they don't know this one lady who they think she is a witch, and they used to burn people because they said "Well, this person is strange, so they are a witch." And so they [the men] are like, "Okay, we don't know anything about women, but all we do know is that we are supposed to be ... in charge." ... And so the women never get to explain themselves.... All they know is what their duties are. They don't really know much about each other.... So that is what I think.

> Julia: They just kind of fulfill roles, and because they are locked in these roles then you have to act out, you can only act out your role when you are in the presence of the opposite sex. Like that? Is that what you mean?

Here Mackenzie engaged in speculation with Julia about the structure of gender at the time and the ways in which that structure constrained social relations. Given Mackenzie's background knowledge—her mother had taken her to feminist lectures and often talked about feminist issues at home—it is not surprising that she felt comfortable asserting her competence here and thus engaging in speculation with Julia. Again, the social codes and practices familiar to Mackenzie were a comfortable match for those she encountered in this classroom.

In another excerpt from the same *April Morning* discussion, Julia directed students' attention to the systems that influence events that students attribute to individual choice. In the following excerpt, Nikki talked at length about what she saw as the theme of this book.

The main point of this book is that ... this book is all about one choice that Adam made. And I was thinking about it and ... you know every day you go through choices, and sometimes I think how can I go wrong, what if I would have said, "Yes, I want to do this and [go] with my dad to the store instead of staying home," you know. You think of all the things that would have happened ... and he [Adam] made this one choice that really changed ... his life completely.... He just said, "Okay, my mom wants me to stay, but you know I want to go to the war," and then all of the sudden he is in the war. And now ... I mean he doesn't say this, but what I understand from what he is saying is "I want to go home." And if he wouldn't have signed the muster book, then he would have just been home right now doing whatever.... I kind of think of this book about just about choices—about how the committee is making choices, and about how he made choices.... I guess everything you do is kind of a choice.

Nikki was referring here to the decision made by the main character, 16-year-old Adam, to go into battle with his father. As the book progressed, Julia, who at first had told the students that "war is not a natural disaster," began to reconsider her perspective. What follows is an excerpt from a journal entry written by Julia. Because this was her first time reading *April Morning*, she had decided to keep a journal along with her students, which she shared with them near the end of occasional discussion sessions. This is an excerpt from the journal entry she wrote after Adam's father died in battle:

And now that the arguments are over, and the shots were fired and the family and friends are dead, this war seems for Adam exactly what I said it wasn't a natural disaster. So Adam is stuck in the smokehouse with his grief and his fear, and it was as if it was the flood or earthquake in LA or something. This is something that has now happened and changed him forever. And originally I said war is a choice, and it was a choice they were making then, but now that it's come, it must feel for Adam and for everybody else just like Bill's death [a reference to Mackenzie's grandfather who had just died]. Any senseless death of someone you love and care about is just a disaster.

Although Julia was not explicit about the systems of domination at work that contribute to the decisions often attributed to "individual choice," she let students in on her reflections as she revised her own thinking about the individual's role within a much larger system. When the group finished *April Morning*, Julia asked the students to write about the book in any way that mattered to them. She referred to Nikki's thesis about important choices and said that this might be something Nikki would want to write about. Reflecting on her own thinking about the book and how that would impact her writing, she mentioned that she saw the choices as imposed on by "external circumstances," that what seems to be "free choice" isn't free at all.

The performative nature of interpretation was clear in this teacher-led group when David read a journal entry in which he said that the Committee-men should have killed a young British soldier who already had been shot and badly injured by their fire. In the same entry he noted that it was diffi-cult for him to write about this because the reader only sees the boy through Adam's point of view. Julia told the group that she found his response "scary" and was surprised that others in the group didn't respond in kind. "Now David is afraid," Mackenzie quipped, perhaps as surprised as I was by the intensity of Julia's response, and knowing that she could challenge Julia with impunity. After further questioning, David said that he thought prisoners of war (POWs) lost all their rights. Julia talked with students about the larger cultural issues again and about the laws that govern treat-ment of POWs. She told David to talk to his parents to find out about the rules that must be honored during war. She mentioned the well-known pho-tograph from the Vietnam War of an officer shooting a man point blank and the outrage that it produced. I was surprised by Julia's passion for this sub-ject and her anger with David, because I had interpreted David to mean that he couldn't bear to think about the young man's suffering and so thought it would be kinder to put him out of his misery. When I asked Julia about her response to David and told her I interpreted his comment differently, she re-plied "That's because you haven't seen him hurt someone as hard as he can," and later added that she interpreted his response as analogous to what he was doing to James at the time, "rubbing him out socially."

Julia read a set of unspoken conditions into the exchange, as did David, who once told me that he sometimes anticipated what Mrs. Davis would want him to say and gave her the response she wanted. He added, "If we get in an argument, and she says 'Well, this is what this book is about.' I say 'yeah,' but I really know what I think it is about—my side of the story." By contrast, when I asked Nikki if she ever said things during discussions that she knew her teacher would want to hear, this was what she had to say:

> No, I don't think so.... I know what she favors, and I try not to let that inter-fere because I've known people who just, you know, say whatever Mrs. Da-vis or another teacher likes. And, you know, I think that is really stupid, because then the teacher thinks you are someone that you aren't.

Bakhtin's (1981) notion of addressivity comes to mind, here, in both Da-vid's and Nikki's responses. They anticipate the expectations and voices of their audience (in this case the teacher) and make decisions about what to say based on that knowledge. Nikki's belief in the essential nature of an individual—that is, there is someone that you are and someone that you are not—is ironic in light of the multiple voices and overlapping roles she herself negotiated during the extended exchange from the *Number* discussion included in chapter 4. Culturally, we promote the concept of the unified self, and as Davies (1993a) argued with regard to gender identity, children strive to fit their multiple selves into this cultural mold. They are uncomfortable with the complex identities they must inhabit and juggle, in part because the unified self is promoted as a natural state.

The credo of the young adolescent to be true to oneself is difficult to attain in either teacher-led or peer-led literature discussions where students must negotiate multiple roles as they interact with audiences who require of them multiple selves. However, during teacher-led discussions, these negotiations go underground, leaving Julia with more visible space for matters of interpretation. The space she inhabited as a member of a literature discussion group was to perform a kind of cultural critique and encourage her students to consider why they believed what they believed. Julia also invited her students to view the text as a historical and social construction, and in so doing, to resist, at times, the pull of the story.

RESISTANT READINGS

> Yevtushanko has this wonderful poem called "It is Wrong to Tell Lies to Children" ... and the thesis of that poem is it is wrong to tell children everything will turn out all right in the end. And of course that is very Russian, to not do that, right? And to say you can't count the cost. And I really think that is true—that they are hungry for, tell me a story ... tell me something that will give me hope, that will help me make sense of my life. But do not tell me a lie. Do not tell me it will all be swell.

In this excerpt from an interview, Julia was responding to her students' common complaint that children's books often had unrealistically happy endings. Tyler told his group that he didn't want *War* to be perfect. When Julia asked him what he meant, because, after all, Willy's father had already died and her mother had been taken away, Tyler said that in *The Island of the Blue Dolphins* (O'Dell, 1960) everything was too perfect and he didn't want that to happen again. He wanted action instead, he told her. Julia responded by making visible the constructed nature of the text: "You are writing this book now. What are you going to write next? You are in charge."

Another student, Steven, had a similar response to *April Morning*. "I hope they all die," he said about the book's characters. When Julia expressed surprise and asked why, he told her, "I want the good guys to die for once. In all the movies and books all the good guys always win." Instead of underscoring the value of the characters' lives, as I might have done, Julia again made visible the constructed nature of texts. (The following exchange includes Julia and several students.)

Julia: That's an interesting notion because the Greeks killed off all their heroes. It's a fine literary tradition to want the hero to die. It's the history of tragedy.

Mark: It makes them seem more like a hero if they give their lives.

Julia: Ooh, ooh, now is that part of what you wanted?

Steven: No, I just want them to die for once ... because it's so *rare.*

Julia: Not in real life, only in childhood books that /

Steven: Like in Cinderella

In both of these examples, the students, Tyler and Steven, performed resistant readings; that is, they read against the grain of the texts. If I were their teacher, I believe I would have responded more sympathetically to Tyler's desire for an imperfect ending than to Steven's more nihilistic desire for death, which I might have understood more as resistant behavior than resistant reading. Had I tried to squelch Steven's response, however, he may well have excluded himself from the conversation. Julia's response to Steven, on the other hand, served several purposes at once: First, it legitimized his contribution; second, it placed his contribution within a historical and cultural context, thus showing Steven that his wish for a character's death comes with a tradition and is rational; and third, it highlighted the constructed nature of texts, foregrounding their ideological functions (e.g., children's stories do not reflect reality but promote a certain version of reality). Her response suggests the malleability of texts, which are constructed and can be reconstructed by readers.

This sense of the constructed text was evident in the way Julia led discussions about *Where the Red Fern Grows* (Rawls, 1961) as well. Written in first-person narration, the book is a fictionalized memoir about the adventures and love shared by a boy and his two dogs. Most of Julia's students loved *Red Fern* and they entered the text world effortlessly. They talked about the book with their friends outside of reading time, and the girls cried whenever the dogs were endangered. It was not the sort of book that engendered doubt or resistance. For one discussion, Julia asked students to consider events in the book from a temporal perspective, deciding how those events were viewed when the story took place compared to how they are viewed now. Julia's purpose was to invite students to question behavior that seems natural and acceptable in the text: actions such as chopping down a tree to catch a coon simply for the sport of hunting. Why might it have been acceptable to take this action at that time, but not acceptable now? Some of the students suggested that if today someone were to drive a nail through the fist of a live animal, as Billy did when he was trapping, animal rights activists would try to stop this action. David pointed out that no one would know about it if it happened way up in the mountains where the story took place. He continued with a comment that related the temporal change to a spatial one.

David: When you say it's now and it's then, you know? Well, the Ozark Mountains [where the story takes place] probably aren't as much as they were, you know. There are probably, like, houses.

Julia: I guess you're right. That's a good point. I should probably say not only just now and then but here and there. That's a good point, David. That, that, that sets of morality accrue to a place as well as a time. That's a real good point.

Although students were, for the most part, easily able to enter the text world of *Red Fern*, Julia's probes and responses moved students to situate the text socially, culturally, and historically, as well as to consider the constructed nature of Billy's life. Following Althusser (1971), Davies (1993a) discussed the need to deconstruct a text's "obviousness," what a text sets up as being natural or taken for granted. Davies argued that "teachers and students need to immerse themselves in text and distance themselves from that text at the same time" (p. 63).

Immersion and distance—a complicated positioning—is achieved by both David and Julia as illustrated by the following conversation. During one discussion of *April Morning*, Julia talked about a scene that struck her as being "absolutely real," and David responded.

David: I think that is what books are really about. It's just trying to write it real.... Books are just trying to convey a message to be real.

Julia: That's what books are about?

David: Yeah. That's all books are just supposed to, you are supposed to look at them and say, "This is real. This sounds real."

Julia: Really?

David: It's a story, but it sounds real.

Julia: You know what I think of? I think of what we were doing in the sound stuff, when we were talking about a sound being a vibration.

David: Yeah.

Julia: You know, that there can be a sound over here and that vibration somehow reaches us.

David: Uh huh.

Julia: I think of that when I read books ... it's, it's almost as if it's resonance, you know. There is some string plucked in me. I know what that note sounds like. I know what this feels like. But I really love that experience. But also I turn to books for experiences I've never had—

David: Yeah.

Julia: that I want to have.

David: Yeah. And it's, it's supposed to just be like a book about a story that, like, something that happens to someone and you are that person.

Julia: Uh huh.

David: So like if I read this book and it's really, really real, I will feel like I am in the Revolutionary War as soldiers. It is like virtual reality.

Julia: Did you do that?

David: Um. Not really.

Julia: It's better than virtual reality. Virtual reality doesn't use enough of *me*. There isn't enough *resonance* set up for me in virtual reality. I don't even like film for that reason. [David laughed.] How's that from the nonvisual teacher to the visual kid.

Despite Julia's claim of difference at the end of this conversation, she and David spoke the same language when it came to what literature meant to them. Both Julia and he liked to enter the text world—evident in their references to feeling the literature and living it—yet both retained some slight distance—the reality was virtual for David and resonant for Julia. Both accomplished what Smith (1992) referred to as *controlled surrender*, a stance that combines detached observation with involved identification, thus opening the way for a developing critical awareness:

> I want, I want to know what they [characters] would do. I want to be able to act out what they were doing in a situation without knowing.... Like if they're in a situation and ... he was gonna either jump off a cliff or stay on a cliff, I would know what he would do because I know his feeling and how he acts and that kind of stuff.

I turn now to an excerpt from a discussion that presents a crystallized performance of resistant reading. This took place during the individuality versus conformity unit I mentioned earlier that included 8 students. The students had all read books about societies where uniformity had become fascist, books that promote individuality over uniformity, even when the latter is easier, less painful, or, in the case of *The Giver* (Lowry, 1993), more communitarian. The communities in each book strive for a sameness among people that leads to death or isolation for those who are different or refuse to conform. *The Giver* is the only book of the three that is about a community that is seductive for the first half of the book. Gradually, what seems like a utopian society reveals a dark underside. The two other books are about communities that are overwhelmingly evil: *Number the Stars* (Lowry, 1989) about the Nazi takeover of Denmark, and *A Wrinkle in Time* (L'Engle, 1962) about a planet that has been taken over by an evil force. The students reading each of these books were moved by them and, for many discussions, talked about the evil in each society.

In the following exchange, Julia moved in a different direction, encouraging students to resist the most accessible readings—those shaped not only by the ideology of the text but by the students' own positions as early adolescents living in an individualistic society. Thus, she asked the group to think about ways in which the communities in their books are better or worse than aspects of our society. Answering how they are worse, Nikki offered the first response in one word—"sameness." Julia used that word as the starting point for a resistant reading in the discussion that follows:

Julia: Okay, now think about inequity in terms of, think about in our society, inequity in terms of education, inequities in terms of educational opportunities, in terms of economic opportunities, in terms of, um, those kinds of things. Do you ever view the unequalness, the unsameness about our culture as being a problem?

Kate, a fifth grader, talked at length about the need for everyone to go to school and how some don't take it seriously enough.

Julia: So we said that sameness is not a good thing, by and large, in these societies. But now Kate is saying, "Well, except I'd like to see everybody go to school." So these are places where we value sameness and Kate values sameness in education.

Most of the students commented on the education issue, after which Julia asked for other positive outcomes of sameness.

Nikki: Like in *The Giver*, they take pills so you can't, so you can't really fall in love with anyone, right? It controls your hormones, right? So it's kind of good that you don't look different, because … I notice some people have really big deals about looks, and I think it … can be a big problem for somebody, you know. And looks aren't really an issue if you have sameness, you know.

Julia, Lisa, and Nikki took several turns on this subject. Then Lisa continued.

Lisa: Yeah, but it's good and bad because you can't fall in love with the person you want to fall in love with.

Kate: But, if you've never experienced love, then you wouldn't really know the difference.

Nikki: Yeah, but it's still bad. I mean—

Kate: We think it's bad, but they probably don't notice it, because they never even felt it.

After several more turns on this topic, Julia invited Jason into the conversation. He had read *Number*.

Julia: Jason, how about you? … We hardly think of … Europe under Hitler as a utopian society, but in fact it was a real attempt on the part of the Germans to reform society in a way that would be good for them. And that is connected to what Nikki said…. They [*The Giver* group] were all having an argument about how society ought to be, and Nikki had an insight. She said, "I realized I designed a society that was good for me." And so Hitler's Germany was a design for the good of Aryan Germany. What are, can you see anything that was good about Germany in those days?

Jason: Hmm. No.

Julia: What about some of the problems that you see in, what problems do you see in Denmark under Hitler?

Jason: The Nazis will come to your house and look for Jews and take them away.

Julia related this to search and seizure without a warrant, about which Mackenzie and David each took a turn. Kate then talked about how difficult it is to think of positive things about what happened in Nazi Germany because now "we are all looking through the eyes of the Jews."

Julia: You raise a very interesting point. Um, especially because as we do history in this country, we tend to ascribe all of World War II to Hitler, to one person. And, in fact, World War II could not possibly have happened if it only had been the idea of one person. It was not only an idea that was palatable to an enormous number of Germans, it was palatable to an enormous number of Europeans, and plenty of Americans as well. And so you have to ask yourself … why did they buy it? Why did this uneducated demagogue get up there and have millions of people following him?

Mackenzie said that she knew why because she had studied Hitler for an independent project in her program for "gifted" students. She shared what she learned about the Jews being used as scapegoats.

David: It wasn't just then that no one liked Jews. They had always had … a bad reputation. Like there were ghettos and there were ( ).

Julia: Um hmm. In fact, there were expulsions from entire countries. And 1492 is famous in Jewish history because all of the Jews were expelled from the country of Spain the same time that Christopher Columbus set out. That's true. This is a long long history of prejudice. Um. James. Anything in the book that you read [*Wrinkle*] that in that society makes you say, "Hey, this might not be such a bad idea?"

James: Well.

Julia: Anything in there that you found kind of appealing?

James: The Black Thing [referring to the "Dark Thing," which represents evil in the book].

Julia: The what?

James: Black Thing.

Julia: Oh. Okay. So what about the Black Thing seemed to you to not relate to anything in our world?

James: Well, it's not real.

Julia: Is there anything that is analogous in our society? Anything that you think is sort of unbelievably evil? What kind of things, what kind of content do you put on the Black Thing? Or is it just sort of a fantasy of evil? James, what do you, anything that you think is just evil, plain and simple?

James: I don't know.

In this exchange, Julia led the students in a discussion that made available to them another way of reading their texts. Most of them, having fully entered the worlds of their texts, had embraced the message conveyed therein that individuality is critical—a message that was reinforced in their music, in other books, among friends, and in the larger culture. They had spent a good deal of time during previous discussions talking about the evils of a society that demands conformity, but this time, Julia wanted to make another way of reading available for her students. Everyone, with the exception of Jason and James, tried on this alternative perspective. Again, on the heels of David's and Mackenzie's responses, both reflecting knowledge gained in other contexts, James's response pointed to his difference from those who, along with Julia, shaped the meaning of interpretive competence.

The difficulty of this kind of critical pedagogy lies in the ease with which it can tip the balance toward teacher-directed practice. Yet the role of the English and language arts teacher has long been ambiguous in that the teacher is cautioned to lead without squelching individual freedom. Moss

(1989, 1995), who wrote about critical theories related to literacy teaching, pointed out that a critical pedagogy is no more ideologically based than a humanistic pedagogy. She argued that as educators we need to acknowledge that we want students to read texts in certain ways because we hope to influence the sort of people our students will become.

When I reread the previous exchange between Julia and her students, I think about the sort of people I want those students to become, and I consider ways to help them understand more about the economic and political conditions that made the Holocaust possible. Indeed, I think that this was what Julia was after when she implicated the United States and all of Europe, indirectly inviting her students to focus on political struggles among countries rather than the struggle between good and evil among individuals. Perhaps I would have wanted to focus more on the structures that created and supported the ideology Julia referred to when she asked why the Holocaust was possible, but Julia was the one making the difficult moment-to-moment decisions, not me. Mackenzie jumped in, wanting to share what she had learned about Jews as scapegoats for a weak economy, and Julia went with the moment. After David added what he knew, Julia framed his comments with earlier history, but did not fully contextualize that history.

Again, the problematic nature of critical teaching rears its head, with teachers like Julia continuously negotiating the nature and degree of their involvement. It is noteworthy that James's statement about the "Dark Thing" represented a resistant reading as well, but not one that would be seen as interpretively competent in this context. He might have responded as he did because celebrating evil was a socially resistant response, and contesting social norms in the classroom was a role he often performed. He might have done so because he understood that he was to say something positive about something normally seen as negative and didn't know quite how to do it. In either case, his response was shaped by the conditions that come together at the moment—the readings available to him, the expectations he did not meet, the role he did accept, the voices of his peers and his teacher.

REFINING THE MEANING
OF INTERPRETIVE COMPETENCE

Social roles are an important dimension of interpretation in any setting, but in the teacher-led setting, with the teacher as active participant, the negotiation and struggle, the meta-awareness of social roles was not prominent. In session after session, what surfaced was the attention paid to the work of interpretation. In heterogeneous groups, students like Mackenzie, David, and Nikki, who shared with Julia similar beliefs about the meaning of literature, constructed the meaning of interpretive competence along with their teacher. In groups consisting primarily of students who were low to middle achieving, students were able to coconstruct with Julia a revised notion of interpretive competence. For instance, during one *War* session, Julia acknowledged that the boys preferred focusing on the book's action, as they repeatedly told her, and she preferred focusing on the characters. Julia came up with a way to combine the two performances that served to deconstruct, to some degree, their binary relationship: The boys would tell her about an important action that occurred and together they would decide how the action affected the characters. Yet, as we saw during the *War* discussions quoted earlier, Julia did maintain her focus on probing the larger culture with the low- and middle-achieving students as well, so the dominant meaning of the teacher-led groups remained stable across ability levels.

In keeping with the focus on why we believe what we believe, Julia often invited students to think about their interpretive processes, and she often modeled her own. In talking with a group of students about what they get out of keeping journals, she stressed the personal over the cultural, yet still invited students to look at themselves from a distance to understand more about who they were and a time in the past and how this influenced who they had become:

> My daughter is doing Shakespeare sonnets. And … I remembered that I had a favorite when I was in eighth grade. One that I loved. And I found it because I remembered the first line of it, and I was amazed. I can't imagine what in the eighth grade me was interested in that poem. And I would like to know.… You will be almost totally different, Tyler, and it would be fun to visit Tyler in fifth grade and see what he thought.

Julia often talked to her students about the value of leaving a written trail of their reading. Although the students weren't generally allowed to write in the books owned by the school, Julia allowed them to do so on one occasion, to talk with them about the value of keeping track of their responses to texts. She asked the students to mark the chapter as they saw fit, but then to write on a sheet of paper the page number and reason for making the mark, so that they could look for patterns among themselves and analyze the reasons for their interpretations. Again, it was the metaknowledge or awareness that she was after—the answer to the question, why do we believe what we believe.

Julia's comments during teacher-led discussions were punctuated with her own experiences, but the experiences most often related to the process of interpretation. When her students were feeling despair about the state of the world, a fairly frequent occurrence, perhaps because many of the books they read were about tragic events (e.g., Holocaust, slavery, war, fascism), she would often give examples from her own life to point to the resourcefulness of human beings, human tenacity, and hope. She provided examples that ranged from a friend's romantic rejection to her father-in-law's experiences with Alzheimer's disease, but the two threads that connected these examples were elements of hope and the process of interpretation. For instance, when she talked about her father-in-law's memory loss, she talked about aspects of him that were "still alive with zero memory." Lisa was indignant:

Lisa: Wait. Is the use of living when you are old and stuff just to make your loved ones and everybody feel happy that you are alive or something because if you died then they are all sad? But is that just the use of living when you are that old?

Julia: Why do we have geraniums in here?

...

Julia: Because they are pretty. I mean that is exactly why we have them in here. And that is of value to me. And there are many things that have a value that is symbolic, that feeds my soul, that nourishes my, my, the reason for getting up in the morning.

...

Lisa: I don't want to be a symbol or anything like that when I get older.

It was typical of Julia to talk about life as a text one must interpret, full of symbols and aesthetic beauty that she felt made life worth living, despite its tragic dimensions.

Like Julia, Nikki was interested in symbolic images and language. After taking some of the children to *Schindler's List* (Spielberg, 1994) one weekend, Julia held two optional, emotionally charged discussions about the film. During one of them, Nikki said that her mother thought that when it was time for a character (a Nazi) to be hung, it was difficult to kick the chair out from under him because this was a symbol of his being not entirely evil. Julia's response characteristically focused on the reader's or viewer's role in the making of symbolic meaning:

The interesting things about symbols are [that] all the weight of meaning in a symbol is in the interpretation. So for your mother, it symbolized that, and, and, if you think about the film, think about the visual images or the lines that made a difference to us, a great deal of the meaning we find there is what we invest it with.

During a conversation that made connections between the Nazis in *Number,* the Dark Thing in *Wrinkle,* and the murder of an infant in *Giver,* Julia talked to students about evil by basing it in what she learned about an object's essence from a college philosophy class.

A philosophy professor when I went to college … was trying to teach us about essence, what an essence is.… We know that a chair is a chair even if they are wildly different in appearance, and even if some are so uncomfortable that you wouldn't even really want to sit down on them. It seems to me that these books are doing that kind of thing with evil—that evil resides in all kinds of shapes and forms. But all these books are talking about evil, something that you identify as having the essence of evil.

Again, Julia used an example from her own life to make a philosophical and interpretive connection to the text under discussion. She modeled a habit of mind that is reflexive (Babcock, 1980) in its use and awareness of the process of interpretation.

For Julia, it was through these habits of mind—the process of interpretation and art of representation—that one could experience hope. This connection of life world and text world is evident in a very long talk she had with students in the *April* group about *Zlata's Diary: A Child's Life in Sarajevo* (Filipovic, 1994), an excerpt of which was published in *Newsweek.* I include a small portion of Julia's comments, which came at the end of a discussion about the ethics of war as it was debated within the plot of *April Morning.*

In *Newsweek,* if your family gets it, there is a wonderful diary by a girl, who has been compared to Anne Frank.… And I will bring it as soon as everybody in my family gets a chance to read it. It has some excerpts from her diary. A child—somebody like you—living in the middle of a contemporary horror, has been so articulate, that she has saved her family.… So for those of you who write and who take issue with the world, take yourself seriously. Some people *do* listen. And read this if you have a chance.… But I thought you might be interested in it because you are reading about … the beginning of another war. And these arguments about … why one ought to fight, should one fight, how much, how many arguments are worth a life?

In teacher-led, small group discussions, the meaning of interpretive competence was refined. The established norms, those that emerged through the first read-aloud, still operated, but in this small group setting, Julia was able to adjust her patterns of interaction, both with texts and students, and expand the range of possibilities. When students moved in new interpretive directions, Julia openly expressed her pleasure. Such was the case when Tyler revealed his understanding of the constructed nature of texts and readers in his discussion of *Number the Stars:*

Tyler: The problem about this book is it doesn't tell how the characters feel. So I just have to guess here. So I guess you have to guess here, so, and I think Ann Marie is feeling important [because she has a package to take to her uncle] and then scared that the soldiers will bomb.

Julia: Tyler, dear, I think I love you. That is so wonderful, because it is so true....

She went on to say that such texts invite readers into the book, "so that I think later on if you are older and you read this book, you might have different feelings." The kind of text that she and Tyler referred to was what Barthes (1975) coined the "writerly" text. Such texts require the reader to take an active role, almost as though they are writing and revising the text as they read. Whereas Tyler saw this writerly quality as problematic, Julia was pleased by it because it moved Tyler to both engage with and distance himself from the text. He had to engage to imagine a character's feelings and distance himself to think about how the book is constructed and how this makes him respond as a reader.

PERFORMING TEACHER-LED DISCUSSIONS: WHY DO WE BELIEVE WHAT WE BELIEVE?

Literature discussions in which Julia participated often probed cultural norms in an effort to examine hidden assumptions, and students were encouraged to view the text as a historical and social construction. Teachers can serve an important function in literature groups, as did Julia, by situating texts and engendering cultural conversations. Her tendency to lead discussions that probed cultural norms and her focus on the text as a constructed artifact opened up roles for literature that students did not often take up on their own. Understanding the ways a text promotes a familiar and unquestioned discourse, the discourse of individuality, for instance, in *The Giver,* and learning to read against the grain, to examine or resist as well as to enter the text world, provides students with another role that literature can serve. This role, exemplified by the underlying question of discussion groups that included Julia—"Why do we believe what we believe?"—is essential if we view the development of a critical social awareness to be an important function of schooling. This approach to interpretation was coconstructed by Julia and her students as they interacted over a text, particularly those students who were the most verbal and confident and whose purposes for reading literature matched those of their teacher.

Peer-led literature groups without teacher participation offer certain advantages. As chapter 4 suggests, they can serve as hybrid communities in which students borrow from the culture of the classroom as well as from youth culture, thus using linguistic constructions and interpretive norms appropriate to both spheres. However, the move to decenter authority in student-led environments is not enough if what we are after is a critically democratic stance, not only because the inequities of the larger culture are reproduced in the classroom, but also because allowing students to choose texts and responses will not challenge familiar and comfortable discourses. Thus, as the next chapter on independent reading shows, young girls left to their own devices may consistently choose to read books that promote desire as it has been constructed within a patriarchal ideology and young boys may choose horror books that promote the discourse of violence, often directed against women. Davies (1993b) argued for the important role of the teacher in providing a forum for critique in the classroom:

> If the language used in classroom text and talk is treated as transparent, it is more likely to become the reader's language through which they fashion the world and themselves. If the metaphors, images, and storylines through which characters are created are not themselves understood as constitutive, the reader cannot turn a critical gaze on that constitutive process. (p. 157)

The teacher's role, according to this scheme, is to teach students to read in search of that constitutive process. Although I would not want to suggest that critically engaged reading is the only kind of reading worth promoting in school, I would suggest that this is an important role of literature that is largely overlooked in school. I envision a role for literature instruction in the classroom that encourages students to "listen" for the multiple voices in texts as they read, those that are promoted by the text as well as those that are silenced.

6

Appropriating Cultural Norms Through Independent Reading: What Will We Accept, Reject, or Reinvent?

Cynthia: How does it make you feel as you read the books when the girls have something [bad] happen to them?

Nikki: I don't know. It's normal, I guess.

I open this chapter on independent reading with an excerpt from an interview with Nikki because her words so aptly represent what many fear—that the regular consumption of narrative storylines that portray girls as victims serves to normalize this position as the most natural one for girls to inhabit. Many girls in the class chose to read series books by R. L. Stine or Christopher Pike whenever they had a chance to choose a book. Regularly, during independent reading, more than half the girls in the class were reading books by one of these two authors. In these books, females are often placed in precarious or dangerous situations, and although they might be involved in extricating themselves from these situations, the male characters ultimately save the day. That this scenario felt "normal" to Nikki would affirm Julia's sense, conveyed to me in an interview, that adolescent novels (she named R. L. Stine novels in particular) seemed to reinforce power structures and position women in submissive ways.

In Julia's classroom, the students used independent reading to appropri-ate elements of the larger culture—dominant and popular cultural symbols and resources. However, it must be understood that this appropriation of larger cultural norms was dependent on elements of the local culture, par-ticularly existing discourses related to gender as described in earlier chap-ters. Throughout this chapter on independent reading, I argue that the practice needs to be situated within a sociocultural context if its role in the classroom is to be understood. A model for this kind of analysis is Tobin's (2000) book on children's responses to media texts in which he contextualizes children's talk about media through a close, careful reading of their responses as they are embedded in local and systemic social and cultural relations. His analysis leads readers beyond the media effects model, which argues that there is a cause-and-effect relation between text and viewer, toward a model of response that takes into account the multivocality of all interaction (textual and social). It is this multivocality, one that acknowledges the many social codes and discourses students nego-tiate, that this chapter on independent reading foregrounds. My analysis of a key event includes an examination of the institutional discourses that shape it (Fairclough, 1995), to understand the ways in which social and in-stitutional discourses intersect and compete (Beach, 1996; Dyson, 1997; Tobin, 2000).

During independent reading, which occurred almost every day, Julia in-vited students to choose their own texts as well as some of the conditions surrounding the reading of these texts (location, pace, form of response), hoping to increase student motivation to read, enjoyment in reading, and authenticity of response. Students would often crawl under desks or into corners with other readers. They recorded what they read and sometimes chose to write in a dialogue journal with their teacher about these books. Occasionally, Julia would have a conference with students about the books they were reading and ask them to read aloud for a bit for a quick compre-hension strategy check, but more often, she would facilitate quick, informal discussions among the students. It is easy to see why the practice of inde-pendent reading would create tensions for teachers (and most adults) who might not want to legitimate the storylines that young people may "choose" to bring into the classroom, which may be violent, perhaps, or sexual. Yet, the nature of the practice is meant to give students choices, and therefore to bring youth culture into the classroom.

In discussing the tensions that surround the practice of independent reading, I draw on work in gender and cultural studies. From the field of gender studies related to literacy, I refer to work that argues that children come to literacy in contexts that support in word, action, and ideology gendered ways of reading (Cherland, 1994; Christian-Smith, 1993; Davies, 1993b; P. Gilbert & Taylor, 1991; Luke, 1994; Moss, 1995). From popular culture studies, I refer to work that argues that popular culture subverts social control, shapes social allegiances, and creates subcultural capital (Fiske, 1989; Thornton, 1996) at the same time that it also exerts a powerful influence over readers' gendered positions (McRobbie, 1990). In what follows, I use these theoretical frames to situate independent reading within the intersecting discourses that shape the practice.

SOCIAL DISCOURSES OF PROTECTION
AND DESIRE

Ten students surrounded Julia at a table in the front of the classroom. They had just finished reading *Alanna: The First Adventure* (Pierce, 1993). There are four books in the series, and having loved the first, the group wanted to read another. Julia told the students that they could not read the book as part of their sanctioned reading time because Alanna, the adolescent main character, has a sexual relationship in this book, and she did not want to promote early sexual activity among teens. One of the students pointed out that Nikki had already read the second book in which Alanna sleeps with someone. Julia told them that she would not impose her views on their free reading time, but would not support teacher and group time spent on these books—that she could not do this in good conscience personally or as a teacher. The students argued with her. They all voted, they told her, and every one of them wanted to read the book. Furthermore, Lisa argued, the *Alanna* books take place during medieval times when people got married at the age of 16 and Alanna is already 16 in the book they just read. Julia appreciated this reasoning but nonetheless gave her final words on the matter. She told them:

> Can you all go to [the name of a local bookstore] tomorrow and buy it? Absolutely! Can you bring it in here and read it? Absolutely! Can you talk about it at recess? Absolutely! ... You can meet at 3:00; you can meet on the front steps; you can read—I mean I'm not telling you that you can't read the book. What I'm telling you is that I won't devote instructional time to it!

I started with the *Alanna* example to make visible some of the opposing social discourses that were patterns in the data on independent reading practices in Julia's classroom. I use social discourses to mean the worldviews and ideologies that regulate and define particular social contexts and activities (Brodkey, 1992; Gee, 1996; Weedon, 1987). In the previous scene, Julia used the social discourse of protection that adults often use when they refer to what they see as dangerous elements of popular culture. Thorne (1987) pointed out that adults construct an image of children as either victims or as threats, yet neither image leads to a contextualized understanding of children's actions. The students, on the other hand, used the discourse of desire—the desire to know what it means to be an adult, what to do, how to act, and how to fit in. Patterns of desire, according to Davies (1993a), are "constituted through discourse and through storyline in particular" (p. 145). For many girls, this means learning how to perform heterosexual relationships (Cherland, 1994; Christian-Smith, 1990; Finders, 1997; Moss, 1989), and for many boys this means learning to understand their place in relation to authority, power, and aggression (Connell, 1987; Connolly, 1995).

In addition to these conflicting discourses of protection and desire, another set of oppositional discourses surfaced in the classroom scenario: the official discourse regarding appropriate material for school consumption represented by the classroom teacher in opposition to the resistant discourse represented by the students who sought to bring the desires just described into the classroom and to subvert institutional norms.

GENDERED READINGS IN THE LOCAL AND LARGER CULTURE

Again, the classroom I studied was one in which girls' reading and response practices were established as the norm for competence. Many researchers (Cherland, 1994; Christian-Smith, 1990; Evans, 1996; Sarland, 1991; Simpson, 1996) have found that when given what we refer to as "free" choice, girls tend to choose fiction that often includes romance with an emphasis on characters, whereas boys choose fiction that may well include violence with an emphasis on plot. Girls tend to choose books based on suggestions from others, whereas boys more often choose books based on their genre. Girls tend to talk about feelings and relationships connected to texts, whereas boys tend to talk about action. Rather than seeing these differences as innate and universal, I hold the view that they are socially and discursively constructed. That is, we come into literacy as children in contexts that support (in word, action, and ideology) particular ways of reading, talking, and writing, and those ways are constituted in gender as well as other social and cultural factors (Luke, 1994). It is this mix of factors that readers will see at work in the key and illustrative events that follow.

Although the gender binary I have described related to literacy practices was evident in this classroom, it was not impermeable. Students performed stances related to gender that were also shaped by social class and peer relationships. Thus, in chapter 3, we saw David responding to literature according to the "feminized" interpretive norms of the classroom, and James sometimes embracing and other times resisting those norms. In a study of the oral narrative texts of two adolescent girls, one working class and one middle class, Gee and Crawford (1998) revealed the very different storylines that shaped each girl's worldview and discourse. Finders' (1997) research on the literacies of working-class and middle-class girls also speaks to the complicated intersection of gender and social class with each group of girls reading and writing in ways that would clearly situate them within their own group and clearly set them apart from the other group. Thus, gender categories are more complicated than they may at first appear. Although we may try to position ourselves according to discursively constructed patterns of desire, those patterns are not clean. So we keep at it, "never totally convincingly" (p. 14), as Tobin suggested (2000), and take up stances in relation to the texts we encounter within and against the gender categories and boundaries represented therein (Enciso, 1998). Other researchers argue, as do I, that the stereotypical gender categories they observed in their studies were not to be essentialized as biological or cognitive in nature, but rather as stances that are socially and discursively produced (Alvermann, Young, Green, & Wisenbaker, 1999; Evans, Alvermann, & Anders, 1998).

As a White, middle-class woman with interests similar to this teacher's, it was easy for me to feel comfortable in this classroom where the kinds of responses to literature that were valued were related to experiences, characters, and ideas rather than to plot and action. Julia emphasized personal responses to reading. In introducing the culminating project for one of the texts read in class, Julia told the students that she wanted them to do "anything to make your book your own." As an example of a personal response to literature, she read one of her daughter's high school English papers that was about understanding honor as it related to her process of self-discovery. In an interview with David at the end of the school year, David expressed his distaste for books that "make you cry," books he marked as female.

Cynthia: Do you ever choose a book ... for independent reading that might be like the kinds of books that ... Mrs. Davis chooses—like a Newberry Award winner, say, or/

David: I don't really like those kinds of books 'cause they're all the
              same I think. They're all, they have different stories, but they're
              all the same feelings, I think. Just maybe in a different time pe-
              riod. They're mostly all about death or suffering in some
              way.... And they're meant to make you cry, and that kind of
              stuff, and I don't know, I just don't like it. I don't like those
              kinds of book.

I pressed on trying to understand why he preferred his choice of
books—usually the *Redwall* series (Jacques, 1987).

Cynthia: Is there suffering in the world [of *Redwall*]?

David: Yeah, well, in this one there is a fever—like a plague. And it
              runs through an abbey and everyone is dying. But it doesn't
              make you want to cry. It just brings the issue into it.

David, readers will recall, was the male student most attuned to
Julia's interpretive expectations, and often, as we have seen throughout
this book, he demonstrated his engagement with the class texts. By the
end of the year, however, ready to move out of elementary school and on
to junior high, he performed his masculinity related to literacy in ways
more aligned to the other boys in the class. His passion for books by
Jacques remained constant throughout the year, but it was only near the
end of the year that he repeatedly complained that Julia favored girls and
he seemed to reject all that he felt was coded female in the classroom.
The local culture of the classroom as it related to gender, then, must be
understood to understand any literacy practice therein. In addition to the
information about the gendered discourse of the classroom provided
here, chapter 3 shows how gender relations were embodied in the classroom culture, and chapter 4 discusses gender as a complicating factor in
the classroom. These previous analyses are significant to my discussion
of independent reading in this chapter and are important for readers to
keep in mind.

It should come as no surprise that the gendered culture of the classroom
was shaped by masculinist culture outside the classroom. The larger culture
of dominant norms beyond the classroom is one in which male violence toward females is widespread, males hold more economic and cultural capital, and male ways of knowing, acting, believing, and being (as constructed
within the gender binary) are normative. This encompassing social discourse or ideological position competed with the local social discourse just
described in a dynamic that was played out during independent reading.

SUBCULTURAL CAPITAL IN THE CLASSROOM: STATUS AND POPULAR CULTURE

Like many teachers, Julia's view of popular culture was on the order of "don't ask, don't tell." That is, she knew her students were very influenced and enamored of popular culture, but she didn't want to know too much about it. She never watched television and purposely stayed out of the loop. She told her students to consider what they wanted to hold as "furniture in the brain." She understood, however, that at this time in their lives, the answer might be R. L. Stine or *Beavis and Butthead*. She remembered having a nun catch her with a book on her lap during class and calling it trash, which led her to want to understand why she liked trash, the beginnings of firmly held beliefs about the difference between "high" and "low" culture. Julia also believed that watching violence made people "more prone to violence," and that reading terrifying material made for more "terrified people." The students were very well aware of Julia's view of popular culture. As Nikki once told me:

> Don't even mention the word Christopher Pike to Mrs. Davis. She's like yuck ... but I think kids are pretty good at just ignoring that. I mean, I try to. I get kind of sick of reading, I don't know, books my mom would want me to read and stuff, you know.

In reviewing some of the precepts of ritual theory (Bell, 1992; McLaren, 1993), we recall that ritualized practices can tolerate internal resistance, reify the social world in which they are embedded, and transform participants' social statuses. In the practice of independent reading in Julia's class, all three seemingly contradictory elements of ritual surfaced, as evident in the key illustrative events depicted here.

There were several times during the year when independent reading took center stage. I focus here on a time during the last month of class when students read independently during reading time. They met in optional discussion groups that divided along gender lines with the girls agreeing that they wanted to hold discussions 3 days a week and the boys preferring 2. Julia allowed them to hold discussions according to these preferences. The boys formed one large group of 12, which met together only a few times on occasions when the teacher insisted that they all participate. Most Tuesdays and Thursdays, the group consisted of 3 or 4 boys. Jason told me that the first time the boys' group met, Julia put Brian in charge, a fifth grader who had behavioral, emotional, and academic difficulties. Jason, readers will recall, did not feel comfortable in groups that focused on discussions of what he called "big ideas" with sixth graders; yet he enjoyed this group and was one of the regular members who attended even when the teacher did not request his participation.

I turn now to three excerpts from a discussion that included 10 boys on a day when Julia asked them all to participate (2 boys were absent). These excerpts revolve around the discussion of a horror series book, *Bobby's Back* (Pickford, 1993), and its relation to horror films. The boys were very animated for most of the discussion, and there was a good deal of overlapping background talk related to the primary dialogue. I refer to the nature of this background talk when it is relevant to my analysis. *Bobby's Back* is the first in a series of books about a young man who seeks murderous revenge on a group of five people (four of them female) who teased him when he was a child. In these excerpts, the boys' discussion works in opposition to the social discourse of this classroom, with its feminized norms for competence, as they relate this book to other horror books and movies they have seen (Lewis, 1998).

Tyler: This [book] is about, well, *this dude/*

Brian: *Bobby's Back.*

Tyler: named Bobby. He, like, gets this group of people—they call themselves the five 'cause it's just five people, and at the beginning, he, this kid Bobby, he wanted to be in their group, but they, they told him that he had to do one test, and then, and it was to go into this old house and just to walk through and go out the back door. Well, so he did. He went, and then I guess, yeah, he fell through a hole/

Brian: and he landed, *and he uh /*

Tyler: *and this rat jumped on him.* And then /

Brian: He was scared. *They left him down there.*

Tyler: *They left him down there* cuz they thought he just chickened out cuz they were waiting on the other side to see if he really had, if he was really gonna come out....

Tyler and Brian collaborated on Tyler's summary of the book for a while, after which several of the boys engaged in a discussion of the main plot line of several other books in the *Bobby* series. About 10 minutes further into the share time, after one of the boys had just shared his summary of another book, James asked Tyler if he could see his copy of *Bobby's Back*. In contrast to James's participation in most literature discussions, during this particular half-hour discussion, James was a central participant, taking more turns than any of the others in the group of 10. However, many of his turns were either disruptive or playful. He made noises into the speaker of the tape recorder and yelled at students who did not follow the procedures he had in mind. For instance, when one student began to share his book by announcing the page he was on, James shouted, "That doesn't matter, just say what happened!" His other comments during the discussion included, "Sounds kinda stupid," and "Okay, you're done; shut up. Come on, Tyler. It's Tyler's turn!" Although these comments had a disruptive element to them, they also showed him to be far more involved in the procedures and talk than he ordinarily was, keeping up with the conversation and moving it forward in his own way. At one point, he asked to see the cover of *Bobby's Back,* initiating a conversation that spun into a discussion of the relative merits of horror films that all the boys had seen.

Brian:	Jason's better than Freddy. Jason kills more people. One movie he kills like fifteen people. The most Freddy ever *killed was five, six.*
James:	*They run from him and they get like* a mile away, and then they turn around and he's right there and he's just walking.
Tyler:	Who cares who kills more people?
Brian:	*Jason doesn't even act real.*
Mark:	The guy is like running away from Jason and he stops and Jason is right in front of him, and he's only walking.
Brian:	They're never even scared.

[James makes the sounds from the theme song for *Friday the Thirteenth*.]

James was the most vocal member of this group, the self-selected facilitator, although technically Brian held that position. Jason, although rather quiet, smiled and laughed with the others, and appeared engaged throughout. However, David, who usually carried more status in the classroom, had less in this context. The social and interpretive norms established by group members worked in opposition to the codes and practices of the classroom that David performed so well. I discuss David's role in this group more fully in the section on performing independent reading.

SOCIAL DISCOURSES BEYOND THE
CLASSROOM: APPROPRIATION AND SUBVERSION

Clearly this conversation was not the sort sanctioned by the social discourse of this classroom. It is, however, in keeping with the social discourse of the larger male-dominated culture, particularly in its violence toward females. In several of the sections I did not include in this excerpt, the boys talked about a girl being hit in the head with a harpoon gun and a mother, who herself was a killer, getting her head chopped off. The boys talked about these events with very little commentary, none of the big ideas that Jason liked to avoid. Horror fiction is part of a regulatory process that positions boys within hegemonic versions of masculinity (Christian-Smith & Erdman, 1997). I suggest, however, that talking about violence and who feels fear in the face of violence is a way of examining and questioning masculinity. In addition, it provided the boys with an opportunity to resist the social discourse of the classroom and regender the discourse.

Urquhart (1996) speculated that boys' uses of popular culture can be especially threatening to female teachers because, as women, the teachers have themselves felt oppressed by masculine identities. Yet, the adult fear of boy culture, McDonnell (1994) argued, accords it with a degree of respect and power not bestowed on girl culture, which tends to be trivialized and, indeed, was trivialized in this class by the boys in particular, who claimed that the girls were foolish to read such obviously formulaic books (cf. Luke, 1994; Moss, 1995; Williamson, 1981–1982).

Although the social discourse of the classroom opposed the discourse of this literary event, this event proceeded by way of certain forms of shared local knowledge among certain members of the classroom culture. Gutierrez et al. (1995) asserted that such forms of local knowledge "include unacknowledged cultural references to popular music, film, and television. In this way, individual students take stances toward the roles they are supposed to play" (p. 451). Indeed, play them they must. The need to fit in—to belong—is strong, and perhaps stronger still for those who need to replace what Bourdieu (1986) called cultural capital—the status middle-class knowledge that is accumulated through upbringing and education—with subcultural capital. Subcultural capital, according to the popular culture theorist Thornton (1996), is about the status one gains from being "in the know" about popular culture. One gains access to this capital through media exposure, not through education. Access to this capital results in allegiances—bonds with other members of the subculture that foreground particular representations of masculinity.

It is interesting to note that Mackenzie and Brooke, two middle-class (and in Brooke's case, quite affluent), high-achieving girls in the class, both expressed some ambivalence about reading series books, as if they did not want to be caught liking them. Once when Brooke told me that she was reading an R. L. Stine book, Mackenzie announced, "Brooke's been reading that R. L. Stine book all year!" Brooke was very indignant about this, and insisted on making it clear to me that she was only reading it as a second book and always had another book going. Mackenzie also expressed ambivalence, telling me that it was important to read a variety of books, books like *Anne of Green Gables* (Montgomery, 1976), along with R. L. Stine. She claimed that to read only Stine would be like eating one kind of food and that the variety makes her a better reader (very much her teacher's and her mother's metaphor). Reading Stine and Pike is easier, she said, but when you read "other kinds of books, you get more of a sense, and a visual image of what is really going on." Yet, Mackenzie admitted that outside of school, reading Stine and Pike was necessary to achieve the kind of subcultural capital I mentioned earlier. She told me about a friend who didn't read these series books and was consequently left out of many conversations.

This finding is in keeping with Dyson's (1997) recent work on children's uses of popular culture in writing, in which she found that the middle-class children also played with cultural material from the popular media, but they distanced themselves from that material in official school contexts. This effort to mark social class was evident in other studies of children's responses to television (Buckingham, 1993) and girls' responses to popular series books (Alvermann et al., 1999) as well. These young people wanted to mark their difference, and possibly their cultural capital, from others—a difference that, for Mackenzie and Brooke in this classroom, connected them to the ethos promoted by their teacher. Other students delighted in the minor subversion of engaging in independent reading at school. One working-class student was most explicit about this. She loved all the Stine and Pike books, having read 20 by Stine and 10 by Pike during the year. She talked at length with me about the social bonds these authors engendered among her friends. When I asked her to describe the difference between these books and the ones that her teacher chose, she replied: "Well, the ones that she picks usually have a meaning that you could learn something from, but R. L. Stine books don't really have anything that you would learn." This girl liked that there was nothing educational about them and when I asked her why, she told me, "Well, I kind of like it because it's different and you get a chance to just, I mean, it's, you're in school but you don't have to be learning something all of the time."

During an interview, Julia told me that adolescent series books often seemed to uphold "attributes of the majority culture." One can read Julia's distaste for such books as a feminist response, but it also serves to support the historical view of women whose consumption of romance literature was seen as a sign of inferiority (Luke, 1994). As she told me on another occasion, "You simply do Little LuLu comic strips until you're sick of it and you can predict with absolute accuracy what's gonna happen next, and you're bored. And then you go on to something a little more challenging." These books, then, carried both status and stigma—the status of social currency, but the stigma of being female and, according to many of the boys, manipulated by formulaic writing, or according to their teacher, controlled by patriarchal and commercial technologies.

Not all of the students read series books for independent reading. In light of the boys' discussion focusing on male aggression, often toward females, it is worth noting that one of the independent reading discussions in which some of the girls, including Nikki, participated focused extensively on the subject of rape. One girl in the group had read *So Far From the Bamboo Grove* (Watkins, 1994) on Julia's recommendation, a memoir about a young Japanese girl's experiences living with her family in Korea at the end of World War II. Parts of the book relay the rape of young Japanese girls at the hands of Korean men. The 4 girls in the group talked about this tragedy in some depth and with a focus on the emotional content of the book. What was striking to me about this discussion was Nikki's interjection after the group had discussed the politics of rape as it occurred in Korea at a particular historical moment.

Nikki: Raping is kind of common.

Lisa: Hmmm?

Nikki: That is what it seems like. Raping is kind of common.

Anne: I know it does.

Lisa: Not in Japanese [meaning Japan, perhaps], it doesn't.

Kate: In wars it is.

Nikki: No, but it seems like nowadays it is common. Like my sister tells me, like, that she went to this forum and, like, this lady—this girl—told them that, like, she got raped a couple of summers ago, and it seems like everybody has.

Social discourses beyond the classroom include versions of masculinity that position females as victims. When we consider the juxtaposition of the girls' focus on rape and the boys' focus on male violence, we can see that these discourses are compelling to early adolescents as they begin to make sense of the stances that are available to them related to gender.

PERFORMING INDEPENDENT READING: WHAT WILL WE ACCEPT, REJECT, OR REINVENT?

Fiske (1989) argued that "popular culture is always in process; its meanings can never be identified in a text, for texts are activated, or made meaningful, only in social relations and in intertextual relations" (p. 3). Another look at the boys' discussion of horror books and films reveals how meanings were constituted in social and intertextual relations.

James: Jason's better. *He carries a chainsaw.*

Tim: *It's really scary.*

Mark: Not always. He uses anything he can find.... [The conversation turned to a movie about Freddy Krueger.]

Tyler: What happened? How does [Freddy] get killed? How does he get killed? [The boys discussed other movies about Freddy Krueger.]

Brian: They conquer him in a video game, like.

Sam: Isn't there a Jason versus Freddy? [The boys discuss other movies about Freddy and Jason.]

Brian: Free Willy scared me. [laughter]

Tyler: Free Willy versus Jaws.

Sam: Care Bears scared me. *They got in a fight with Mr. Unhappy Person.*

Tyler: *Oh, free Willy versus Jaws. Oh!*

Brian: The Smurfs versus Jason.

[Several boys repeat this, laughing as they speak.]

Brian: The Flinstones could bash his face in.

James: *Bam bam bam bam.*

Sam: Bambi versus the Smurfs.

Tyler: Free Willy versus Jaws.

Sam: Willy versus Shamu.

James: Tyler versus Mark.

Brian: Free Willy versus Jaws.

Brian: Mark versus Tyler.

[James is making noises reminiscent of the soundtrack from *Jaws,* the part that marks the approach of the shark.]
         ...

Sam: This dummy on the cover versus Jaws.

Sam: We started out talking about *Bobby's Back.* Now we're talking about Bambi versus Spiderman! [laughter]

Although this conversation again opposed the social discourse of the classroom, I want to make a case for the social work these students engaged in. First, James and most of the other students who spoke in this segment (and others in this half-hour discussion) were academic outsiders within their classroom; a few were social outsiders as well. Here they were animated, engaged, and participatory, a stance that was highly uncharacteristic for them and one they maintained throughout this literary event. Second, the language used throughout this excerpt is playful, parodic, and performative in ways that allowed the students, in Dyson's (1997) words, "to play with each other and with powerful societal images" (p. 283). In this case, and earlier in the conversation as well, the boys brought up the issue of fear. Earlier, we heard Brian say admiringly that the characters in the film were never even scared. Here, another student admits that Jason's chainsaw was scary, and soon after that the parodic exchange began, an exchange that was almost entirely related to fear.

Perhaps this conversation served as a way for the boys to abstract themselves from the fears they had being members of a culture in which they were supposed to be fearless in the face of monstrous opponents. Connell (1987) described "hegemonic masculinity" as one that aims to dominate femininity as well as other masculinities through "power, authority, aggression, and technology" (p. 187). It would be scary, I suspect, to take on those attributes, and the boys dealt with this condition through parody and performance. They juxtaposed something scary with something that was not (*Free Willy* vs. *Jaws*), then something not scary with themselves ("Care Bears scare me!"), and finally one of them against another—but in play, not aggression. The tone was lively, quick, and innovative. In other parts of the discussion, the boys engaged in clever, if sometimes off-color word play. "Instead of *Bobby's Back,* Bobbit's back," Sam contributed to the conversation at one point, delighting his peers with a reference to the man in the news at the time whose spouse had dismembered him. The boys were collaborators in performance and in audience. Indeed, being an audience member was to be a part of the performance itself, so entwined were the two. This was an emergence of text in context, as anthropologists Bauman and Briggs (1990) described such performances. Together, the boys acted as a performance team (Goffman, 1959).

To take Goffman (1959) further here, and to make an important point about opposing social discourses, I argue that the boys were engaged in both front-stage and backstage performance sites. The front stage is the metaphorical site where the performance is given, and this was clearly a joyful performance for each other. Within the classroom context, it was a backstage performance as well—a site where suppressed selves can appear. Within the context of the classroom, then, this was a subversive event with a social discourse in opposition to the social discourse of the classroom, yet allowable within it. The social and interpretive boundaries in the classroom culture were permeable enough to allow for this transgression, and to allow the students to appropriate and subvert, to some degree, the larger social discourse of hegemonic masculinity.

Within a classroom there are multiple audiences for any performance, audiences that have competing expectations for what it means to be a competent communicator. Brooke (1991), in discussing identity negotiation in college writing classes, noted the complexity of forming an identity in light of the various contexts and sanctioned roles that impinge on the life of every student in the class. Brooke invoked Goffman's (1959) concept of the underlife (backstage performances) that resists officially assigned roles.

Critiquing the notion of the stable self, "the 'little me' inside that opposes the efforts of parents, peers, authorities, and other social groups to alter its basic nature" (p. 15), Brooke acknowledged instead the socially constructed self that comes into being through cultural interaction.

With a focus on the same rich discussion, several illustrations of the performance of self as described by Goffman (1959) and Brooke (1991) come to mind. Each boy took a turn to describe the plot of a book he was reading. Sam was reading *The Diary of a Young Girl* (Frank, 1993). Obviously, this was a book quite unlike the horror book that had sparked such an animated discussion. I was interested to see how the other boys would respond, and was not surprised to find that they managed to fit the book into the maintenance and regulation of gender as it had been consistently performed in the group.

Sam: Shut up [several boys had been talking over him]. I'm on page 29 of The Diary of Anne Frank.

James: That doesn't matter! *Just what happened!*

Sam: And, um what's happening is, they're getting forced out of their home and into another one. It's about the Holocaust. It's the diary of a girl.

Tyler: Is it good?

Sam: Uh, yeah, it's okay. Cuz, it's like, it's like I'm reading someone else's personal life.

James: It's like reading your sister's diary.

[Overlapping talk and laughter.]

Tyler: He probably goes through the trash.

Even though this book is the sort of book Julia would want students to read, one that "makes you cry," as David might put it, the boys were not about to frame it as such. Instead, they situated this book within their immediate performance of gender, which included the maintenance of the gender binary, with males imposing themselves on females, physically and emotionally (reading secret diaries, violating personal space), yet using the group, in part, to explore what it means for males to be in control and lack fear. Sam never brought up the very real fear that Anne Frank faced while in hiding or how her diary may have represented a way for her to retain some control over her life.

David's position in this group was not as clearly defined as that of most of the boys. He did not attempt to discuss his book (*Ghost in the Mirror,* Bellairs, 1993) using his considerable repertoire of interpretive conventions. Instead, he quickly provided a plot summary, as expected in this context, and did not seem to mind when James interrupted, saying it was time to move on to another student. He laughed on occasion with the others and commented now and then, but for the most part remained aloof. David's interactive style was not a good match for this group, to the point that on one occasion he mentioned that a peer's humor was not funny.

One could say that he did not meet the social and interpretive norms established by this group and controlled primarily by James. Even though it was shortly after this discussion that David told me he did not like the books that Julia chose, he certainly seemed more at home during discussions of those books. The one time during this discussion that David appeared to be engaged was shortlived. Sam had read *Moss Flower* (Jacques, 1998), one of the books by David's favorite author. David jumped in several times to provide clarification during Sam's retelling of the plot, and when James tried to move the conversation along to the sort of books with which he was more familiar, David continued a quiet conversation with a few students about the characters that run through the *Redwall* series. Apart from this exchange, he was uncharacteristically subdued throughout. Interestingly, the two times when he spoke most (during his own book description and during the *Moss Flower* description) were the rare times in this discussion that did not serve the purpose of gender maintenance or exploration.

Rather than using class discussion time to discuss their favorite series books, the girls talked about the books by R. L. Stine and Christopher Pike during free moments at school and often outside of school. The books carried a certain status that resulted in important allegiances and bonds among the girls. When I asked Nikki why the girls in her class read Stine and Pike, but the boys did not, she related the question to herself:

> I guess 'cause it has to do with, um, people a little older than me, but in the age I'm interested in and just … they're cool. They're kind of scary but they're mysteries too.

Here, Nikki suggested that these books related to her life in that the characters are the age she was looking forward to, suggesting, perhaps, that the books provide a sense of belonging to the world of adolescence that she had just begun to enter. Yet, I would not be doing Nikki justice if I were to suggest that these books represented a reality for her. Nikki understood these books to be constructed artifacts, and she was fully capable of analyzing the construction:

Nikki: … like in all the Chrisopher Pike books, it's usually … a girl in the series I'm reading, a girl gets killed and then, like um, there's a main character that's a girl and a boy, but more girls are gonna get killed.

Cynthia: Okay. Why is it that more girls than boys get killed in those books, do you think?

Nikki: Well … maybe it's 'cause they're slightly sexist, you know, I think maybe they like to show the male as being more the hero or something, especially in the R. L. Stine books. In the R. L. Stine books, the boyfriend always comes and, like, rescues the girl in the end.

Nikki was clever enough to know what I was driving at in my heavy-handed way, so she provided what seemed to me to be a response a teacher would want to hear. In the next segment, however, she continued to demonstrate her understanding of how these series books are structured:

… in most of the Christopher Pike books, it seems to me there is, like, a boy that's really strong, you know, and then there's a boy … he's like nice and all, but, and he's really, like, smart or something, but, and he would *try,* but you know, he probably wouldn't win 'cause he's not very muscular or anything.

She had the formula for the series worked out, but this did not spoil her enjoyment. In fact, if we consider the young girls and women who participated in studies of romance and series fiction conducted by Christian-Smith (1990, 1993), Cherland (1994), and Radway (1984), mastering the formula is part of the pleasure, resulting in feelings of competence and agency. This is not to dismiss the fact that as Cooper (1993) suggested, such gender formulas are marketed to girls starting at a very young age so that the gender and power relations set up in these books seem—as Nikki put it at the start of this chapter—normal.

In their study of read and talk clubs, Alvermann et al. (1999) cited Brodkey (1989) to explain the way that a female participant in their study used a cultural stereotype about females (the trivialization of "girl talk") to her own advantage. Mackenzie's response to my question about why the girls read Stine and Pike, whereas the boys in her class did not reveals a similar strategy:

Most of the main characters are girls. Like, the girls are the ones that have the problems and they are the ones with the boyfriends that kill them and things like that. So it's basically ... it puts boys in a bad position to read about guys killing girls.

From my perspective as a teacher, I was not able to imagine any ways in which "guys killing girls" could be empowering to girls and disempowering to boys. Yet, something about these books allowed Mackenzie to feel in control of male violence and in touch with female perceptions of that violence. Often, it seems, the contradictory nature of popular culture is related to its appeal (Lewis, 1998). Males killing females would not seem to place girls in control, yet Mackenzie used what many of us would see as an antifemale storyline to command authority, both in terms of how she was willing to read this text and in terms of how she would interpret the boys' tendency to dismiss these series books. Although males often denigrate females for reading and enjoying series and romance books (and this classroom was no exception), she was able to interrupt this commonplace trivialization of female activity by pointing out that boys do not want to read such books because they do not want to see themselves in a negative light.

What I suggest throughout this chapter is that the social and political uses of popular narratives (both horror and romance) during independent reading must be examined. In this classroom, students used such narratives to create allegiances, marking the boundaries of who was in and who was out and enabling those with less power to make their own tactical use of those who hold more (de Certeau, 1984).

It is an interesting irony, I think, that what we call "independent reading" is actually social in such complicated ways, and what we call "free choice," in terms of students choosing the books they want to read, is clearly not free of the need to establish particular social identities in relation to what Fairclough (1989, 1995) called local and institutional discourses. Theorists of popular culture argue that the common pedagogical response to popular culture—to worry over its effects on students who are seen as passive consumers—is mistaken, given that readers actively reproduce rather than passively consume texts. I think we can see this happening in the examples included in this chapter.

Despite this sense of agency, the boys' desire for aggression and fearlessness and the girls' desire for protection and romance are constructed through dominant ideological discourses that also must be examined. For example, whereas I was encouraged by Mackenzie's response to R. L. Stine because it pointed to ways in which she revised the storyline to protect her own interests, I was not as hopeful about another part of our conversation in which she told me that reading about girls in dangerous situations taught her to be careful: "I read a book where a girl was walking down the street and a guy was chasing her, and so now I'm walking down the street, you know, looking, making sure no one's chasing me." Who benefits from this lesson? Not Mackenzie, who had learned, in this case, to feel powerless in the face of male violence. How is it that this popular text worked with other media texts and dominant cultural ideologies to shape Mackenzie as a reader who felt she must protect herself from males as an ordinary part of her day?

Earlier in this chapter, I pointed out that the practice of independent reading, like other ritualized practices, can tolerate internal resistance, reify the social world in which it is embedded, and transform participants' social statuses. Throughout this chapter we see the intersection of all three elements of ritual. Social statuses rose and fell with popular narratives as currency; social codes and discourses that opposed those of the classroom were negotiated in relation to the larger discourses in which they were embedded. Students grappled with the texts and contexts, trying to negotiate what to accept, reject, or reinvent. Mackenzie positioned herself as one who read popular narratives but only with a wink and a nod, making sure that I knew she didn't really value these texts. She also reinvented her position as a female reader of texts that victimize girls. Nikki accepted the victimization of girls as "normal," but understood how the popular texts she read were structured to position girls in this way. James and his peers used horror texts to accept but also reinvent (through playful juxtapositions) popular versions of masculinity, as well as their own status in the classroom. These findings hold implications for teachers and researchers to critically examine the practice of independent reading in all of its social complexity. Such examination can help us to determine when to make room for play and appropriation of dominant, and sometimes repressive, cultural symbols and norms and when, on the other hand, to promote critical analyses of these symbols.

III

Reflections
and Implications
for Pedagogy

7

Literary Practices as Social Acts

In this book, I set out to represent the depth of context that shaped cultural meaning related to literary practices in one fifth- and sixth-grade classroom, but now, at the book's end, I find myself thinking about conditions of meaning that I left out, the defining gaps. As I have argued throughout, in any classroom, at any time, the rituals and routines are dynamic, their meanings dependent on one's position and agency as enacted and reenacted through moment-to-moment interaction. So, for example, in chapter 4, I briefly noted Nikki's relationship with Lisa and its shaping influence on the peer-led literature discussions in which they took part, but I left out the complicated dance these students did as they attempted to reestablish their friendship across unanticipated boundaries: Lisa needing to shape an identity as a sixth grader, but feeling drawn to Nikki and their shared vision; Nikki, negotiating new friendships of her own, yet wanting to reaffirm her shared history and intellectual kinship with Lisa. I made a passing attempt to acknowledge this tension, but in the end found myself—as researchers do—summarizing the most salient features of their discussions.

Thus, some of the particulars, even in a study that claims to attend to them, get reduced to a minor segment of an illustrative event or, perhaps, to a quick aside. I draw attention here to what has been left out to bring home the important point that social drama in the classroom is complex and inevitable. Although we would not want to unravel the threads of social life that create the classroom culture, we must acknowledge the material constitution of its fabric, the ill-matched patterns and clashing colors as well as its harmonious design.

SHIFTING PRACTICES AND LITERARY
MEANINGS

Like other features of classroom life, the literary culture of a classroom is created through social codes and practices that authorize particular worldviews. Rituals related to literature are enacted and reenacted as practices that shift in meaning from setting to setting but exist within the boundaries of social and interpretive competence established by the members of the classroom culture. This book's focus has been the multiple contexts through which such codes and practices are produced. Before moving to a discussion of the study's pedagogical implications, I summarize the findings related to each literary practice. Again, it is important to remember that these practices were constituted in the local culture of the classroom and community as well as in cultural norms and symbols beyond the classroom.

Read-Aloud: What Do We Have in Common?

- The ritual of read-aloud was an attempt to enact the classroom culture as the teacher and many of her students wished it to be lived, thus creating an ethos for life in the classroom that centered on the importance of common bonds.
- Through the use of ritual, this practice engaged students and teacher in the construction of social and interpretive competence as it was to be understood in the classroom.
- Students gave meaning to the ritual in multiple ways, depending on their social positions related to power and status in and out of the classroom.
- In an attempt to claim a community, the read-aloud practice also revealed tensions and contradictions related to power and status. Such tensions and contradictions were visible particularly in the clearly embodied contrast between the girls and boys in relation to the teacher, to the text, and to each other.

Peer-Led Literature Discussions: What Are Our Social Roles?

- The negotiation of social roles and identities took place in peer-led groups in ways that both sustained and interrupted normative and hierarchical elements of the local culture of classroom and community.

- Students used peer-led discussions to comment, directly or indirectly, on the constraining and enabling features of social and interpretive competence as constructed in the classroom.

- Textual interpretation was shaped by moment-to-moment interaction embedded in sociocultural conditions and contexts.

Teacher-Led Literature Discussions: Why Do We Believe What We Believe?

- Probing social codes and cultural norms was central to the teacher-led discussions, which focused on resistant reading and critical stances.

- Whereas the meaning of peer-led discussions was shaped primarily by the local culture of classroom and community, the meaning of teacher-led discussions was shaped by broad cultural knowledge and resources as well as dominant cultural norms.

- During teacher-led discussions, the negotiation of social roles went underground as students and their teacher focused on textual interpretation.

Independent Reading: What Will We Accept, Reject, or Reinvent?

- "Free choice" of texts for independent reading was not free of the need to establish particular social identities in relation to local and institutional discourses; thus independent reading was a profoundly social activity.

- The knowledge of popular narratives displayed during independent reading served as subcultural capital, a currency that, in some cases, worked to transform social status.

- During independent reading, social codes and discourses that opposed those of the classroom were played out in relation to the larger discourses in which they were embedded (e.g., codes and discourses related to gender).

Each of these contexts made available to students particular opportunities for social interaction and literary interpretation. Providing students with varied contexts for reading and discussing literature was important in that it allowed students to position themselves differently in relation to peers, teacher, and text, given the dominant meaning of each practice.

THE SOCIAL POLITICS OF LITERARY CULTURE

As the literature events described in this book reveal, students and teacher manipulated the social codes available to them as they engaged in each literary practice. The meanings of social and interpretive competence in this classroom, as coconstructed by the teacher and many of her students, resulted in expectations for appropriate action and interaction within or against which students performed. Evident in the data is the somewhat fluid nature of these performances. Although Jason's performative stance during peer-led discussions was, more often than not, to disappear, and James's, more often than not, to resist, both students performed more engaged roles during teacher-led discussions. Furthermore, just as context shaped performance, ongoing performances continually shaped and reshaped classroom context, such as when Brooke was in charge of the *Red Fern* discussion, only to have her interpretive competence called into question. In this case, Lisa's performance interrupted Brooke's authority, creating an open space for cultural change.

I would argue that such open spaces occur most often when students are given opportunities to negotiate social positions without teacher surveillance, times when their activities are liminal in the sense that they are truly "betwixt and between" (Turner, 1969, p. 95), partially coopting the role of teacher, partially embracing the role of student, friend, or rebel. Although there are disadvantages to opening such spaces to students, disadvantages I discuss in the next section, there are significant advantages as well. The social drama that exists in any classroom will surface during peer-led discussions, creating opportunities for students to negotiate social positions. Such discussions also provide a space for interruptions of power to occur and for students to form alliances that create an alternative to power as it is ordinarily constructed—that is, the power of those who display social and interpretive competence according to classroom norms. James's relationship with David was just such a positive alliance. Their friendship often served to bring James into the discussion, required him to display a degree of learner engagement, and allowed him to bask in David's attention. Julia's work to reestablish this alliance midyear revealed her awareness of its significance to James as a learner.

In addition to fostering the negotiation of roles, peer-led discussions also enabled students to try on and display a wider range of roles. During teacher-led discussions, students either performed as engaged learners (or willing to appear engaged), passive learners, or, less often, resistant learners. During peer-led discussions, however, students took up these positions plus others, such as the role of leader, risk taker, and friend. They used the group to create solidarity and delineate boundaries, both related to the interpretation of literature. In addition, as noted in chapter 4, peer-led groups existed as hybrid communities, using lexical and interpretive norms keyed to a variety of contexts.

Although Julia sometimes intervened in peer-led discussions, occasionally modeled group processes, and frequently assigned a leader, she generally allowed the groups to work alone once their work had begun. Although some would argue that established collaborative learning procedures, such as heterogeneous grouping and assigned roles for each student—or more modeling of social norms—should be implemented to avoid the power plays that occurred in these groups, I would argue against these regulatory moves.

In this classroom, peer-led discussions represented one literary practice out of four. Most of the school day, in this school as in most, was structured by teachers; yet, if classrooms are going to function—at least some of the time—as sites for social negotiation and change, conflict and difference need to be visible rather than hidden dimensions of the classroom. In peer-led groups, students engaged in metadiscourse about the meaning of social and interpretive competence in the classroom. It was a time when multiple voices in the classroom came into contact with one another, leading to greater awareness of power, difference, and the control of meaning in the classroom. The heteroglossic nature of these peer-led groups brought to the surface the competing identities students needed to address within themselves and others, the multiple roles they played within the social networks of their classroom, their families, and their communities.

Both the literature on student-centered classrooms and much of the literature on critical pedagogy tend to idealize the communities created in classrooms where teachers release power to students. As the results of this study make clear, however, when the teacher gives up power, particular students will take up the slack. Cherryholmes (1988) quoted Florio (1983) on this subject: "Put simply, I came to the realization that in a social world that is unequal, you don't get a democratic or open conversation simply by saying that everybody's free to talk" (p. 8). The decentering of authority that occurred in peer-led groups had its advantages, as just described, but it had its drawbacks as well These drawbacks included the marginalization of students who were seen as having less social and interpretive competence, the recentering of authority in the form of students who embraced or accepted the role of teacher, and the emphasis placed on social roles at the expense of textual interpretation.

In a similar vein, forming heterogeneous groups, thus decentering the authority of "ability" as it is often defined in classrooms, did not appear to be the panacea collaborative learning advocates claim. Indeed, in this classroom, groups that consisted of students whose social and interpretive competence were well matched often functioned to democratize power relations in ways that heterogeneous groups did not. I am reminded here of Fox's (1994) depiction of heterogeneous groups as a kind of structured oppression with a dominator in every group. Clearly, some of what Julia and I both noticed happening in these groups earned that depiction.

Throughout the year, my interviews with students were peppered with references to friendships. Intellectual and social solidarity were important elements of the classroom. Indeed, this study suggests that whether or not, as David said of Nikki, "She always thinks the same thing as me," whether or not one feels included or excluded from the conversation, whether or not one is authorized by teacher or peers, makes a difference. Factors such as allegiance, status, perceived ability, age, and gender shape who speaks, how they are received, and what they understand and say about texts.

As in recent work on student perceptions of discussions about content reading, my focal students reported to me that their experiences in literature groups were shaped in part by other members of their literature groups (Alvermann et al., 1996). Jason was intimidated by sixth graders, James did not like to be in groups with the girls who he felt the teacher favored, Nikki wanted to have "meaty" discussions with sixth graders, Mackenzie found that peer-led groups created too much pressure to conform, and David believed he had to please his teacher when she participated in literature discussions. Students reported acting differently in different groups, depending on their sometimes complicated relationships with group members or their teacher. In addition, they used the groups to create solidarity and delineate boundaries, to vie for power and interrupt authority, all related to their engagement with and interpretation of literature. Conquergood (1995) discussed the ways in which Turner (1982) transformed the commonly held view that to perform roles was to be inauthentic—to engage in fakery. Turner proposed, instead, that to perform roles was to engage in social action, acknowledge multiple identities and layered contexts, recognize positions of power, and, always, to continually create culture.

THE TEACHER'S ROLE:
IMPLICATIONS FOR PEDAGOGY

Teachers can play an important role in helping students work through the social drama that surfaces during literature discussions. Acting as participants in such groups, they can lead students in metadiscussions of power and difference within the classroom context. Julia participated in these ways on several occasions, drawing attention in one case, for instance, to the dominance of female voices in a particular group. Another time, in the discussion of death and marriage related to *Number the Stars,* Julia talked with students about why their turn taking was not equitable. She legitimized and extended both Nikki's and Jason's interpretations of the text, inferring possible reasons for their responses that did not get voiced during the actual discussion.

A pedagogy that keys into the intersecting network of social relations within and beyond the classroom, one that makes available to students new roles to take up and new ways of constructing a self in the classroom, may lead to individual growth as well as growth within the classroom culture. A student like James, for instance, can offer resistant readings of texts not available to other students. However, because of his role as a student resistant to the social ethos of the classroom, his comments were often disregarded, effectively silencing his vision of the text world. When he announced in his peer-led group's discussion of *A Wrinkle in Time* that "The Dark Thing's cool," his peers did not respond. Indeed, it may have been difficult for his peers to take the comment seriously because such a vision of the Dark Thing (evil in L'Engle's [1962] Christian belief system) represented too much of a break with their reality.

Luke and Freebody (1997) advocated a critical literacy, one that would involve teachers and students in examining the discourses they embrace, enact, and resist. Davies (1997), too, argued for the important role of the teacher in "giving students some skill in catching language in the act of formation and in recognising and assessing the effects of that formation" (p. 29). James's comment can be seen as just the sort of resistant reading that, if extended, could move students toward a critical awareness about the ways in which children's literature naturalizes a White, middle-class, Christian worldview. Social drama may surface in peer-led groups, but the teacher, even when not present, is very much a part of that drama in terms of defining what it means to engage in classroom practices and to be seen as a competent member of the classroom. Although social conditions constitute discursive practices, new discursive practices can transform social conditions (Fairclough, 1989), and both teachers and researchers need to know more about the teacher's role in achieving such transformation.

Teachers can serve an important function, as did Julia, by culturally situating texts and promoting critical awareness of dominant cultural norms. Her tendency to lead discussions that probed cultural assumptions opened up a role for literature that was rarely available during the peer-led discussions, and her focus on the text as a constructed artifact made visible the ways that texts promote particular interests. Discussing the ways a text promotes a familiar and unquestioned discourse, the discourse of individuality, for instance, in *The Giver,* and learning to read against the grain, to examine or resist as well as to enter the text world, provides students with another role that literature can serve.

Our roles as teachers should include teaching students to probe and resist popular cultural texts in the same way that we teach students to interact with canonized texts. Instead of persuading students to revere all that has been deemed "great literature" and forsake the movies, books, and television shows they love, we need to engage students in conversations about the uses they have for a range of texts in their lives. We might also ask students to examine how particular popular narratives work on readers to sustain and fulfill patterns of desire. For this reason, one of the most important roles a teacher can serve when she or he participates in literature discussions is to mediate the literature in critical ways, helping students to traverse social and institutional discourses—the discourse of popular narratives as well as the official and unofficial discourses of the classroom.

This chapter argues that the meanings of literary practices shift from setting to setting, shaped by discourse and ritual within the classroom and by social codes and cultural norms beyond the classroom. In this classroom, as in all classrooms, there existed a social organization that privileged certain social and interpretive ways of being over others. Often teachers committed to equity and social justice disclaim personal authority and insist that no ways of being, acting, believing, and evaluating are favored over others in their classrooms. Yet, as Delpit (1988) cogently argued, when teachers disclaim authority in the name of equity, that which is already most powerful in the larger society becomes the norm against which all ways of being are judged. Given that a classroom serves as a temporary culture, it is inevitably a site where particular acts and behaviors will become normative.

Close readings of actual classroom talk can help teachers achieve a delicate balance: on the one hand, to acknowledge and teach existing local norms and those expected in the larger dominant culture, and on the other, to ensure that classroom norms are permeable enough for students to take up a range of positions in the classroom and potentially transform the classroom culture. Close readings of this sort can be conducted by teachers through action research or simply as a regular process of inquiry and reflection. Such readings can be useful to teachers in the following ways: First, a close analysis of interaction and of the conditions surrounding the interaction can lead teachers reflecting on their own practice to a better understanding of the social and power relations that influence the ways students speak and act. Second, an examination of specific interactions can help educators discern which students' interests are served by particular classroom literacy practices and which students' interests are not. Third, such analysis and reflection can lead to changes in instructional practices and classroom contexts.

As the literature events in this book make clear, literary interpretation depends on moment-to-moment performances that are embedded in sociocultural conditions and contexts. Any attempt to understand the transaction between reader and text must include an examination of the many social conditions that shape how students engage with literature. As teachers, we can create spaces within which students can negotiate and comment on social roles and reenact the social drama that exists just beneath the surface in any classroom. We can also take responsibility for guiding students in readings of literature that examine the text's social and cultural constitution and invite students to experience, in Julia Davis's words, "a dialogue with the book."

Appendix

Methodology

This appendix includes additional information about my research method not included in the main chapters of this book.

RESEARCH SETTING AND PARTICIPANTS

The site for this study was an elementary school in a Midwestern university town. Emerson School is situated in an older neighborhood of mixed-income residents, a neighborhood that prides itself on its architectural history and its strong community bonds. Just a few blocks from the school, one tree-lined street is noted for its stately, elegant, and expensive homes. Most of the neighborhood, however, consists of modest wood-frame homes, many of them cottages and bungalows built in the early 1900s.

Enrollment at the school at the time of this study (1993–94) was 366 students, 12.8% of whom were students of color. The percentage of students on free and reduced lunch in 1993–94 was 16.9%, compared to the 13.7% on free and reduced lunch districtwide. Emerson has a stable student population, resulting in long-term friendships among children who attend school together throughout their elementary years.

Emerson underwent substantive change in 1986 when it switched to a multiaged unit format. Most of the teachers who taught at the school when change was underway left for more traditional schools; consequently, all of the 1993–94 teachers had taught at the school for 7 years or less. The principal was new to the school as well, having assumed his position at the start of the 1993–94 academic year. His previous positions included administration of a rural elementary school and 18 years of elementary teaching experience. There were 29 teachers on the staff, including a counselor and literacy specialist, both serving additional buildings, and 19 support staff.

In many ways, Emerson School can be viewed as an idealized setting, located in a neighborhood that, although not affluent, was considered to be comfortable and safe. Attendance for most students was regular; parental involvement, more often than not, was consistent; and student motivation to succeed in school was strong. Yet, according to Julia, the school was not considered among her colleagues to be one of the "prestige schools" in the district. She described her school as a comfortable school where teachers did not feel the pressure from colleagues, administrators, and parents that teachers felt in several other district schools. Those schools, she explained, employed more teachers who had leadership roles in the district, and served parent populations that demanded and received more curricular input.

As described in my theoretical framework, my own assumptions as a researcher include a belief that context is dynamic, shifting, and manifold. Although the site for this study lacked diversity as it is often defined (i.e., ethnic or racial diversity), my goal has been to examine this context in ways that reveal its complexity and reconsider the meaning of diversity. Given that context is shape-shifting and multidimensional, I needed to examine the ways in which this classroom was embedded within the broader contexts of school, district, and community. I focused most directly on the classroom (i.e., on the beliefs and actions of the students and their teacher), but I also examined how classroom context was constituted within a broader framework.

After spending 10 hours per week in the classroom (divided among three weekly classroom visits) for a period of 2 months, I chose 5 focal students for this study. I chose students who were representative of the classroom population, yet who would provide contrasting characteristics as described in Table 2.1. The column labeled #LDG lists the number of literature discussion groups in which I was able to observe each focal student participate. The (T) following SES and Ability represents teacher and signifies that student designation in these categories is from the point of view of the classroom teacher.

RESEARCHER'S ROLE

As an adult in an elementary classroom, my presence was met with a set of assumptions both from students and from the teacher. Julia was accustomed to having adults in the class as learners (student teachers), as evaluators (principals), or as helpers (parent volunteers). The adult as researcher role is unfamiliar to most teachers, including Julia, and perhaps especially confusing when the researcher hopes to establish herself as a participant-observer.

When I first called Julia to ask her to participate in the study, she expressed eagerness to have another adult in her room, someone with whom to share insights, humor, and frustration. She also mentioned that she would appreciate any feedback I might have because she finds it valuable to reflect on her practice. I explained that I had contacted her because of her reputation as an exemplary literature-based teacher who allowed for much student talk and decision making. I told her that I planned to describe the classroom context as she and her students constructed it together, but that I did not see myself as an evaluator or agent for change. Julia agreed to participate and seemed comfortable with my explanation. In retrospect, this original statement of intent and expression of the boundaries of my relationship with Julia and her students seems naive in its simplicity. I hope that the following description of the ways in which the study evolved will make clear that research is shaped by a web of relationships akin to those that shaped the classroom interactions I observed.

I knew from previous research projects and from my own experiences as a teacher that it can be difficult to have another adult in one's classroom, especially an adult who is trained in one's field, without expecting some sort of commentary on how things are going. From the beginning, Julia rarely asked me what I thought about what I observed. Yet, when we talked informally and when I interviewed her in November, she expressed to me how much she enjoyed having another adult in the room and reiterated that she would like it if we could plan together or if I could offer her suggestions for improvement. She always added, however, that she understood why this was not possible given my research project.

Due to the nature of my study, I didn't feel I could be the collaborative partner she was hoping for; yet, because I felt that her request was fair and because I wanted to reciprocate the openness she had shown me, I decided to make occasional suggestions unrelated to literature discussions. I shared with her some materials I had developed while working on a portfolio assessment project, for instance, and we discussed our views regarding the teacher's role in Writer's Workshop. I was concerned that if I were to participate in peer-led discussions as a teacher or even as an experienced reader, my responses might carry an authority about them that would have altered the way that patterns of interaction in this classroom shaped student characterizations of literature discussions. If I led a whole class discussion or regularly collaborated with Julia on activities with which to engage reluctant readers, I might alter her characterization of what is important in the reading and discussing of literature. Moreover, had I established this "teacherly" stance, students may well have been more guarded in sharing their beliefs with me. Yet, I kept feeling a pull toward more active involvement, and began to consider my role in shaping the context of Julia's classroom.

As I reconsidered my position in the classroom, I thought about situating myself as a participant who enacted the role of student rather than teacher. Yet, as I mentioned in chapter 1, my presence was met with a set of assumptions not only from the teacher, but from students as well. Like teachers, students also are accustomed to the roles adults usually play in their classroom, and for them, too, the role of participant-observer is not familiar. They are used to interacting with adults as authority figures, so that my passivity in terms of discipline, especially when I was the only adult to witness the misbehavior, confused some of them. Student responses to my chosen stance were varied. When I observed during peer-led literature discussions, my refusal to claim authority frustrated some who felt responsible for the group and wanted the discussion back on track; it delighted others who would sneak furtive glances at me after making bold statements usually deemed inappropriate for school. Others were casual about my presence, either ignoring me or helping out by setting up the tape recorder or speaking the date into the microphone.

Surely age differences between researchers and students affect the level of involvement a researcher can have. It probably did not work to my advantage that, although I always called myself Cynthia when talking with or writing notes to the students, Julia persisted in referring to me as Mrs. Lewis when she spoke of me to the class. When I asked a focal student, Nikki, if she thought of me as a teacher when I observed her peer-led discussion that day, she replied:

Nikki: Yeah, typically, since you're a lot older. I just think of anybody older as a teacher and anybody younger as a student.

Cynthia: OK.

Nikki: Or else, like, I don't really think of the college students that come in because /

Cynthia: Because they're not old enough?

Nikki: Yeah, they're not like, that old so ...

Being *that* old, then, restricted the level of participation I could have as a student. Bogdan and Biklen (1992) suggested that given the challenge of re-

searching children, the best option may be to establish oneself not as an authority figure, and not as a peer, but as a "quasi-friend" or "tolerated insider
in children's society" (p. 88). This stance best describes the one I gradually
found my way into as one of my focal students, David, affirmed:

Cynthia: How would you describe my role in the classroom?

David: You were more our friend than the other people [referring to
            practicum students from the university].

For the first week of class, I attended every day and stayed for all subjects
other than math and science, giving me a sense of the flow of the school day,
its work time and "down" time. It was important for me to see how Julia and
her students coconstructed a way of being together in this classroom, a way
of taking control and sharing it, cooperating and resisting, forming allegiances and establishing boundaries. In an article on the intertextual nature
of classroom life, Dixon, de la Cruz, Green, Lin, and Brandts (1993) suggested that researchers develop an understanding of how classroom context
is constructed across events and time, noting that too narrow a focus can
distort the way researchers represent the opportunities students have for
learning in a classroom. I allowed myself time to observe the unfolding in
Julia's classroom before narrowing my focus.

After the first week, I attended class regularly on Mondays, Wednes-
days, and Fridays during reading, but usually stayed longer on Fridays for
writer's workshop, lunch, and recess. By December, I had dropped my regular lunch and recess visits, and made only sporadic visits to writer's workshop. I had, by then, identified focal students and felt sufficiently immersed
in the classroom culture to hone in on the parts of the day most relevant to
my research questions.

Early on, I suggested to Julia that I would like to read aloud to the students some time. I reasoned that this would help me to establish a relationship with the students without placing me in a teacherly role. Adults
occasionally came to read to Julia's class, and I knew I could assume that
parents had come to read to most of them in earlier grades. When I read to
them the first time, Julia was absent, and I asked the substitute to tell the students to gather around "Cynthia." I wanted to be sure that I was not placed in
the role of facilitator and was careful during my reading not to ask questions
about the text. This experience, however, led Julia to ask me to read a particular medieval book to the students on a day in October, during a medieval
unit, when she would be absent. She wanted me to help the students to make

connections between the book and what they had been learning about medieval times. I agreed out of deference to Julia, but privately worried that this would alter the nonteaching role I had so carefully established early on. On the same day Julia asked me if I would keep an eye on one of my focal students and I struggled, once again, with my research position (as described in chap. 1). I had done my part, Julia had done hers, and the students theirs, to construct a new role for me in the classroom.

If Julia asked me how a discussion group I observed had progressed without her, for instance, I offered some observations. On a few occasions, when a student given to disruptive behavior during discussions infringed substantially on the rights of others in the group and ignored peers' requests to stop, I told him to stop. After Julia gave several "quiet down" reminders to a group I observed, I asked them to remember Julia's request. When Julia voiced her concern that the discussions were too often off the topic, I did not want to offer a strong opinion in favor of continuing peer-led small groups, but did loan her the book *Talking About Books: Creating Literate Communities* (Short & Pierce, 1990), which addresses the issue of off-topic talk among children. I wrote notes to students about their writer's workshop pieces when they shared them with me, I comforted a student I found crying in the bathroom, I interjected a question on rare occasions during literature discussions if it related to something students had already addressed, and, once or twice, I asked students to listen to a child who had not been able to get a word in during an animated discussion.

In all of these cases, I accounted for my actions and what effect I could document, and was humbled by how little authority I seemed to have over anyone in that room. I was not seen as an evaluator by Julia, who told me several times that I didn't need to call her if I was unable to attend because my presence didn't affect her planning, and the students would pursue or not pursue a question I put on the table as it pleased them. They did what children do when they are together despite my presence—interrupting, giggling, talking about things an adult might consider inappropriate for school, and yelling for others to "shut up." Although I did not become a full participant in the classroom, over time the students more often requested my responses, not only during literature discussions but during routine social exchanges as well. Their public performances were shaped by a context of which I was an expected part, and all of us produced and reproduced that context through our interactions.

For former public school teachers, ethnographic research inverts the ethnographic commonplace to "make the strange familiar." When former teachers enter schools as ethnographers, they must, instead, try to make the familiar strange. Although the culture of a particular classroom may be unfamiliar to the researcher, the culture of schooling will be familiar. The researcher may know about schooling from a variety of perspectives: that of a student, parent, teacher, and teacher educator. This makes for a relationship between researcher and informant unique to school ethnographies. Other ethnographers studying unfamiliar cultures are not viewed as experts when they begin to participate in the culture. School ethnographers, on the other hand, are often viewed by teacher informants as experts due to their previous positions as teachers and current positions, in many cases, as teacher educators. Thus it is common for informants to ask researchers about the meaning (especially evaluative meaning) they would give to particular classroom practices, making it difficult for the researcher to focus on the cultural meanings held by informants.

These issues were foregrounded at various times in the course of conducting my study. Julia occasionally wanted to know what I thought about strategies she used or responses students gave. Although a very confident teacher, she would, at times, position herself as a nonexpert about the teaching of reading and writing and underscore the expertise she felt I could offer. I came to realize that it was senseless for either of us to act as though I were a stranger to this culture, yet it would have been just as disingenuous for me to claim expertise in implementing theory and research in this new and complex setting. I had to acknowledge the conditions that situated me as researcher and Julia as teacher, and the different degrees of autonomy afforded to each. Julia was tied to her classroom, whereas I could choose to come and go as my research, school, and home needs dictated. Although I always tried to arrange interviews according to Julia's schedule, I was the one who initiated and defined the parameters of the interviews. I shared time and space with Julia and her class all year, but she and I both knew that eventually I would work alone to write my interpretation of her classroom, her students, and her beliefs.

The purpose of ethnography is to "explain cultural representations" (Athanases & Heath, 1995, p. 267), yet the politics of representation as discussed by postmodern and feminist ethnographers (Behar & Gordon, 1995; Clifford & Marcus, 1986) suggest that such explanations can never be innocent. The researcher's position in relation to informants and the informants' positions in relation to each other have everything to do with what gets represented and how. Near the end of the study, Julia often wondered aloud what I would make of all this data, and would fill me in over the telephone about things that happened while I was away, events I might want to consider for my study. How did she choose what to tell me at these times, or what self she would present in answer to one of my questions? How did I determine what to share about my observations or when to align myself more with students as opposed to Julia? Rabinow (1977) referred to the partial understandings that are the most one can hope for between researcher and informants, the small ways in which we can or cannot understand the historical conditions that constitute "otherness." If I am to interpret the classroom through a performative lens then I must interpret the relationships I developed within the classroom as performance as well. Just as the students had to juggle multiple selves as they interacted with peers and teacher, Julia and I had selves to negotiate as well.

On my last day of observation, Julia told her students that she probably would not have left them on their own during literature discussions as often as she did if it had not been for me. I worried over Julia's remarks about my having influenced her instructional decisions. I had felt torn throughout the study about whether or not to ask her to allow for more peer-led groups than she was inclined toward. I opted for occasionally asking when she might arrange for a particular literature group to discuss on their own again, but stopped short of advocating for one approach over the other. Although I was very interested in observing peer-led groups, I did not want to influence the way Julia would ordinarily do things. However, it became increasingly clear to me that my very presence altered the setting to some respect, and that, as in any relationship, my comments were "read" by Julia through the politics of our relationship and the partial understandings that our interactions produced. Probyn (1993) argued that researchers must interrogate their subject positions to understand the conditions that constitute a relationship between researcher and researched:

> I want to posit a self as a speaking position that entails a defamiliarization of the taken-for-granted. It is a speaking position that, in contrast to the ethnographers I have discussed, is firmly based in an epistemological questioning of how it is that I am speaking. Speaking myself thus should render me uneasy in my skin ... as it decentralizes any assurance of ontological importance. (p. 80)

"Uneasy in my skin" aptly describes, for me, what is was like to be a researcher in another teacher's classroom, enmeshed as I was in my own identity as a teacher and my own way of being with children. Although I felt overwhelmingly comfortable just spending time with Julia and my focal students, the role of researcher always created a healthy tension, one that kept me questioning my motives and revising my position.

DATA SOURCES AND COLLECTION

In conducting this study, I worked to achieve "data triangulation" (Denzin, 1970, p. 237) by employing multiple data sources to provide for a variety of perspectives in examining both student interactions and the nature of the school, district, and community. Data sources included audiotaped literature discussions; interviews with students, teacher, parents, and administrators; field notes taken throughout the year; students' written responses to literature; and student sociograms delineating their friendship circles. Interviews with parents and administrators were most useful in answering my third question regarding contexts beyond the classroom. All other data sources were used in answering my first two research questions.

My three weekly classroom visits included participant-observation during reading, a weekly writer's workshop session, and occasional lunch and recess periods. Students spent much of their reading time during the year in teacher-led or peer-led small groups. I observed each focal student throughout his or her participation in at least four literature discussion groups, audiotaping discussions three times per week (a total of 79 audiotaped discussions). In addition, I audiotaped comments Julia made to introduce themed literature units or particular book discussions.

I audiotaped semistructured formal interviews with all participants, using question guides to compare data from multiple participants. I held semistructured interviews with Julia in August, November, March, and June, focusing on her purposes for reading and teaching literature, her goals for literature discussions, and her views about focal students. I held two semistructured interviews with each focal student, one in January and another in June, focusing on their social networks, their choice of key events during literature discussions, and their opinions about literary practices in their classroom. I audiotaped semistructured interviews with parents at the beginning and end of the year, focusing on literacy practices at home, connections to school, and views about social and literacy growth. I held one interview with the director of curriculum, one with the school principal, and one with a literacy specialist, focusing in each on beliefs about the reading and discussion of literature and literary practices at Emerson and in the district. Informal interviews were an important data source and were conducted regularly. Held throughout the year with the teacher and with individuals or groups of students, informal interviews were brief, often audiotaped, conversations that took place in spare moments during my visits to the classroom.

DATA ANALYSIS

At a time when those of us who do qualitative research have begun to examine our own positions in relation to contexts, participants, and sources, recognizing that interpretation is constituted in positionality, we often hold on to the notion that true findings will eventually "emerge" from the data. Troubled by this view of analysis, I looked for an alternate view, and was intrigued by what Brantlinger (1993) called a *hermeneutic interpretive* approach, one that acknowledges one's own interpretive stance at the same time that one becomes immersed in the perspectives of participants. With this approach in mind, I tried to acknowledge the multiple perspectives represented by research participants while reflecting throughout the process on the sources of the theory I generated. Erickson (1986) argued that theory is not generated simply from the ground up, but rather that theory generated inductively from data is simultaneously sifted through the researcher's "culturally learned frames of interpretation" (p. 140).

During data collection, I made repeated passes through interview transcripts to help me plan future interactions with participants in follow-up conversations. I listened to the audiotapes of literature discussions regularly and logged each tape using a format adapted from Merriam (1988). Field notes, typed and expanded weekly, were a source of ongoing analysis, with an eye toward recurrent patterns that I began to label using key words (Glasser & Strauss, 1967). These patterns provided a lens through which to observe future interactions.

Approximately every 6 weeks, I wrote an analytical memo in which I examined in more depth the patterns I had noticed and began to theorize what they might mean in terms of my interpretive frame. The themes I considered evolved over the course of the study as depicted in Table A.1. For example, the first set of themes, developed during data collection, referred to the roles students took up during literature discussions. These themes were shaped by my theoretical predisposition toward performative theories of literacy and social interaction. Because I was interested in how contexts af-

TABLE A.1

Evolution of Themes

Themes developed during data collection

1. Student roles during literature discussions

   Achievement/intellectual engagement

   Playing the game

   Resisting

   Disappearing

   Social allegiance

2. Probing cultural knowledge and assumptions within a reader response framework during teacher-led discussions

Themes developed after data collection

3. Organizational themes suggested by research questions

   Classroom culture

   Performative roles

   Meanings given to literary practices

   Contexts beyond the classroom

4. More specific themes with many subcategories

   Status and solidarity

   Performative roles

   Meanings ascribed to the reading of literature

   Literary understanding

   Classroom culture

   Culture of school and district

   Culture of home and neighborhood

   Teacher probes and questions

Table A.1 *(Continued)*

5. Three analytic categories regarding the literary culture
   of the classroom

   Characterizations of literature discussions

   Performative roles enacted during discussions

   Interactions that reveal the purposes and expectations of literary discussions in various settings

---

fected the roles students accepted, rejected, or embraced in class, I began to categorize performance settings (e.g., group peer-led discussions organized by the teacher) and the roles that students played within each setting (e.g., resisting or disappearing). After data collection was complete, I identified general themes suggested by my research questions: classroom culture, performative roles, meanings given to literary practices, and contexts beyond the classroom. Having organized field note data into these four categories, I developed a list of analytic categories and subcategories to use for coding interview transcripts and tape logs (Table A.1). However, I soon abandoned this coding process, which included, for example, nine subcategories under the heading "literary understanding," because it led me to approach my data in isolated segments rather than as contextualized events.

Eventually, I developed a few major categories that would help me analyze the literary culture of the classroom and make connections between important literature discussions and the social positions of the participants. Three analytic categories informed my analysis of specific literature events, defined as any school activity related to the reading or discussion of literature: (a) characterizations of literature discussions, (b) performative roles enacted during discussions, and (c) interactions that reveal the purposes and expectations of literature discussions. Using methods of discourse analysis described in chapter 1 (Gee, Michaels, & O'Connor, 1992), I focused my closest analysis on two categories of events: (a) key events—those that research participants characterized as particularly significant, and (b) illustrative events—those that depicted performative roles that were repeatedly documented in field notes and audiotapes. All of the themes or categories were part of the process of analysis, bringing me progressively closer to what I came to see as the dominant meaning of each of the four main literary practices in the classroom, fully described throughout this book.

References

Alloway, N., & Gilbert, P. (1997). Boys and literacy: Lessons from Australia. *Gender and Education, 9,* 49–58.

Almasi, J. F. (1995). The nature of fourth-graders' sociocognitive conflicts in peer-led and teacher-led discussions of literature. *Reading Research Quarterly, 30,* 314–351.

Althusser, L. (1971). *Lenin and philosophy and other essays.* New York: Monthly Review Press.

Alvermann, D. E. (1996). Peer-led discussions: Whose interests are served? *Journal of Adolescent and Adult Literacy, 39,* 282–289.

Alvermann, D. E., Young, J. P., Green, C., & Wisenbaker, J. M. (1999). Adolescents' perceptions and negotiations of literacy practices in after-school read and talk clubs. *American Educational Research Journal, 36,* 221–264.

Alvermann, D. E., Young, J. P., Weaver, D., Hinchman, K. A., Moore, D. W., Phelps, S. F., Thrash, E. C., & Zalewski, P. (1996). Middle and high school students' perceptions of how they experience text-based discussions: A multicase study. *Reading Research Quarterly, 31,* 244–267.

Athanases, S. Z., & Heath, S. B. (1995). Ethnography in the study of the teaching and learning of English. *Research in the Teaching of English, 29,* 263–287.

Atwell, N. (1987). *In the middle: Writing, reading, and learning with adolescents.* Portsmouth, NH: Boynton Cook/Heinemann.

Babcock, B. A. (1980). Reflexivity: Definition and discriminations. *Semiotica, 30,* 1–14.

Baker, C. D. (1991). Literacy practices and social relations in classroom reading events. In C. D. Baker & A. Luke (Eds.), *Towards a critical sociology of reading* (pp. 161–188). Amsterdam: John Benjamins..

Baker, C. D., & Freebody, P. (1989). Talk around text: Constructions of textual and teacher authority in classroom discourse. In S. de Castell, A. Luke, & C. Luke (Eds.), *Language, authority, and criticism: Readings on the school textbook* (pp. 263–283). London: Falmer.

Bakhtin, M. M. (1981). *The dialogic imagination* (C. Emerson & M. Holquist, Trans.). Austin: University of Texas Press.

Bakhtin, M. M. (1984). *Rabelais and his world* (H. Iswolsky, Ed. & Trans.). Bloomington: Indiana University Press.

Bakhtin, M. M. (1986). *Speech genres and other late essays* (V. W. McGee, Trans.). Austin: University of Texas Press.

Barthes, R. (1975). *The pleasure of the text* (R. Miller, Trans.). New York: Hill & Wang.

Barton, D., & Hamilton M. (2000). Literacy practices. In D. Barton, M. Hamilton & R. Ivanic (Eds.), *Situated literacies: Reading and writing in context* (pp. 7–15). New York: Routledge.

Barton, D., Hamilton, M., & Ivanic, R. (Eds.), *Situated literacies: Reading and writing in context.* New York: Routledge.

Bauman, R. (1977). *Verbal art as performance.* Prospect Heights, IL: Waveland.

Bauman, R., & Briggs, C. (1990). Poetics and performance as critical perspectives on language and social life. *Annual Review of Anthropology, 19,* 59–88.

Beach, R. (1993). *A teacher's introduction to reader-response theories.* Urbana, IL: National Council of Teachers of English.

Beach, R. (November 1996). *Early adolescents' construction of gendered identities through social practices of selection and exclusion in group discussion.* Paper presented at the 46th Annual Meeting of the National Reading Conference, Charleston, SC.

Beach, R., & Lundell, D. (1998). Early adolescents' use of computer-mediated communication in writing and reading. In D. Reinking, M. C. McKenna, L. D. Labbo, & R. D. Kieffer (Eds.), *Handbook of literacy and technology* (pp. 93–112). Mahwah, NJ: Lawrence Erlbaum Associates.

Behar, R., & Gordon, D. A. (1995). (Eds.). Women writing culture. Berkeley: University of California Press.

Bell, C. (1992). *Ritual theory, ritual practice.* Oxford, UK: Oxford University Press.

Bennett, T. (1979). *Formalism and Marxism.* London: Methuen.

Bloome, D. (1983). Reading as a social process. In B. A. Hutson (Ed.), *Advances in reading/language research* (Vol. 2, pp. 165–195). London: JAI.

Bloome, D., & Bailey, F. (1992). Studying language and literacy through events, particularity, and intertextuality. In R. Beach, R. J. Green, M. Kamil, & T. Shanahan (Eds.), *Multidisciplinary perspectives on literacy research* (pp. 181–210). Urbana, IL: National Council of Teachers of English.

Bloome, D., & Egan-Robertson, A. (1993). The social construction of intertextuality in classroom reading and writing lessons. *Reading Research Quarterly, 28,* 305–333.

Bogdan, R. C., & Biklen, S. K. (1992). *Qualitative research for education: An introduction to theory and methods* (2nd ed.). Boston: Allyn & Bacon.

Bourdieu, P. (1977). *Outline of the theory of practice* (R. Nice, Trans.). Cambridge, UK: Cambridge University Press. (Original work published 1972)

Bourdieu, P. (1986). The forms of capital. In J. G. Richardson (Ed.), *Handbook of theory and research for the sociology of education* (pp. 241–258). New York: Greenwood.

Bourdieu, P. (1990). *The logic of practice* (R. Nice, Trans.). Cambridge, UK: Polity.

Bratlinger, E. (1993). Adolescents' interpretation of social class influences in schooling. *Journal of Classroom Interaction, 28,* 1–12.

Brodkey, L. (1989). On the subjects of class and gender in "The literacy letter." *College English, 54,* 125–141.

Brodkey, L. (1992). Articulating poststructural theory in research on literacy. In R. Beach, R. J. Green, M. Kamil, & T. Shanahan (Eds.), *Multidisciplinary perspectives on literacy research* (pp. 293–318). Urbana, IL: National Council of Teachers of English.

Brooke, R. E. (1991). *Writing and sense of self: Identity negotiation in writing workshops.* Urbana, IL: National Council of Teachers of English.

Bruner, J. (1986). *Actual minds, possible worlds.* Cambridge, MA: Harvard University Press.

Buckingham, D. (1993). Boys' talk: Television and the policing of masculinity. In D. Buckingham (Ed.), *Reading audiences: Young people and the media* (pp. 89–115). New York: St. Martin's.

Butler, J. (1990). Performative acts and gender constitution: An essay in phenomenology and feminist theory. In S. Case (Ed.), *Performing feminisms: Feminist critical theory and theater* (pp. 270–282). Baltimore: John Hopkins University Press.

Cai, M. (1997). Reader-response theory and the politics of multicultural literature. In T. Rogers & A. O. Soter (Eds.), *Reading across cultures: Teaching literature in a diverse society* (pp. 199–212). New York: Teachers College Press.

Calkins, L. M. (1983). *Lessons from a child: On teaching and learning of writing.* Portsmouth, NH: Heinemann.

Cazden, C. (1988). *Classroom discourse.* Portsmouth, NH: Heinemann.

Cherland, M. R. (1994). *Private practices: Girls reading fiction and constructing identity.* Bristol, PA: Taylor & Francis.

Cherryholmes, C. H. (1988). *Power and criticism: Poststructural investigations in education.* New York: Teachers College Press.

Christian-Smith, L. K. (1990). *Becoming a woman through romance.* New York: Routledge.

Christian-Smith, L. (Ed.). (1993). *Texts of desire: Essays on fiction, femininity and schooling*. London: Falmer.

Christian-Smith, L. K., & Erdman, J. I. (1997). "Mom, it's not real!" Children constructing childhood through reading horror fiction. In S. R. Steinberg & J. L. Kincheloe (Eds.), *Kinder-culture: The corporate construction of childhood* (pp. 129–152). Boulder, CO: Westview.

Clifford, J., & Marcus, G. (1986). (Eds.). Writing culture: The poetics and politics of ethnography. Berkeley: University of California Press.

Connell, R. W. (1987). *Gender & power.* Stanford, CA: Stanford University Press.

Connolly, P. (1995). Boys will be boys? Racism, sexuality, and the construction of masculine identities amongst infant boys. In J. Holland & M. Blair, with S. Sheldon (Eds.), *Debates and issues in feminist research and pedagogy* (pp. 169–195). Philadelphia: The Open University.

Conquergood, D. (1989). Poetics, play, process, and power: The performative turn in anthropology. *Text and Performance Quarterly, 1,* 82–95.

Conquergood, D. (1995). Of caravans and carnivals: Performance studies in motion. *The Drama Review, 39,* 137–141.

Cook-Gumperz, J., & Gumperz, J. (1982). Communicative competence in educational perspective. In L. C. Wilkinson (Ed.), *Communicating in classrooms* (pp. 13–24). New York: Academic.

Cooper, D. (1993). Retailing gender: Adolescent book clubs in Australian schools. In L. Christian-Smith (Ed.), *Texts of desire: Essays on fiction, femininity and schooling* (pp. 9–27). London: Falmer.

Corcoran, B. (1994). Balancing reader response and cultural theory and practice. In B. Corcoran, M. Hayhoe, & G. M. Pradl (Eds.), *Knowledge in the making: Challenging the text in the classroom* (pp. 3–23). Portsmouth, NH: Boynton/Cook.

Cox, C., & Many, J. E. (1992). Stance towards a literary work: Applying the transactional theory to children's responses. *Reading Psychology, 13,* 37–72.

David, M. E. (1989). Schooling and the family. In H. Giroux & P. McLaren (Eds.), *Critical pedagogy, the state, and cultural struggle* (pp. 50–65). Albany: State University of New York Press.

Davies, B. (1993a). Beyond dualism and towards multiple subjectivities. In L. K. Christian-Smith (Ed.), *Texts of desire: Essays on fiction, femininity and schooling* (pp. 145–173). London: Falmer.

Davies, B. (1993b). *Shards of glass.* Cresskill, NJ: Hampton.

Davies, B. (1997). Constructing and deconstructing masculinities through critical literacy. *Gender and Education, 9,* 9–30.

Davies, B., & Harré, R. (1990). Positioning: The discursive production of selves. *Journal for the Theory of Social Behaviour, 20,* 43–63.

de Certeau, M. (1984). *The practice of everyday life.* Berkeley: University of California Press.

Delpit, L. D. (1988). The silenced dialogue: Power and pedagogy in educating other people's children. *Harvard Educational Review, 58,* 280–298.

Denzin, N. K. (1970). The research act: A theoretical introduction to sociological methods. Chicago: Aldine.

Dias, P. (1990). A literary-response perspective on teaching reading comprehension. In D. Bogdan & S. B. Straw (Eds.), *Beyond communication: Reading comprehension and criticism* (pp. 283–299). Portsmouth, NH: Boynton Cook/Heinemann.

Dixon, C., de la Cruz, E., Green, J., Lin, L., & Brandts, L. (1993). Do you see what we see? The referential and intertextual nature of classroom life. *Journal of Classroom Interaction, 27,* 29–36.

Dyson, A. H. (1992). The case of the singing scientist: A performance perspective on the "stages" of school literacy. *Written Communication, 9,* 3–45.

Dyson, A. H. (1997). *Writing superheroes: Contemporary childhood, popular culture, and classroom literacy.* New York: Teachers College Press.

Edelsky, C. (1994). Education for democracy. *Language Arts, 71,* 252–257.

Eder, E. (1986). Organizational constraints on reading group mobility. In J. Cook-Gumperz (Ed.), *The social construction of literacy* (pp. 138–155). Cambridge, UK: Cambridge University Press.

Enciso, P. (1998). Good/bad girls read together: Young girls' coauthorship of subject positions during a shared reading event. *English Education, 30,* 44–62.

Erickson, F. (1982). Classroom discourse as improvisation: Relationships between academic task structure and social participation structures in lessons. In L. C. Wilkinson (Ed.), *Communicating in the classroom* (pp. 153–181). New York: Academic.

Erickson, F. (1986). Qualitative methods in research on teaching. In M. C. Wittrock (Ed.), *Handbook of research on teaching* (3rd ed, pp. 119–161). New York: Macmillan.

Evans, K. S. (1996). Creating spaces for equity? The role of positioning in peer-led literature discussions. *Language Arts, 73,* 194–202.

Evans, K. S., Alvermann, D., & Anders, P. L. (1998). Literature discussion groups: An examination of gender roles. *Reading, Research, and Instruction, 37,* 107–122.

Fairclough, N. (1989). *Language and power.* New York: Longman.

Fairclough, N. (1995). Critical discourse analysis: The critical study of language. New York: Longman.

Felman, S. (1993). *What does a woman want? Reading and sexual difference.* Baltimore: Johns Hopkins University Press.

Fetterley, J. (1977). *The resisting reader: A feminist approach to American fiction.* Bloomington: Indiana University Press.

Finders, M. (1997). *Just girls: Hidden literacies and life in junior high.* New York: Teachers College Press.

Fiske, J. (1989). *Understanding popular culture.* New York: Routledge.

Floriani, A. (1994). Negotiating what counts: Roles and relationships, texts and contexts, content and meaning. *Linguistics and Education, 5,* 241–274.

Florio, S. R. (1983). *The written literacy forum: An analysis of teacher/researcher collaboration.* Paper presented at the annual meeting of the American Educational Research Association, Montreal, Canada.

Foley, D. E. (1989). *Learning capitalist culture: Deep in the heart of Tejas.* Philadelphia: University of Pennsylvania Press.

Foucault, M. (1980). *Power/knowledge: Selected interviews and other writings 1972–1977.* New York: Pantheon.

Foucault, M. (1990). *The history of sexuality: An introduction. Vol. 1.* (R. Hurley, Trans.). New York: Vintage Books. (Original work published 1978)

Fox, T. (1994). Race and gender in collaborative learning. In S. B. Reagan, T. Fox, & D. Bleich (Eds.), *Writing with: New directions in collaborative teaching, learning and research* (pp. 111–121). Albany: State University of New York Press.

Freebody, P., Luke, A., & Gilbert, P. (1991). Reading positions and practices in the classroom. *Curriculum Inquiry, 21,* 436–457.

Galda, L. (1982). Assuming the spectator stance: An examination of the responses of three young readers. *Research in the Teaching of English, 16,* 1–20.

Gee, J. P. (1992). *The social mind: Language, ideology, and social practice.* New York: Bergin & Garvey.

Gee, J. P. (1996). *Sociolinguistics and literacies: Ideology in discourses* (2nd. ed.). New York: Falmer.

Gee, J. P. (1999). *An introduction to discourse analysis: Theory and method.* London: Routledge.

Gee, J. P., Michaels, S., & O'Connor, M. C. (1992). Discourse Analysis X. *The handbook of qualitative research in education.* New York: Academic Press.

Gee J. P., & Crawford, V. (1998). Two kinds of teenagers: Language, identity, and social class. In D. Alvermann, K. Hinchman, D. Moore, S. Phelps, and D. Waff (Eds.), *Reconceptualizing the literacies of adolescents' lives* (pp. 225-245). Hillsdale, NJ : Erlbaum.

Gilbert, P. (1987). Post reader-response: The deconstructive critique. In B. Corcoran & E. Evans (Eds.), *Readers, texts, teachers* (pp. 234–250). Upper Montclair, NJ: Boynton/Cook.

Gilbert, P., & Taylor, S. (1991). *Fashioning the feminine: Girls, popular culture and schooling.* North Sydney, Australia: Allen & Unwin.

Gilbert, R., & Gilbert, P. (1998). *Masculinity goes to school.* New York: Routledge.

Giroux, H. A. (1992). Textual authority and the role of teachers as public intellectuals. In C. M. Hurlbert & S. Totten (Eds.), *Social issues in the English classroom* (pp. 304–321). Urbana, IL: National Council of Teachers of English.

Glasser, B., & Strauss, A. L. (1967). *The discovery of grounded theory: Strategies for qualitative research.* Chicago: Aldine.

Goffman, E. (1959). *The presentation of self in everyday life.* New York: Doubleday.

Goffman, E. (1981). *Forms of talk.* Philadelphia: University of Pennsylvania Press.

Goodenough, W. (1971). *Culture, language, and society.* Reading, MA: Addison-Wesley.

Graff, G. (1987). *Professing literature: An institutional history.* Chicago: University of Chicago Press.

Graves, D. (1983). *Writing: Teachers and children at work.* Portsmouth, NH: Heinemann.

Green, J. L., & Meyer, L. A. (1991). The embeddedness of reading in classroom life: Reading as a situated process. In C. D. Baker & A. Luke (Eds.), *Towards a critical sociology of reading pedagogy* (pp. 141–160). Philadelphia: John Benjamins.

Green, J. L., & Weade, R. (1986). In search of meaning: The sociolinguistic perspective on lesson construction and reading. In D. Bloome (Ed.), *Literacy and schooling* (pp. 3–34). Norwood, NJ: Ablex.

Gutierrez, K. (1995). Unpacking academic discourse. *Discourse Processes, 19,* 21–37.

Gutierrez, K., Rymes, B., & Larson, J. (1995). Script, counterscript, and underlife in the classroom: James Brown versus Brown v. Broad of Education. *Harvard Educational Review, 65,* 445–471.

Hall, S. (1993). What is this "Black" in Black popular culture? *Social Justice, 20*(1–2), 104–114.

Harker, W. J. (1987). Literary theory and the reading process: A meeting of perspectives. *Written Communication, 4,* 235–252.

Harris, J. (1989). The idea of community in the study of writing. *College Composition and Communication, 40,* 11–22.

Heap, J. L. (1991). A situated perspective on what counts as reading. In C. D. Baker & A. Luke (Eds.), *Towards a critical sociology of reading pedagogy* (pp. 103–139). Philadelphia: John Benjamins.

Heath, S. B. (1983). *Ways with words: Language, life, and work in communities and classrooms.* Cambridge, UK: Cambridge University Press.

Holdaway, D. (1979). *Foundations of literacy.* Sydney, Australia: Ashton Scholastic.

Hollindale, P. (1988). Ideology and the children's book. *Signal, 55,* 3–32.

hooks, b. (1991). Narratives of struggle. In P. Mariani (Ed.), *Critical fictions: The politics of imaginative writing* (pp. 53–61). Seattle, WA: Bay Press.

Hruby, G. G. (2001). Sociological, postmodern, and new realism perspectives in social constructionism: Implications for literacy research. *Reading Research Quarterly, 36*(1), 48–62.

Hymes, D. (1972). Introduction. In C. B. Cazden, V. John, & D. Hymes (Eds.), *Functions of language in the classroom* (pp. xi–lv). New York: Teachers College Press.

Hynds, S. (1997) *On the brink: Negotiating literature and life with adolescents.* New York: Teachers College Press.

Johnston, P., Guice, S., Baker, K., Malone, J., & Michelson, N. (1995). Assessment of teaching and learning in "literature-based" classrooms. *Teaching & Teacher Education, 11,* 359–371.

Kapchan, D. A. (1995). Performance. *Journal of American Folklore, 108,* 479–508.

Knoblauch, C., & Johnston, P. (1990). Reading, writing, and the prose of the school. In R. Beach & S. Hynds (Eds.), *Developing discourse practices in adolescence and adulthood* (pp. 318–333). Norwood, NJ: Ablex.

Kozol, J. (1991). *Savage inequalities.* New York: Crown.

Langer, J. A. (1993). Discussions as exploration: Literature and the horizon of possibilities. In G. E. Newell & R. K. Durst (Eds.), *Exploring texts: The role of discussion and writing in the teaching and learning of literature* (pp. 23–43). Norwood, MA: Christopher-Gordon.

Langer, J. A. (1995). *Envisioning literature: Literary understanding and literature instruction.* New York: Teachers College Press.

Lankshear, C., with Gee, J. P., Knobel, M., & Searle, C. (1997). *Changing literacies.* London: Open University Press.

Lareau, A. (1987). Social class differences in family–school relationships: The importance of cultural capital. *Sociology of Education, 60,* 73–85.

Laws, C., & Davies, B. (2000). Poststructuralist theory in practice: Working with "behaviourally disturbed" children. *Qualitative Studies in Education, 133,* 205–221.

Lehr, S. (1988). The child's developing sense of theme as a response to literature. *Reading Research Quarterly, 23,* 337–357.

Lensmire, T. J. (1994). *When children write: Critical revisions of the writing workshop.* New York: Teachers College Press.

Lewis, C. (1997). The social drama of literature discussions in a fifth/sixth-grade classroom. *Research in the Teaching of English, 31,* 163–204.

Lewis (1998a). Literary interpretation as a social act. *Journal of Adolescent and Adult Literacy, 42,* 168–177.

Lewis, C. (1998b). Rock'n'roll and horror stories: Students, teachers, and popular culture. *Journal of Adolescent and Adult Literacy, 42,* 116–120.

Lewis, C. (1999). The quality of the question: Probing culture in literature-discussion groups. In C. Edelsky (Ed.), *Making justice our project: Teachers working toward critical whole language practice* (pp. 163–190). Urbana, IL: National Council of Teachers of English Press.

Lewis, C., Ketter, J., & Fabos, B. (2001). Reading race in a rural context. *International Journal of Qualitative Studies in Education, 14*(3).

Luke, A. (1991). Literacies as social practices. *English Education, 23,* 131–147.

Luke, A. (1992). The body literate: Discourse and inscription in early literacy training. *Linguistics and Education, 4,* 107–129.

Luke, A. (1994). On reading and the sexual division of literacy. *Journal of Curriculum Studies, 26,* 361–381.

Luke, A. (1995). Text and discourse in education: An introduction to critical discourse analysis. In M. W. Apple (Ed.), *Review of research in education* (Vol. 21, pp. 3–48). Washington, DC: American Educational Research Association.

Luke, A,. & Freebody, P. (1997). The social practices of reading. In S. Muspratt, A. Luke, & P. Freebody (Eds.), *Constructing critical literacies* (pp. 185–225). Cresskill, NJ: Hampton.

Marshall, J. (2000). Research on response to literature. In M. L. Kamil, P. B. Mosenthal, P. D. Pearson, & R. Barr (Eds.), *Handbook of reading research* (Vol. 3, pp. 381–402). Mahwah, NJ: Lawrence Erlbaum Associates.

McCormick, K. (1994). *The culture of reading and the teaching of English.* New York: Manchester University Press.

McDermott, R. P. (1977). The ethnography of speaking and reading. In R. W. Shuy (Ed.), *Linguistic theory: What can it say about reading?* (pp. 153–185). Newark, DE: International Reading Association.

McDonnell K. (1994). *Kid culture: Children and adults and popular culture.* Toronto: Second Story Press.

McLaren, P. L. (1993). *Schooling as ritual performance: Towards a political economy of educational symbols and gestures* (2nd ed.). London: Routledge.

McMahon, S. I. (1992). *Book club: A case study of five students as they participate in a literature-based reading program.* Unpublished doctoral dissertation, Michigan State University, Lansing, MI.

McRobbie, A. (1990). *Feminism and youth culture: From 'Jackie' to 'just seventeen.'* Boston: Unwyn Hyman.

Merriam, S. B. (1988). Case study research in education: A qualitative approach. San Francisco: Jossey-Bass.

Millard, E. (1994). Stories of reading. In B. Corcoran, M. Hayhoe, & G. M. Pradl (Eds.), *Knowledge in the making: Challenging the text in the classroom* (pp. 245–258). Portsmouth, NH: Boynton/Cook.

Moore, S. F., & Myerhoff, B. G. (1977). Introduction. In S. F. Moore & B. G. Myerhoff (Eds.), *Secular ritual: Forms and meanings* (pp. 3–24). Amsterdam: Van Goreum.

Morgan, W. (1997). *Critical literacy in the classroom: The art of the possible.* New York: Routledge.

Moss, G. (1989). *Un/popular fictions.* London: Virago.

Moss, G. (1995). Rewriting reading. In J. Holland, M. Blair, & S. Sheldon (Eds.), *Debates and issues in feminist research and pedagogy* (pp.157–168). Bristol, PA: The Open University.

Newkirk, T. (1997). *The performance of self in student writing.* Portsmouth, NH: Boynton/Cook.

Newman, J. (1985). (Ed.). *Whole language: Theory in use.* Portsmouth, NH: Heinemann.

Nodelman, P. (1996). *The pleasures of children's literature* (2nd ed.). White Plains, NY: Longman.

O'Connor, M. C., & Michaels, S. (1993). Aligning academic task and participation status through revoicing: Analysis of classroom discourse strategy. *Anthropology and Education, 24,* 318–335.

O'Neill, M. (1993). Teaching literature as cultural criticism. *English Quarterly, 25,* 19–25.

Pathey-Chavez, G. (1993). High school as an arena for cultural conflict and acculturation for Latino Angelinos. *Anthropology and Education Quarterly, 24,* 33–60.

Patterson, A., Mellor, B., & O'Neill, M. (1994). Beyond comprehension: Poststructuralist readings in the English classroom. In B. Corcoran, M. Hayhoe, & G. M. Pradl (Eds.), *Knowledge in the making: Challenging the text in the classroom* (pp. 61–72). Portsmouth, NH: Boynton/Cook.

Phelps, L. W. (1988). *Composition as a human science: Contributions to the self-understanding of a discipline.* New York: Oxford University Press.

Pineau, E. L. (1994). Teaching is performance: Reconceptualizing a problematic metaphor. *American Educational Research Journal, 31,* 3–26.

Pradi, G. M. (1996). *Literature for democracy: Reading as a social act.* Portsmouth, NH: Boynton/Cook.

Pratt, M. L. (1987). Linguistic utopias. In N. Fabb, D. Attridge, A. Durant, & C. MacCabe (Eds.), *The linguistics of writing* (pp. 48–66). Manchester, UK: Manchester University Press.

Probyn, E. (1993). Sexing the self: Gendered positions in cultural studies. New York: Routledge.

Purcell-Gates, V. (1991). On the outside looking in: A study of remedial readers' meaning-making while reading literature. *Journal of Reading Behavior, 23,* 235–251.

Puro, P., & Bloome, D. (1987). Understanding classroom communication. *Theory Into Practice, 26,* 26–31.

Quantz, R. A. (1999). School ritual as performance: A reconstruction of Durkheim's and Turner's uses of ritual [20 pages]. *Educational Theory* [On-line serial], *49*(4) . Available via FTP: Hostname: ebscohost: ehostvgw3.epnet.com. Access number 2738052.

Rabinow, P. (1977). Reflections on fieldwork in Morocco. Berkeley: University of California Press.

Radway, J. (1984). *Reading the romance: Women, patriarchy, and popular literature.* Chapel Hill: University of North Carolina Press.

Reynolds, N. (1993). Ethos as location: New sites for understanding discursive authority. *Rhetoric Review, 11,* 325–338.

Rosaldo, R. (1989). *Culture and truth: The remaking of social analysis.* Boston: Beacon.

Rosenblatt, L. M. (1978). *The reader, the text, the poem: The transactional theory of the literary work*. Carbondale: Southern Illinois University Press.

Rosenblatt, L. M. (1988). *Writing and reading: The transactional theory* (Tech. Rep. No. 416). Champaign, IL: Center for the Study of Reading.

Rosenblatt, L. M. (1991). Literary theory. In J. Flood, J. M. Jensen, D. Lapp, & J. R. Squire (Eds.), *Handbook of research on teaching the English language arts: Sponsored by the International Reading Association and the National Council of Teachers of English* (pp. 58–61). New York: Macmillan.

Rosenblatt, L. M. (1995). *Literature as exploration* (4th ed.). New York: Modern Language Association.

Routman, R. (1991). *Invitations: Changing as teachers and learners K–12*. Portsmouth, NH: Heinemann.

Sarland, C. (1991). *Young people reading: Culture and response*. Bristol, PA: Taylor & Francis.

Schechner, R. (1988). *Performance theory*. New York: Routledge.

Short, K., & Pierce, K. (1990). *Talking about books: Creating literate communities*. Portsmouth: Heinemann.

Simpson, A. (1996). Fictions and facts: An investigation of the reading practices of girls and boys. *English Education, 28,* 268–279.

Smith, M. W. (1992). Submission versus control in literary transactions. In J. Many & C. Cox (Eds.), *Reader stance and literary understanding* (pp. 143–160). Norwood, NJ: Ablex.

Soja, E. (1989). *Postmodern geographies: The reassertion of space in critical social theory*. London: Verso.

Spradley, J. P. (1980). *Participant observation*. New York: Harcourt Brace Jovanovich.

Stallybrass, P., & White, A. (1986). *The politics and poetics of transgression*. Ithaca, NY: Cornell University Press.

Street, B. (Ed.). (1993). *Cross-cultural approaches to literacy*. Cambridge, UK: Cambridge University Press.

Swartz, D. (1997). *The sociology of Pierre Bourdieu*. Chicago: University of Chicago Press.

Taxel, J. (1989). Children's literature as an ideological text. In H. A. Giroux & P. McLaren (Eds.), *Critical pedagogy, the state, and cultural struggle* (pp. 205–221). Albany: State University of New York Press.

Thorne, B. (1987). Re-visioning women and social change: Where are the children? *Gender & Society, 1,* 85–109.

Thornton, S. (1996). *Club cultures: Music, media, and subcultural capital*. Hanover, NH: University Press of New England

Tobin, J. (2000). *"Good guy's don't wear hats": Children's talk about the media*. New York: Teachers College Press.

Tompkins, J. P. (Ed.). (1980). *Reader-response criticism: From formalism to post-structuralism*. Baltimore: Johns Hopkins University Press.

Turner, V. (1969). *The ritual process: Structure and anti-structure*. Chicago: Aldine.

Turner, V. (1974). *Drama, fields, and metaphors: Symbolic action in human society*. Ithaca, NY: Cornell University Press.

Turner, V. (1982). *From ritual to theatre: The human seriousness of play*. New York: Performing Arts Journal.

Urquhart, I. (1996). "You see all blood come out": Popular culture and how boys become men. In M. Hilton (Ed.), *Potent fictions: Children's literacy and the challenge of popular culture* (pp. 150–184). New York: Routledge.

Walkerdine, V. (1985). On the regulation of speaking and silence: Subjectivity, class and gender in contemporary school. In C. Steedman, C. Unwin, & V. Walkerdine (Eds.), *Language, gender and childhood* (pp. 203–241). London: Routledge & Kegan Paul.

Walkerdine, V. (1990). *Schoolgirl fictions*. New York: Verso.

Walkerdine, V. (1997). Redefining the subject in situated cognition theory. In D. Kirshner & J. A. Whitson (Eds), *Situated cognition: Social, semiotic, and psychological perspectives* (pp. 57–70). Mahwah, NJ: Lawrence Erlbaum Associates.

Walmsley, S. (1992). Reflections on the state of elementary literature instruction. *Language Arts, 69,* 508–514.

Weedon, C. (1987). *Feminist practice and poststructuralist theory.* Oxford, UK: Blackwell.

Wertsch, J. (1991). *Voices of the mind: A sociocultural approach to mediated action.* Cambridge, MA: Harvard University Press.

Wiencek, J., & O'Flahavan, J. F. (1994). From teacher-led to peer discussions about literature: Suggestions for making a shift. *Language Arts, 71,* 488–498.

Williamson, J. (1981/1982). How does girl number twenty understand ideology? *Screen Education, 40,* 80–87.

Willinsky, J. (1990). *The new literacy: Redefining reading and writing in the schools.* New York: Routledge.

Wolf, S. A., Mieras, E. L., & Carey, A. A. (1996). What's after "What's that?": Preservice teachers learning to ask literary questions. *Journal of Literacy Research, 28,* 459–497.

Zebroski, J. (1989). The social construction of self in the work of Lev Vygotsky. *The Writing Instructor, 8,* 149–156.

Children's Fiction Mentioned in the Text

Bellairs, J. (1993). *Ghost in the mirror.* New York: Puffin.

Collier, J. (1974). *My brother Sam is dead.* New York: Scholastic.

Collier, J. L., & Collier, C. (1983). *War comes to Willy Freeman.* New York: Dell.

Crichton, M. (1969). *The Andromeda strain.* New York: Knopf.

Fast, H. (1961). *April morning.* New York: Bantam.

Filipovic, Z. (1994). *Zlata's diary: A child's life in Sarajevo* (C. Pribichevich-Zoric, Trans.). New York: Scholastic.

Frank, A. (1993). *The diary of a young girl.* New York: Bantam.

Jacques, B. (1988). *Moss flower.* New York: Philomel.

Jacques, B. (1987). *Redwall.* New York: Philomel.

Kelly, E. (1928). *The trumpeter of Krakow.* New York: Macmillan.

L'Engle, M. (1962). *A wrinkle in time.* New York: Dell.

Lindgren, A. (1983). *Ronia, the robber's daughter.* New York: Viking.

Lindgren, A. (1985). *The brothers lionheart.* New York: Puffin.

Lowry, L. (1989). *Number the stars.* New York: Dell.

Lowry, L. (1993). *The giver.* Boston: Houghton Mifflin.

Montgomery, L. (1976). *Anne of green gables.* Toronto: Bantam.

O'Dell, S. (1960). *The island of the blue dolphins.* Boston: Houghton Mifflin.

Paulsen, G. (1985). *Dog song.* New York: Bradbury.

Pickford, T. (1993). *Bobby's back.* New York: Bantam.

Pierce, T. (1983). *Alanna: The first adventure.* New York: Knopf.

Rawls, W. (1961). *Where the red fern grows.* New York: Bantam.

Skurzynski, G. (1988). *The minstrel in the tower.* New York: Random House.

Speare, E. G. (1958). *The witch of blackbird pond.* Boston: Houghton Mifflin.

Spielberg, S. (1994). *Schindler's list* [Film]. Universal City, CA: MCA Universal Home Video.

Watkins, Y. (1986). *So far from the bamboo grove.* New York: Lothrop, Lee & Shepherd.

Yep, L. (1975). *Dragonwings.* New York: Harper & Row.

Yolen, J. (1992). *Encounter.* New York: Harcourt Brace Jovanovich.

Author Index

A

Alloway, N., 94
Almasi, J. F., 95
Althusser, L., 139
Alvermann, D. E., 95, 155, 161, 168, 178
Anders, P. L., 155
Athanases, S. Z., 188
Atwell, N., 67

B

Babcock, B. A., 148
Bailey, F., 77
Baker, C. D., 10, 17
Baker, K., xi
Bakhtin, M. M., 13–14, 15–16, 84, 115, 116, 117, 121, 136
Barthes, R., 149
Barton, D., 10
Bauman, R., 13, 15–16, 165
Beach, R., 16, 17, 114, 152
Behar, R., 188
Bell, C., 71, 85, 117, 157
Bellairs, J., 167
Bennett, T., 16, 114
Biklen, S. K., 6, 185–186
Bloome, D., 10, 16, 77
Bogdan, R. C., 6, 185–186
Bourdieu, P., 11, 30, 45, 160
Brandts, L., 186
Bratlinger, E., 191
Briggs, C., 13, 15–16, 107, 165
Brodkey, L., 12, 154, 168
Brooke, R. E., 16, 105, 106, 165–166
Bruner, J., 12
Buckingham, D., 94, 161
Butler, J., 6, 13

C

Cai, M., 17
Calkins, L. M., 51, 67
Carey, A. A., 3
Cazden, C., 12, 77
Cherland, M. R., 6, 10 fn. 3, 111, 153, 154, 168
Cherryholmes, C. H., 177
Christian-Smith, L. K., 153, 154, 160, 168
Clifford, J., 188
Collier, C., 122, 123
Collier, J., 55
Collier, J. L., 122, 123
Connell, R. W., 154, 165
Connolly, P., 154
Conquergood, D., 13, 105, 178–179
Cook-Gumperz, J., 77
Cooper, D., 168
Corcoran, B., 17
Cox, C., xi
Crawford, V., 155
Crichton, M., 63

D

David, M. E., 45, 46, 139
Davies, B., 13, 17, 90, 137, 150, 153, 154, 179
de la Cruz, E., 186
deCerteau, M., 169
Delpit, L. D., 180–181
Denzin, N. K., 190
Dias, P., xi
Dixon, C., 186
Dyson, A. H., 13, 14, 15 n. 4, 16, 152, 161, 164

Subject Index

Index conventions: fig. following a page number indicates a figure; tab. following a page number indicates a table, an fn. following a page number indicates a footnote

A

Addressivity, 136–137
Alanna (Pierce), 30, 31, 89, 102, 103, 104, 108, 113, 120–121, 153–154
Andromeda Strain (Crichton), 63
Andy (student), and teacher-led reading discussion, 124–125, 126, 127–128
Anne of Green Gables (Montgomery), 161
April Morning (Fast), 39, 89–90, 94, 112, 126, 134, 138, 148

B

Backstage performance, 165
Beavis and Butthead, 81, 157
Bobby's Back (Pickford), 158–160
Book choice, 135, 150, 154–155, 175
Boys reading group, 111, 133, 157–160, 163, 164, 166, 167, 170
Brian (student), 157, 158, 159, 163, 164
Brooke (student), 64, 93, 176
    and peer-led discussion, 90, 97, 101, 102, 103, 105, 106–107, 108, 109–110
    independent reading of, 161
    violent conflict with David, 107
Brothers Lionheart (Lindgren), 59–60, 68, 74–77, 79, 80

C

Classroom culture
    and age relationship to status/power, 90–91
    collective dimension of, 73–80
    gender relations in, 6, 72–73, 91–95, 154–156
    interpretive expectations in, 64–70
    perceived ability within, 87–90
    social expectations, shaping, 61–64
    social order, reification of, 81–82
    status/popular culture in, 91–95, 157–160
    student-centered, 14, 90, 122, 177–178
Close reading, 68–69
Collaborative learning, 62
Columbus, Christopher, 62
Communitas, 14–15, 84
Constructivism, 11
Controlled surrender, 141
Creases, 15
Critical teaching, problematic nature of, 144–145
Cultural critique, reading position, 121–137
Cultural norms, larger/local culture, 8, 94–95, 112, 152, 154–157
Culture, defined, 12
Curriculum director, at Emerson School, 52, 54